Benjamin

Preserving Evangelical Unity

Preserving Evangelical Unity

Welcoming Diversity in Non-Essentials

MICHAEL J. MEIRING

EDITOR

WIPF & STOCK · Eugene, Oregon

PRESERVING EVANGELICAL UNITY
Welcoming Diversity in Non-Essentials

Wipf & Stock
A Division of Wipf and Stock Publishers
199 W. 8th Ave., Suite 3
Eugene, OR 97401
www.wipfandstock.com

ISBN 13: 978-1-60608-268-3

Manufactured in the U.S.A.

List of Contributors

Adrio König
Barbara Wannemacher
Benjamin R. Webb Jr.
Colin Maxwell
Craig Branch
Dereck F. Stone
Diana Valerie Clark
Eric Severson
James D. Hernando
L. L. (Don) Veinot Jr.
Willem Berends

Contents

Introduction

IF YOU WERE TO pray for the Christian church, what would you specifically pray for? Perhaps you would pray for her purity and victory over sin or maybe for her progress in world evangelism. I'm praying that Jesus's prayer would become a reality in the life of his body:

> My prayer is not for them [the disciples] alone. I pray also for those who will believe in me through their message, that all of them may be one, Father, just as you are in me and I am in you. May they also be in us so that the world may believe that you have sent me. I have given them the glory that you gave me, that they may be one as we are one: I in them and you in me. May they be brought to complete unity to let the world know that you sent me and have loved them even as you have loved me. (John 17:20–23)[1]

The Lord Jesus Christ prayed for all who would ever believe in him that they "may be brought to complete unity" so the world would know that God sent his Son and that he loves us. The Christian church can only be effective in evangelism, in sharing the good news that God the Father demonstrated his love for us by sending his Son to be the Savior of the world, when all believers are united in love. The complete union between the Father and the Son—*I in them and you in me*—should be seen in the lives of those who are the recipients of God's saving love and grace. Matthew Henry wrote, "The good fruit of the church's oneness . . . will be an evidence of the truth of Christianity, and a means of bringing many to embrace it."[2]

I can understand why Jesus prayed for unity among believers, because the stark reality is there are so many divisions within the body of Christ that the following verse of an old hymn seemingly remains just a pipe-dream:

---

1. Unless otherwise indicated, all Scripture quotations in this introductory chapter, including chapters one and two, are taken from the *New International Version*.

2. Henry, *Matthew Henry's Commentary in One Volume*, 1,609.

> We are not divided,+
> All one body we,+
> One in hope and doctrine,+
> One in charity.[3]+

One Protestant author suggested that the verse be changed to:

> We are all divided,+
> Not one body we,+
> One lacks faith, another hope,+
> And all lack charity.[4]+

This was not always the case. For the first few centuries of her existence, the persecuted Christian church demonstrated unity in its faith. The early Church Father, Tertullian, recorded the following observation from the unbelievers: "See how these Christians love one another."[5] After Emperor Constantine legalized Christianity in the Roman Empire (AD 312), Christians remained united in preserving the doctrine of God. Several councils were held to defend the doctrine of the Trinity and deity of Christ against the Arian and Nestorian "heretics."

TWO GREAT SCHISMS IN CHURCH HISTORY

The first great schism to occur within the Christian church took place in AD 1054 when the Western branch of the church (in Rome) excommunicated the Eastern branch (in Constantinople). This split happened because the Eastern Church refused to accept the Western's *filioque* doctrine, viz., the Holy Spirit eternally proceeds not only from the Father but also from the Son. I agree with Wayne Grudem that this "obscure point of doctrine" did not warrant such a great schism in the church.[6]

Centuries later, another schism took place. I am referring to the birth of the Protestant Reformation when Martin Luther publicly con-

3. *Onward Christian Soldiers*, written by Sabine Baring-Gould (1865).

4. McAfee Brown, *The Spirit of Protestantism*, quoted in Calver and Warner, *Together We Stand*, 2.

5. Calver and Warner, *Together We Stand*, 2. Unfortunately, it appears that Tertullian lacked charity when he dealt with his brothers in Christ who disagreed with him: "Tertullian was happy attacking practically everyone with whom he disagreed: not simply pagans and persecutors of Christianity, but also those within the Church whose doctrines he considered erroneous" (Hill, *The History of Christian Thought*, 31).

6. Grudem, *Systematic Theology*, 247. Grudem also points out that ultimately the underlying issue was the East's refusal to acknowledge the authority of the Pope (p. 246).

demned the Roman Catholic Church's practice of selling indulgences (AD 1517). Unfortunately, it wasn't long before the Reformers began to argue vehemently among themselves over a certain point of doctrine. It had been only twelve years since the Reformation, but already a meeting was held in Marsbourg Colloquy in an attempt to unite the German and Swiss Reformers. They agreed on all points of the Christian faith except for the presence of Christ in the Lord's Supper. Martin Luther and the German reformers believed in the real, physical presence of Christ in the elements, while Zwingli and the Swiss reformers believed that Christ was represented in the elements symbolically. Sadly, after the meeting, Luther refused to shake Zwingli's hand.[7]

The Swiss reformers were more gracious in their dispute with Luther. John Calvin attempted to gain Luther's approval and unite the reformers by writing to him and calling him "my much respected father."[8] But Luther disregarded these efforts of unity and charity, believing that the devil had influenced the Swiss reformers: "Cursed be such charity and such unity to the very bottom of hell, since such unity not only miserably disrupts Christianity, but makes sport and foolishness of it in a childish manner."[9] Ironically, it was Luther's bitter quibbling and divisive actions that made "sport and foolishness" of the Christian faith in the eyes of her adversaries.[10]

PRESENT-DAY DIVISIONS WITHIN EVANGELICALISM

The apostle Paul said that God has given his church teachers and pastors "to prepare God's people for works of service, so that the body of Christ may be built up until we all reach unity in the faith and in the knowledge of the Son of God and become mature" (Eph 4:12–13). Yet it seems that some evangelical Christians today, especially those in the discernment ministries, are simply not willing to reach unity in the faith.[11] Instead of being united in the essentials of the Christian faith,[12] they argue and

---

7. Hill, *The History of Christian Thought*, 183.

8. Calvin, *Letters of John Calvin*, 71.

9. Green, *Luther and the Reformation*, 170.

10. Although I've pointed out Luther's divisive attitude toward his Swiss brethren that doesn't mean I'm trying to demean the man.

11. I was director of a doctrinal discernment ministry for eight years.

12. Such as the Trinity, the incarnation, death, and resurrection of Jesus Christ, the

bicker over secondary issues, accusing each other of holding to heretical and unbiblical doctrines on minor points, such as the mode of baptism, end-time views, the miraculous gifts of the Spirit, predestination
and free will, women ordination, and the list could go on. I've personally
heard Christians from a discernment ministry speak out bitterly against
a couple of brothers and sisters in Christ because they had disagreed with
them on their interpretation of the millennium in Revelation 20: *"It is our
prayer that our brethren who have been spiritually seduced by the devil into
this error and deception will return to the teachings of the Bible."*

Evangelicals have even argued over trivial issues, such as whether or
not men should wear a tie in church, whether drums and guitars should
be used in the worship group, whether church services should be sinner/
seeker-sensitive or traditional, and, again, the list could go on.

A few years ago, a feud broke out when a certain Reformed counter-cults ministry stated that one had to know that Jesus was God before
one could be converted to Christ. Another counter-cults ministry claimed
that one did not have to know that Jesus was God at the moment of conversion, but that such knowledge would eventually be revealed to them as
they grew in the knowledge of their Lord.[13] Neither group denied the deity of Christ, yet the Reformed ministry accused their brothers in Christ
of preaching a different gospel, calling them "heretics." Just imagine if
anti-Trinitarians witnessed these arguments! They would no doubt think,
*"Just look at these born-again Christians. They keep telling us that Jesus is
God, and yet they can't even agree among themselves as to when one must
believe that Jesus is God!"*

---

transforming power of the Holy Spirit, salvation by grace, the resurrection of the dead,
and the return of Christ.

13. I would agree with the latter view because knowledge does not save a person.
Rather, it is the "new birth" or "regeneration"—that inward, supernatural, sovereign act
of God whereby the Holy Spirit imparts to us spiritual life (John 3:7–8). However, at
regeneration we are not fully aware of all the essential doctrines of the Christian faith.
That is why those who are regenerated are also renewed by the Holy Spirit (Titus 3:5). In
other words, after we become born again our new self is continually being restored in
the image of God in all righteousness, holiness, and knowledge (Eph 4:24; Col 3:10). It
is during our sanctification (being made more like God) that we "grow in the grace and
knowledge of our Lord and Savior Jesus Christ" (2 Pet 3:18). As we grow in the grace and
knowledge of our Lord we come to know and love the truths of our faith.

A couple of years ago Peter[14] refused to have fellowship with me because I had merely disagreed with his attitude on non-essential doctrines. On his website Peter identified the names of Christian churches and pastors in his area he could not have fellowship with because they taught "vital error," which he listed as the teachings of Arminianism, cessationism, paedobaptism, and dispensationalism. He believed we would be "participating in their sin" if we went to these churches or had fellowship with those believers. I gently explained to Peter that we should never stop having fellowship with Christians whom we disagree with on secondary issues. Despite my efforts, he angrily responded, "As long as you hold to this majors-minors philosophy of yours there can be no pretense of fellowship." He later added my name and ministry to his "Hall of Shame" web page along with the other churches.[15]

A Christian once wrote, "I have reached the conclusion that lack of unity may be the single biggest problem in the universal church and, of course, in our individual church . . . We talk about multiplication of our ministry, but we seem to only really understand division. If a house divided cannot stand, it will have an even harder time attracting enthusiastic crowds."[16] I agree. Wasn't it Jesus and not the devil who said, "Every kingdom divided against itself will be ruined, and every city or household divided against itself will not stand" (Matt 12:25)?

Of course the divisions and arguments between Christians do not go unnoticed by unbelievers. *Who would want to be part of a divisive, slanderous, and bitter community of religious fundamentalists who claim to live a life of love?* Is it little wonder that many people have become disillusioned with the Christian church, maintaining that it is an institution comprised of hypocrites who are no different than the "heathens"? Charles Templeton, once an exponent of mass evangelism who toured with Billy Graham in the 1940s and 1950s, later rejected the Christian faith and became an agnostic. Of the Christian faith, he wrote:

14. Not his real name.

15. I have also noticed this unfortunate trend of publicly "exposing" other ministries and Christian pastors among the doctrinal discernment ministries in North America. Others have even filed lawsuits against each other despite Paul's rebuke: "how dare you go before the heathen judges instead of letting God's people settle the matter" (1 Cor 6:1 TEV). I feel it's prudent not to mention any names here or to provide specific examples.

16. Burchett, *When Bad Christians Happen to Good People*, 34.

> Despite the fact that Jesus enjoined his followers to love one an-
> other, most don't, each believing that only they have seen the true
> light of the Gospel and that all the others are in error . . . One of
> the paradoxical aspects of the Christian church (with its emphasis
> on love) is that, throughout history, Christians have contended
> vigorously with each other in internecine quarrels over points of
> doctrine or practice . . . Raised in a particular denomination or
> group, many judge others' behaviour by their acceptance or rejec-
> tion of certain "proof texts" or by their form of worship and often
> brand as heretical or apostate those who differ from them.[17]

Templeton was right on this point. Jesus said, "By this all men will
know that you are my disciples, if you love one another" (John 13:35).
Templeton's words are also a sound rebuke to the Christian church. As
Brennan Manning said, "The greatest single cause of atheism in the world
today is Christians who acknowledge Jesus with their lips then walk out
the door and deny him by their lifestyle. That is what an unbelieving
world simply finds unbelievable."[18]

BUT THERE IS HOPE

Clive Calver, former director of the *Evangelical Alliance*, wrote, "This [com-
mand of Jesus to love one another] was no unachievable pipe-dream."[19]
Therefore, it is the purpose of this book to exhort all Christians to "do
[their] best to preserve the unity which the Spirit gives by means of the
peace that binds you together" (Eph 4:3 TEV).

In order to accomplish this purpose, without turning to a pluralistic
unity-at-all-costs belief, the first part of *Preserving Evangelical Unity* will
identify four recurring dangers to evangelical unity, especially pertaining
to non-essential doctrines (chapter 1). Having identified the root cause
of ungodly divisions, we will then be able to lay down the foundation
of biblical unity, which, as I will explain, is grounded in the gospel of
Jesus Christ, in the essential doctrines of the Christian faith, and in our
freedom to "agree to disagree" over the non-essential doctrines (chapter
2).[20] Because I pointed out the unhealthy divisions within the discern-

17. Templeton, *Farewell to God*, 129, 135.

18. Quoted in Burchett, *When Bad Christians*, 13.

19. Calver and Warner, *Together We Stand*, 2.

20. Exactly how we can discern between the "essentials" and the "non-essentials" will
be explained in chapter two.

ment ministries above (and also will in my first chapter), I have asked two apologists to contribute a chapter on unity and respond to my two chapters where necessary: Reverend Craig Branch, director of the *Apologetics Resource Center*—a ministry that aims to equip Christians with a culturally relevant defense of the faith;[21] and Reverend Don Veinot, president of a well-known counter cults ministry in North America, *Midwest Christian Outreach*.[22] Both of these scholars clearly express their desire to maintain a balance between truth and unity (chapters 3 and 4).

The second part of the book will be a debate section between evangelical theologians from diverse denominations dealing with five non-essential doctrines that have previously led to ungodly divisions within the body of Christ (chapters 5–14). These are fruitful discussions that include responses from both sides. Some of the contributors agreed to compile a short counter response to clarify any misunderstandings. Most of the contributors include a section in their essays dealing with some misrepresentations of their views. Although the contributors are convinced that their view is in harmony with Scripture, they recognize the fact that Christians can agree to disagree on these issues without resorting to a break-up in Christian fellowship. The book concludes with a statement of faith that each contributor helped me to compile, which includes our signatures.

21. See http://www.arcapologetics.org/mission.htm.
22. See http://www.midwestoutreach.org.

Part One

Unity in Essentials

1

Why There is Disunity

D O YOU RECALL THE times when someone asked you a question but
then didn't stick around for an answer? "What is truth?" Pilate asked
Jesus. However, without waiting for an answer, he dashed off to tell the
Jews he found no basis to charge the accused (John 18:38–39). Perhaps
Pilate was being facetious in asking the question, believing that there was
no single truth. Yet in whatever age or culture one lives, people ask that
same question, and it is the task of the church to provide the answer.

Evangelicals have long been noted for their high regard for truth, and
the precious word is usually included in a name of a ministry that seeks to
help Christians "walk in the truth" or "discern truth from error." But with
my experience in seeing so much disunity between Christians in the discernment ministries, I am now wary of such "Truth" ministries because, as
Rob Warner pointed out, a high regard for truth brings with it a "recurring
danger" that brings about disunity.[1] In this chapter I will expose *four* recurring dangers that cause so much disunity within the body of Christ.

A SECTARIAN/FUNDAMENTALIST ATTITUDE:
VIEWING UNITY AS UNIFORMITY

> Now there are diversities of gifts, but the same Spirit. And there
> are differences of administrations, but the same Lord. And there
> are diversities of operations, but it is the same God which worketh
> all in all . . . For the body is not one member, but many . . . Now ye
> are the body of Christ, and members in particular. (1 Cor 12:4–6,
> 14, 27 KJV)

1. Calver and Warner, *Together We Stand*, 60.

"Diversities" and "differences" are two words not usually associated with unity. Nevertheless, Paul uses them to show that the members of the body of Christ (the church) are *united in diversities*: They have been given diverse and different gifts from the Spirit, ultimately for the edification and unity of the church (cf. Eph 4:7ff).

I believe this underlying principle, "unity in diversity," also applies to our diverse and different interpretations of non-essential doctrines. But this belief is either neglected or totally rejected by a sectarian attitude that confuses unity with uniformity and diversity with disunity. G. W. Bromiley refers to the "constant perversion of unity into uniformity and diversity into disunity."[2] In other words, the sectarian attitude believes that to be united in the truth we must all believe the same doctrines, the same practices, the same views, and the same traditions. For them diversity means that there are grounds for "biblical" divisions or disunity.

For example, *Ministry A* is Pentecostal, Arminian, and premillennial in their view of the end times. Then there is *Ministry B*, which is Calvinistic, amillennial, and cessationist in their view of the revelatory gifts of the Spirit. Believing that unity is uniformity, *Ministry A* holds with suspicion that *Ministry B* does not agree with their view of the gifts of the Spirit or their interpretation of the millennium of Revelation 20. And believing that diversity is disunity, *Ministry A* refuses to have fellowship with *Ministry B* unless they agree with their views. (And the same attitude could be found in *Ministry B*.)

A sectarian or fundamentalist attitude can be defined as "my (or my group's) refusing to allow for diversity in others and demanding conformity with all my views, as if my view (in full detail) alone had divine sanction. It is the notion that I, or my own specific group, alone has a market on the truth, to the exclusion of others."[3]

Some extreme evangelical fundamentalists believe that those who do not share their views are not Christians.[4] However, even if "moderate" fundamentalists view others with whom they disagree as Christians, they will still project an attitude that "*we* are right, and *they* are wrong." This eventually leads to a rejection of involvement with other believers who do not accept their views.

---

2. Bromiley, *The Unity and Disunity of the Church*, 20.

3. Koivisto, *One Lord, One Faith*, 44–45.

4. Calver and Warner, *Together we Stand*, 19.

Fortunately, evangelicals from across the globe have addressed this sectarian attitude. The article, *The Chicago Call: An Appeal to Evangelicals*, states:

> We deplore the scandalous isolation and separation of Christians from one another. We believe such division is contrary to Christ's explicit desire for unity among his people and impedes the witness of the church in the world. Evangelicalism is too frequently characterized by an ahistorical, sectarian mentality.[5]

And the *Manila Manifesto*, accepted by the *Lausanne Committee for World Evangelization*, states:

> Jesus prayed that his people's oneness might reflect his own oneness with the Father, in order that the world might believe in him, and Paul exhorted the Philippians to "contend as one person for the faith of the gospel." In contrast to this biblical vision, we are ashamed of the suspicions and rivalries, the dogmatism over non-essentials, the power-struggles and empire-building which spoil our evangelistic witness.[6]

A BROADENING OF ORTHODOX DOCTRINE

Besides differences over the doctrine of the millennium and the gifts of the Spirit, the evangelical church faces diversities and differences over many doctrinal issues. For example, can the divine foreknowledge and sovereignty of God in relation to human freedom be understood and upheld consistently by holding to either Calvinism or Arminianism? Are the Old Testament promises to Israel fulfilled in the New Testament church? Can women be ordained as pastors and teachers? Can infants be baptized along with believers? What is the destiny of the unevangelized? What is the nature of hell?[7] Is Christ going to return before or after the Great Tribulation?[8] How should we understand the Lord's Supper? The list could go on, and for every subject there are three, four, or even five views. Instead of strict uniformity on all points of doctrine (as is the case in most of the sects), evangelicalism provides the Christian with many options.

---

5. Packer and Oden, *One Faith*, 115.
6. Ibid., 112.
7. See Crockett, *Four Views on Hell*.
8. See Gundry, *Three Views on the Rapture*.

However, the evangelical fundamentalist believes that only one view of a particular doctrine is biblical (always their view), whereas the other options are at best "unbiblical" or "false," and at worse "heretical." So, for example, when an evangelical with a premillennial understanding of Revelation 20 says that postmillennialism and amillennialism (end-time views that have been held by many Christians throughout church history) "are clearly heretical," he is deeming not only those views as being unbiblical but placing them and their adherents outside the circle of orthodoxy. A broadening of Christian orthodoxy thus occurs, and these doctrines are strongly upheld as "the essentials" of the Christian faith. This attitude gives birth to full-blown sectarianism, causing a break in Christian fellowship while the sectarian questions the salvation of those who disagree: "Sectarianism may be defined as a *narrowing of the ground of acceptable Christian fellowship and cooperation due to a broadening of what is considered orthodox doctrine.*"[9]

Is it any wonder that Christian apologist, Robert M. Bowman Jr., repeatedly states in his book, which deals with doctrinal discernment, the urgent need for Christians to discern between essentials and non-essentials?

> One of the most crucial functions of Christian theology, and one of the most neglected, is to sort out the really important—the *essential*—from the less important and even the irrelevant (see Rom. 14) . . . [A] balanced understanding of doctrine can help Christians divided by doctrinal differences to be reconciled as they learn which points are minor or unsound and which are not (1 Tim. 6:3–5; Titus 1:9–14). It turns out that shallow understanding of doctrine easily promotes disunity among Christians, while deepening understanding of doctrine tends to foster greater Christian unity . . . It is lamentable that the church has allowed itself to be divided over nonessential issues.[10]

The "most troublesome question," as Bowman points out, is, "*Who should determine the standard [of orthodoxy]?*"[11] Or to put it in another way: *How do we determine which doctrines are essential and which are nonessential?* I will endeavor to answer this pertinent question from Scripture in the next chapter, suffice it to say that this question has been used as a

9. Koivisto, *One Lord, One Faith*, 44.

10. Bowman, *Orthodoxy and Heresy*, 16, 18, 48.

11. Ibid., 48.

tool by evangelical fundamentalists to ridicule and reject, in their own words, the "majors-minors philosophy" and "the practice of dividing the word of God into essentials and non-essentials." For them, non-essential doctrines simply do not exist. Why they believe this will become apparent as I now reveal the third recurring danger to unity.

CONFUSING THE ISSUE: HERMENEUTICS, ILLUMINATION, AND INSPIRATION

Depending on which side of the fence you may sit, there is always the temptation to say, "The Holy Spirit, through God's grace, revealed to me that Calvinism/or Arminianism is true!" The problem with such a statement is that if the Holy Spirit did reveal this to you, it necessarily would follow that the other view is untrue, and therefore false, unbiblical, and even heretical, which brings one back to full-blown sectarianism. Yet this would precisely be the fundamentalist's argument against the evangelical who attempts to discern between essentials and non-essentials. They would argue in this way:

(A)   God's word is truth.

(B)   Truth is absolute, unchanging, and eternal.

(C)   Jesus promised to send the Holy Spirit to guide us into all truth.

(D)   The Holy Spirit illumines our minds so that we may understand all that is written in God's word, the Bible.

(E)   Therefore, there can only be one correct interpretation of a particular doctrine. Otherwise, why would the Holy Spirit impress diverse and different views into the minds of Christians, which has led to so much disunity?

In support of premises *C* and *D*, the evangelical fundamentalist would then cite the following Scriptures:

> But when he, the Spirit of truth, comes, he will guide you into all truth (John 16:13); But God has revealed it to us by his Spirit. The Spirit searches all things, even the deep things of God . . . We have not received the spirit of the world but the Spirit who is from God, that we may understand what God has freely given us. This is what we speak, not in words taught us by human wisdom but in words taught by the Spirit, expressing spiritual truths in spiritual words (1 Corinthians 2:10, 12–13); As for you, the anointing you received

> from him remains in you, and you do not need anyone to teach
> you. But as his anointing teaches you about all things and as that
> anointing is real, not counterfeit—just as it has taught you, remain
> in him (1 John 2:27).

Therefore, in the fundamentalist's understanding, if a Christian denies premise *E* above, then he can no longer believe in the "absolutes of Scripture" (premises *A* and *B*); he has thus moved, in their thinking, to a "mild form of ecumenism," or worse, "liberalism." The problem with this line of reasoning is that many evangelicals—those who accept the fact that there are non-essential doctrines by which we can "agree to disagree"—firmly believe in premises *A* and *B* (i.e., the absolute truthfulness and inspiration of Scripture), and to a large extent, premise *D* (i.e., the illumination of the Spirit). For example, Reformed scholar, Richard Pratt, wrote, "In a word, the Spirit illumines our minds so we may apprehend and appropriate Scripture . . . Without his enlightenment our interpretative efforts are hopeless."[12] Of course, illumination does not rule out careful study on our part, as Pratt later admits.

Nevertheless, my point is that believing in premises *A*, *B*, and *D* does not lead one to the conclusion as stated in *E*. The issue is not about one's view of truth and inspiration; it is a hermeneutical issue (i.e., interpretative). It is rather important to understand how the illumination of the Spirit works in relation to non-essential doctrines. What I propose is a re-working of premises *C* and *D* that will lead one to an entirely different conclusion of *E*, which I will do in the next chapter.

APPLYING HERMENEUTICAL RULES THROUGH
OUR SPECTACLES OF TRADITION

The final "recurring danger" to the unity of the body of Christ applies to all of us who are evangelical Christians (whether one has a sectarian attitude or not).

Believing in the inspiration of Scripture, it should always be our goal to faithfully interpret God's word. Many scholars have written on the subject of hermeneutics (i.e., the science of interpretation) and given us "rules" for biblical interpretation. Reformed theologian Edward Gross cites three rules from Charles Hodge: "Scripture is to be interpreted in its grammatical historical sense, Scripture must interpret Scripture and can-

---

12. Pratt, *He Gave us Stories*, 5.

not contradict itself, and the guidance of the Holy Spirit must be sought to interpret Scripture."[13] Beyond a shadow of a doubt, these rules of interpretation are necessary for any Bible reader, but then Gross concludes, "If Christians would constantly unite a thorough investigation with these simple rules, *differences of interpretation would practically disappear*."[14]

The problem with Gross's concluding statement should be obvious. Christians *have* engaged in thorough investigations, applying these three rules of hermeneutics, and yet they have *still* come up with differences of interpretation. This will become plain later in this book when, for example, Colin Maxwell and I discuss our differences regarding divine sovereignty and human responsibility. However, even in our disagreements I would never be so presumptuous as to accuse Colin of not applying one of the three rules of hermeneutics or failing to engage in a comprehensive study of the subject at hand. "The obvious truth," says Jack Deere, "is that a lack of comprehensive study of the Scriptures and dissimilar hermeneutical principles cannot account for the vast majority of modern theological differences."[15]

What accounts for our theological differences over non-essential doctrines will be stated in the next chapter, but for now it must be noted that in most cases it is our theological and denominational traditions and cultural backgrounds that plays an important role in our diverse interpretations. Deere gives a classic example:

> The truth is, if you take a student who has no position on the millennium and send him to Westminster Seminary, he will probably come out an amillennialist. If you take that same student and send him to Dallas Seminary, he is even more likely to come out a premillennialist. There will be few exceptions to this rule. Our environment, our theological traditions, and our teachers have much more to do with what we believe than we realize. In some cases, they have much more influence over what we believe than the Bible itself.[16]

Of course there are exceptions to this rule, as testimonies exist of many Christians who later discarded, for example, their church's teaching of premillennialism in favor of amillennialism. I made such a transition

13. Quoted in Deere, *Surprised by the Power of the Spirit*, 54.

14. Ibid. Emphasis mine in *italics*.

15. Ibid.

16. Ibid., 47.

when I discarded Calvinism, which I had been taught the first ten years of my Christian life, in favor of Arminianism, and when I replaced my cessationist view of the miraculous gifts of the Spirit for an "open but cautious" position.[17] However, I understand that such a transition from my theological roots does not make my view more "biblical" than the Christian who has always believed in Calvinism. My point is that our theological backgrounds play an important part in our interpretation of Scripture—even when we claim to have arrived at a purely objective view on certain non-essential doctrines. And when we recognize that our theological traditions play a pivotal role in our interpretative efforts, we should refrain from making comments like, "my view is biblical," which will inevitably lead to disunity.[18]

CONCLUSION

Contrary to popular belief, denominationalism is not the root cause of disunity; it is sectarianism or fundamentalism. And the evangelical church is not immune to this disease. Some Christians have in the past and up to now shown a sectarian attitude, believing that unity means conformity to all their views and "refusing to allow for diversity in others." They have broadened Christian orthodoxy by breaking fellowship with any other Christian who disagrees with them on non-essentials doctrines, which is fuelled by their belief that the Holy Spirit illumines their minds to understand everything that is written in the Bible. There is, however, a subtle danger that *all* of us must face in our effort for unity. We must be aware that when we apply principles of interpretation, we are approaching Scripture with our presuppositions, influenced by our environment and theological traditions.

17. See Saucy, "An Open but Cautious View," 95ff.

18. I'm always reminded of George Ladd's expressed frustration in response to Herman Hoyt's chapter on dispensationalism: "Hoyt's essay reflects the major problem in the discussion of the millennium. Several times he contrasts nondispensational views with his own, which he labels 'the biblical view.' If he is correct, then the other views, including my own, are 'unbiblical' or even heretical. This is the reason that over the years there has been little creative dialogue between dispensationalists and other schools of prophetic interpretation." (Ladd, "A Historic Premillennial Response," 93.)

2

Toward a Biblical Unity

MICHAEL J. MEIRING

THE FIRST STEP TOWARD UNITY: SORTING OUT TERMINOLOGY

THE WELL-KNOWN CHRISTIAN APOLOGIST, C. S. Lewis, once wrote, "[God] will make the feeblest and filthiest of us into a god or goddess."[1]

An evangelical fundamentalist once accused C. S. Lewis of holding to theistic evolution for saying this.[2] However, in context, Lewis was applying the term "gods" to glorified believers in Christ. Lewis was merely touching on the doctrine of *theosis*—a teaching once held by the early Church Fathers[3] and that is still held today by the Eastern Orthodox Church, including some Catholics and Protestants.

The doctrine of *theosis* is simply this: That Christians, by grace and the redeeming work of Christ, will become "gods" in the sense that they "participate in the divine nature" by becoming "like God in true righteousness and holiness," and by taking on immortality at the resurrection (2 Pet 1:4; Eph 4:24; 1 Cor 15:53). And so in the fourth century the Church Father, Athanasius, wrote, "The Word was made flesh in order that we might be enabled to be made gods."[4] But Athanasius was quick to point

---

1. Lewis, *Mere Christianity*, 170.

2. I do not know why this person made a connection between theistic evolution and deification!

3. E.g., Iraeneus, Justin Martyr, and Athanasius—the latter being the great defender of monotheism, the Trinity and deity of Christ.

4. Athanasius, *Against the Arians*, 1.39, quoted in Robinson, *Are Mormons Christians?* 61.

out that this participation in the divine nature did not mean that we will become equal in nature to God the Son because "things which partake cannot be identical with or similar to that whereof they partake."[5]

Understanding the doctrine of *theosis* helps us understand what Lewis meant when he said that God would make believers into gods. In the afterlife God will make us like himself: perfect in holiness, completely righteous, and without sin. Only in this sense will we become "gods." By no stretch of the imagination can anyone say that Lewis or the early Church Fathers believed that Christians would eventually become equal to God or inherit his divine incommunicable attributes (e.g., omniscience, omnipotence, etc.). In fact, in his same work, Lewis denied this when he wrote, "What Satan put into the heads of our remote ancestors [i.e., Adam and Eve] was the idea that they could 'be like gods'—could set up their own as if they had created themselves—be their own masters—invent some sort of happiness for themselves outside of God, apart from God."[6]

Whether one agrees with the doctrine of *theosis* or not, my point is that if we understand terminology as stated in their context, we will then be able to overcome any misconceptions and avoid misrepresenting what other Christians believe.[7]

For the purpose of this book it is necessary to define the eterminology that I employ, especially when I refer to "essentials" and "non-essentials." First, when I use the term "essentials," I'm not denying that every doctrine in the Bible is essential or necessary. Rather, when I refer to the essentials of the Christian faith, I'm talking about those doctrines that must be accepted by *all* who claim to be Christians. And when I employ the term "non-essentials," I am not saying that those doctrines are unimportant or irrelevant. Instead, I am referring to those doctrines that need not be accepted by all Christians.

---

5. Athanasius, *Ad Afros*, 7, quoted in White, *Is the Mormon my Brother?* 227.

6. Lewis, *Mere Christianity*, 41.

7. This is why I gave the opportunity to the contributors of this book to include a section in their essays called "Avoiding Misrepresentations." A misrepresentation is an inaccurate or distorted presentation of someone else's belief.

THE SECOND STEP TOWARD UNITY:
AVOIDING THE FIRST TEMPTATION

C. S. Lewis was correct when he said that Satan had put into the minds of Adam and Eve that they could be their own masters, apart from God: "ye shall be as gods, knowing good and evil" (Gen 3:5 KJV). In one sense, Satan was telling the truth when he said that they would become like God in knowing good and evil if they ate the forbidden fruit (cf. Gen 3:22). But what Satan didn't tell them was that they would know evil in a very personal way; in other words, they would *know* evil by *doing* evil. Moreover, their knowledge of God would become deficient, and this would be passed down to all their descendants: "Although they knew God, they neither glorified him as God" (Rom 1:21). I believe that this same temptation is directed at believers in Christ today: We are tempted to believe that we can become like God in knowing everything there is to know about Christian doctrine and theology.

In the previous chapter I stated that the evangelical fundamentalist would vehemently oppose any kind of differentiation between "essentials" and "non-essentials" by arguing in the following way:

(A)   God's word is truth.

(B)   Truth is absolute, unchanging, and eternal.

(C)   Jesus promised to send the Holy Spirit to guide us into all truth.

(D)   The Holy Spirit illumines our minds so that we may understand all that is written in God's word, the Bible.

(E)   Therefore, there can only be one correct interpretation of a particular doctrine. Otherwise, why would the Holy Spirit impress diverse and different views into the minds of Christians, which has led to so much disunity?

The problem with this kind of argumentation, as I stated, is that many evangelicals who delineate between "essentials" and "non-essentials" also hold to premises A and B. The issue is thus not about the truth and inspiration of Scripture; it is a hermeneutical one. And the main problem with premises C and D is that they are based on a faulty interpretation of the illumination of the Spirit in relation to our formulated principles of interpretation. First of all, Jesus did not promise to send the Holy Spirit to guide us into all truth. Our Savior's words are directed exclusively to his disciples (John 16:13–15 cf. 14:26). The apostles would receive the Holy Spirit in such a way that the Spirit of truth would remind them of everything that Jesus had personally taught them so that they would later speak forth the very words of God and record them down as inspired Scripture (1 Thess 2:13; 2 Pet 1:20–21). No Christian today is inspired by the Spirit in this sense to record Scripture and add to the biblical canon.

Second, the notion in premise D that Christians today, by the illumination of the Spirit, can know and understand everything written down in God's word is based on a misinterpretation of 1 Corinthians 2:10–13 and 1 John 2:27, which I cited in chapter one. Looking at the former passage in its context, the apostle Paul begins with the statement that the "message of the cross is foolishness to those who are perishing" and that "none of the rulers of this age understood it, for if they had, they would not have crucified the Lord of glory" (1:18; 2:8). In contrast to this lack of understanding the gospel from a worldly point of view, Paul says that God has given his Spirit to believers so that we can "understand what God has freely given us" (2:12). So when Paul says, "This is what we speak" (2:13), he is referring to the gospel—the message regarding "Jesus Christ and him crucified" (2:2). God has revealed this message to us by his Spirit (2:10). He has therefore given us his Spirit to understand everything we need to know about the gospel—not about doctrine and theology.

In the latter passage, the apostle John refers to the "anointing" received by believers in order to teach us about "all things." In context, this anointing refers to knowing the truth that Jesus is the Christ, the Son of the Father (vv. 20–23)—it does not concern every point of Christian doctrine.[8]

Therefore, premises C and D, including the concluding premise E, can be formulated as follows:

(C)   Jesus promised to send the Holy Spirit to his disciples in order to guide them into all truth, concerning his teachings, in preparation for the proclamation and recording of the Gospels.

(D)   The Holy Spirit illumines our minds so that we may understand the gospel of Jesus Christ as recorded in God's word, the Bible.

(E)   Therefore, there can only be one correct version of the gospel (cf. Gal 1:6–8).

---

8. Later I will contend that the Holy Spirit illumines our minds to (1) the truths found in the gospel as recorded in Scripture and (2) the essential doctrines of the faith which are either explicitly or implicitly stated in Scripture, but which were formulated by the early Church Fathers in order to sustain the gospel of Jesus Christ.

Finally, the reader must understand that certain theological differences between Christians is not the result of one group of believers (or denomination) receiving the "anointing of the Spirit," while another is grounded on human reason or interpretation. Instead, the two main factors that cause Spirit-led Christians to differ over the "non-essentials" follow:

First of all, we have a sinful and imperfect nature. Paul says, "Now we see but a poor reflection as in a mirror, then we shall see face to face. Now I know in part; then I shall know fully, even as I am fully known" (1 Cor 13:12). So there are theological issues that we will not fully understand on this side of glory (cf. 2 Pet 3:16). When the perfect comes, then we will fully understand. And though God has given us his inspired word for us to know him, to believe in his Son, and to live godly lives in Christ, there are just some issues that we won't know fully in our mortal state because we are not gods (in the true sense of the word). Only God can know everything (1 John 3:20).

Second, it is possible that God does not want us to understand everything, for example, about end-time prophecies, or how his sovereignty relates to human responsibility. What is more essential? For us to be faithful when our Savior returns (Matt 24:44), or for us to know when and how long the Great Tribulation will be, and if Christ will return before or after the millennium (Rev 20:1ff)? Is it not required of us to use our God-given gifts to edify the church, instead of arguing and dividing over whether the miraculous gifts have ceased or continued?

THE THIRD STEP TOWARD UNITY: DISCERNING THREE LEVELS OF ORTHODOXY

How do we determine which doctrines are essential and which are non-essential? This is the most crucial question to be answered. If we get it right, believers in Christ will be able to reach unity in the faith. If we get it wrong, we will continue to cause unnecessary and ungodly divisions within the body of Christ.

What we need to identify, first and foremost, is a "mere" Christianity. In other words, says C. S. Lewis in his *magnum opus*, *Mere Christianity*, we need to "explain and defend the belief that has been common to nearly all Christians at all times."[9] Reflecting on Lewis's portrayal of "mere" Christianity, Rex Koivisto wrote, "It is the essential doctrinal core, from

9. Lewis, *Mere Christianity*, vi.

which diversity must be disallowed."[10] Koivisto then goes on in his book to differentiate between a "level one orthodoxy" (i.e., "saving orthodoxy") and a "level two orthodoxy" (i.e., "sustaining orthodoxy") that makes up the "core orthodoxy" that must unite all Christians. Being in basic agreement with Koivisto, I will provide a brief description of each level in my own words and add a third level of orthodoxy that allows for diversity.

Level One Orthodoxy: "Saving Orthodoxy"

The apostle Paul states that Christ's church is "built on the foundation of *the* apostles and prophets, with Christ Jesus himself as the chief cornerstone" (Eph 2:20).[11] He then goes on to refer to the "mystery" of God's grace that was revealed to these New Testament apostles and prophets (3:2–5). This "mystery," says Paul, is that through the gospel "the Gentiles are fellow heirs and fellow members of the body, and fellow partakers of the promise in Christ Jesus" (v. 6 NASB). Therefore, the foundation of the Christian faith is built on the gospel of Jesus Christ. Without this foundation, the church would collapse. Elsewhere Paul affirms, "by this gospel you are saved" (1 Cor 15:2). He then gives a brief definition of this "saving orthodoxy":

> For what I received I passed on to you as of first importance: that Christ died for our sins according to the Scriptures, that he was buried, that he was raised on the third day according to the Scriptures, and that he appeared to Peter, and then to the Twelve. (1 Cor 15:3–5)

Later, in his letter to the Colossian Christians, Paul provides a lengthier definition of the gospel. Here are a few statements from this definition:

> [The Son] is the image of the invisible God, the firstborn over all creation. For by him all things were created . . . And he is the head of the body, the church . . . For God was pleased to have all his fullness dwell in him, and through him to reconcile to himself all things . . . by making peace through his blood, shed on the cross. Once you were alienated from God and were enemies in your minds because of your evil behaviour. But now he has reconciled you by Christ's physical body through death to present you holy

10. Koivisto, *One Lord, One Faith*, 181.

11. Emphasis mine in italics. The use of the definite article shows that Paul has in mind specific apostles and prophets; namely, the New Testament apostles and prophets (cf. 3:2, 5).

in his sight, without blemish and free from accusation—if you continue in your faith . . . This is the gospel that you heard. (Col 1:15–16, 18–23)

Correlating other texts of Scripture, the gospel can be equally defined as such: *God loves the world and sent his Son, Jesus the Christ, into the world, born of a woman, born under law;*[12] *he lived a sinless life,*[13] *died as an atoning sacrifice for our sins,*[14] *and was raised to life for our justification,*[15] *so that whoever believes in him has eternal life, but whoever rejects the Son will not see life.*[16] *He ascended to heaven, sent the Holy Spirit to empower, edify (through gifts), and sanctify his church but will return in the same manner to judge the living and the dead.*[17]

In providing a similar summary of the gospel, Koivisto points out that there are some obvious presuppositions in each of the statements.[18] For example, when we say, *God sent his Son*, we are referring to the "God" as revealed in the Old Testament Scriptures, the God of Abraham, Isaac, and Jacob, the one true God (Deut 6:4). Likewise, when we refer to God's "Son," we are identifying him not only as a man but also as one who is God, the exact representation of God the Father's being, having the fullness of Deity in bodily form (John 1:1; Col 2:9; Heb 1:3).[19]

A couple of other statements in the definition above have the following presuppositions: *born of a woman, born under law.* The incarnation is pivotal to the gospel—it refers to the Word who became human (John 1:14). *He lived a sinless life, died as an atoning sacrifice for our sins.* The presupposition here is that all human beings are sinful and under condemnation, which is why the Son was sent as an atoning sacrifice. The word "atone" means to "make amends," and the word "atonement" can be

12. John 3:16; Galatians 4:4.

13. 1 Corinthians 5:21.

14. 1 John 4:10.

15. Romans 4:25.

16. John 3:36.

17. Ephesians 4:7–13; 1 Corinthians 12:12–13; Romans 2:16.

18. Koivisto, *One Lord, One Faith*, 197.

19. Commenting on Colossians 1:15 and Hebrews 1:3, the *New Dictionary of Biblical Theology* states, "Jesus is thus an exact copy of God's being; if the invisible God could be seen, he would look like Jesus" (Alexander and Rosner, *New Dictionary*, 601).

understood to mean "expiation" (i.e., cleansing from sin)[20] and/or "propitiation" (i.e., turning aside the wrath of God).[21]

"Saving orthodoxy" thus refers to the gospel of Jesus Christ because it is this gospel that brings salvation to humankind. And it is because of this gospel that the apostle Paul exhorted the Philippian Christians to resolve their disunity and "stand firm in one spirit, contending as one man for the faith of the gospel" (Phil 1:27).

Level Two Orthodoxy: "Sustaining Orthodoxy"

Rex Koivisto defines "sustaining orthodoxy" as "the church's subsequent reflection on the implications of the Gospel and its elements."[22] In other words, sustaining orthodoxy builds upon (but does not add to) the gospel; it helps to sustain the core elements of the gospel in the face of heresy. This level of orthodoxy thus comprises the essential doctrines of the Christian faith.

Some of the essential doctrines are explicitly stated in the Scriptures, while others are implicit, formulated by the early Church Fathers to avoid any kind of aberrant teachings that would distort the gospel of Jesus Christ. I would like to expound on three essential doctrines that sustain the gospel.

The Trinity. Although the word "trinity" is nowhere explicitly stated in Scripture,[23] it is a doctrine that is consistent with the gospel message concerning the one true God who sent his Son, who was also God (Isa 9:6; John 20:28).[24] For in reading the definition of the gospel, the question is often asked: *If there is only one God, then how can the Father be God while at the same time Jesus, who is a separate person from the Father, also be God?* The answer lies in the doctrine of the Trinity. When one reads

---

20. Cf. Leviticus 16:30.

21. Cf. Exodus 12:21–23; John 3:36b.

22. Koivisto, *One Lord, One Faith*, 201.

23. The Trinity is implied in the following Scriptures: Genesis 1:26; Isaiah 63:8–10; Matthew 28:19; Luke 1:35; 3:22; John 10:30; 14:11, 16, 26; 16:7–10; 1 Corinthians 12:4–6; 2 Corinthians 13:14; 1 Peter 1:2; Jude 1:20–21.

24. The first early Church Father to use the word "Trinity" in his writings was Tertullian in the second century. He wrote, "All of them [Father, Son and Holy Spirit] are One, by unity of substance; while we still keep the mystery of the distribution which spreads the Unity into a Trinity, placing them in their order the three Persons—the Father, the Son, and the Holy Spirit" (Hill, *The History of Christian Thought*, 34).

the Christian creeds of the early Church Fathers, one will notice that they were primarily concerned with defending and explaining the deity of Christ, his dual natures, and the unity of essence between the Father and the Son. Yet their creeds also helped safeguard the biblical teaching of monotheism[25] and the distinction of personalities between the Father and Son from the aberrations of Tritheism[26] and Modalism.[27]

> [*The Nicene Creed*, AD 325:] We believe in . . . one Lord Jesus Christ, the only-begotten of the Father, that is, begotten of the substance of the Father, God from God, light from light, true God from true God, begotten not made, of the same substance as the Father.[28]

> [*The Chalcedon Creed*, AD 451:] [We] believe in one and the same Son, our Lord Jesus Christ, at once complete in his divinity and complete in his humanity, true God and true man; of one substance with the Father as far as his divinity goes, and at the same time of one substance with us as far as his humanity goes . . . the distinction of the natures being in no way compromised by the fact that they are united, but the qualities of each nature being kept and united to form one person, not divided or separated into two persons.[29]

> [*The Athanasian Creed*, AD 381:] But the Godhead of the Father, of the Son, and of the Holy Spirit is all one, the glory equal, the majesty coeternal. Such as the Father is, such is the Son, and such is the Holy Spirit. The Father uncreated, the Son uncreated, and the Holy Spirit uncreated . . . The Father eternal, the Son eternal, and the Holy Spirit eternal. And yet they are not three eternals but one eternal . . . So likewise the Father is almighty, the Son almighty, and the Holy Spirit almighty. And yet they are not three almighties, but

---

25. E.g., "This is what the LORD says, I am the first and I am the last; apart from me there is no God." (Isa 44:6)

26. The belief that the Father, Son, and Holy Spirit are three separate Gods. This aberration is held today by The Church of Jesus Christ of Latter-day Saints (a.k.a. Mormonism).

27. The belief that God is only one Person. In other words, besides being the Son, Jesus is also the Father and the Holy Spirit. This aberration is held today by Oneness Pentecostal Churches (a.k.a. Jesus Only).

28. Hill, *The History of Christian Thought*, 59–60.

29. Ibid., 93.

> one almighty. So the Father is God, the Son is God, and the Holy
> Spirit is God; And yet they are not three Gods, but one God.[30]

Today, all evangelical confessions of faith affirm monotheism, as well
as the distinction of persons and equality of essence/nature between the
Father, Son, and Holy Spirit:

> We further believe that the one God exists externally in Three
> Persons—the Father, the Son, and the Holy Spirit—all three hav-
> ing the same nature, attributes and perfections but each executing
> distinct but harmonious operations in the work of creation and
> redemption (*Tyndale University College and Seminary*); There is
> one true God, eternally existing in three persons—Father, Son,
> and Holy Spirit—each of whom possesses equally all the attri-
> butes of Deity and the characteristics of personality (*Campus
> Crusade for Christ*).[31]

Original sin. The term was first coined by St. Augustine (AD 354–430),
and by it he meant that "universal sinfulness had a historical beginning
and cause."[32] The historical beginning of sin into the world is recorded
in Genesis chapter three and is often referred to by Christians as "the
Fall." The doctrine of original sin, however, said something much more
than simply about the historical fact of Adam's sin. The sixteenth-century
Reformer, John Calvin, a great admirer and devotee of Augustinian theology, defined the doctrine as the "hereditary depravity and corruption of
our nature, diffused into all parts of the soul, which first makes us liable to
God's wrath, then also brings forth in us those works which Scripture calls
'works of the flesh' (Gal. 5:19)."[33] The doctrine of original sin thus dealt
with the effects that the first sin had upon Adam's descendants.

Still, Augustine's doctrine went further to answer the philosophical
question as to *how* sin was transmitted from generation to generation.
It is here that John Calvin and other Protestant Reformers disagreed
with Augustine's view, for the latter taught that the pollution and guilt
of Adam's sin was inherited by his descendants via sexual transmission
(a.k.a. as the seminal view of original sin).[34] However, this question

---

30. "The Athanasian Creed." Online: http://www.ccel.org/creeds/athanasian.creed.html.
31. Packer and Oden, *One Faith*, 60.
32. Blocher, *Original Sin*, 18.
33. Calvin, *Institutes of the Christian Religion*, II.1.8.
34. The sixteenth-century Reformers, especially Calvin, propagated a federal view of

runs into the category of secondary/non-essential doctrines. Instead, I would like to highlight in Augustine's statement—"in that man [Adam] who first sinned, in whom we all died, and from whom we are all born in misery"[35]—those principles of the doctrine of original sin that help sustain the gospel teaching that through Jesus' atoning death we are delivered from sin:

All of us are sinners. Sin is universal: "There is no difference, for all have sinned and fall short of the glory of God" (Rom 3:22–23). All of Adam's descendents have been affected by the Fall: "Therefore, just as sin entered the world through one man, and death through sin, and in this way death came to all men, because all sinned" (Rom 5:12).[36]

All of us have a sinful nature. Remember that in Paul's definition of the gospel, he writes that, before becoming Christians, we were "alienated" from God and were his "enemies in [our] minds" as shown by our evil behavior (Col 1:21). Elsewhere, he says that we were "by nature" objects of God's wrath (Eph 2:3). Whichever view one takes as to how sin was transmitted to Adam's descendants, the fact is we all have a sinful nature.[37]

Salvation by grace. In the Bible the meaning of "salvation" is *comprehensive*. It synonymously refers to our "redemption," "renewal," and "restoration." Salvation does not begin and end at the point of our faith in Christ but continues throughout our new life in Christ until we are glorified in him. It does not simply mean that we have been delivered

original sin, viz. God imputed Adam's guilt to our account because Adam stood as the federal representative of the human race. Actually, this view could be seen as a development of Augustine's seminal view because Augustine also expressed the participation and co-responsibility of Adam's descendants to his wrong choice. Augustine wrote, "In the misdirected choice of that one man all sinned in him, since all were that one man . . . all sinned in Adam on that occasion, for all were already identical with him in that nature of his which was endowed with the capacity to generate them" (Kelly, *Early Christian Doctrines*, 364).

35. Augustine, *Confessions*, 249.

36. The Latin translation of Romans 5:12—the only translation that Augustine had access to—reads, "*in whom* all sinned." Augustine built on this phrase, "in whom," to propagate his seminal view of original sin.

37. I agree more or less with the Wesleyan view of original sin, which states, "Man is not responsible for the depraved nature with which he is born. Hence, no guilt or demerit attaches to it. Man is not guilty of inbred sin when he comes into the world. He becomes responsible for it only after having rejected the remedy provided by atoning blood. In this way he ratifies it as his own" (Culbertson and Wiley, *Introduction to Christian Theology*, 178).

from sin through repentance, but that we have received something: "For in the gospel a righteousness from God is revealed, a righteousness that is by faith from first to last" (Rom 1:17). We receive a righteousness from God. First, when we hear the gospel and believe in Christ, God *declares* us righteous (i.e., justifies us) by faith: "This righteousness from God comes through faith in Jesus Christ to all who believe" (Rom 3:22). Therefore, it is by God's grace that we are saved through faith and not by works (Eph 2:8–9). I love the way that St. Augustine put it:

> [God] extends his mercy, not because they know him, but in order that they may know him; he extends his righteousness whereby he justifies the ungodly, not because they are upright in heart, but that they may become upright in heart.[38]

Second, God not only declares us righteous in his sight, but he also *makes* us righteous, and again, by his grace. We receive the Holy Spirit who enables us to "put on the new self, created to be like God in true righteousness and holiness" (Eph 4:24). In this sense, salvation is a gradual process as we persevere in good works: "he who stands firm to the end will be saved" (Matt 24:13). But it must be understood that our works of righteousness—a righteousness that was received from God—is motivated by our faith in Christ and the love that God has poured out into our hearts (Rom 5:5; Phil 3:9).

Finally, "salvation" can be spoken of in terms of a future state. When Christ returns to judge the living and the dead, his church will be saved from "the wrath to come" and receive immortality so that when "he appears we shall be like him" (1 John 3:2). Our good works on the day of Judgment will testify to God's grace, his love, and his Spirit in our lives, through the gospel of Jesus Christ:

> And whatsoever we ask, we receive of him, because we keep his commandments, and do those things that are pleasing in his sight. And this is his commandment, That we should believe on the name of his Son Jesus Christ, and love one another, as he gave us commandment. And he that keepeth his commandments dwelleth in him, and he in him. And hereby we know that he abideth in us, by the Spirit which he hath given us (1 John 3:22–24); Now the God of peace, that brought again from the dead our Lord Jesus, that great shepherd of the sheep, through the blood of the everlast-

---

38. Augustine, *De spir. et litt.*, 11.7, quoted in Wilken, "Salvation in Early Christian Thought," 69.

ing covenant, make you perfect in every good work to do his will, working in you that which is well pleasing in his sight, through Jesus Christ; to whom be glory for ever and ever. Amen (Hebrews 13:20–21 KJV).

Level Three Orthodoxy: "Secondary Issues / Non-Essentials"

We've seen above that the gospel of Jesus Christ ("saving orthodoxy") and the essentials of the Christian faith ("sustaining gospel") encompass the "core orthodoxy" that must unite all Christians. To deny the gospel of Christ is to believe in a different gospel that does not save (Gal 1:6–8). And to deny the Trinity, original sin, and salvation by grace, is to distort the gospel by which we are saved. Naturally, then, the non-essentials of the faith, important as they are to the believer, are nevertheless those doctrines that do not affect one's salvation. Rex Koivisto lists some of these non-essentials when he writes:

> Christians who agree on the Gospel as God's unique tool to grant complete forgiveness to sinners through the shed blood of the incarnate and resurrected Son of God will differ on the frequency and the sacramental value of the Lord's Supper; they will disagree on how the church should be organized and run. They will differ on matters pertaining to human free will and its relation to divine sovereignty; they will differ on the function of spiritual gifts today, and whether a believer, once saved, is kept saved. Genuine Christians will also differ from each other on matters of eschatology.[39]

Besides the differences listed above, John Stott includes:

- *Baptism.* "Should we baptize only adult believers or their infants as well? And by immersion or affusion?"
- *Women.* "Are all ministries open to them or does Scripture-preclude certain functions? What does masculine 'headship' mean, and how does it apply today?"
- *Sanctification.* "What degree of holiness is possible for the people of God on earth?"[40]

What characterizes these issues as being non-essentials is the fact that these differences arise, as I argued in chapter one, from one's inter-

39. Koivisto, *One Lord, One Faith*, 210–11.
40. Stott, *Evangelical Truth*, 140.

pretation of Scripture through the lenses of our theological and denominational traditions and cultural backgrounds, and not because the Spirit illuminated our mind to an absolute "truth" of a particular view.

Yet I also stated that it is important to "understand how the illumination of the Spirit works in relation to non-essential doctrines," because these issues are nevertheless important for one's faith. I propose that the Holy Spirit illumines our minds to a particular view if it helps us become "better" Christians. For example, if believing in Calvinism would help one to experience a fuller sense of joy, peace, and assurance of faith, then the Holy Spirit will prompt one's conscience to hold to this theological tradition. But if, in my case, the same fruits of the Spirit work for the opposing view, the Spirit will prompt me to believe in Arminianism. I do not make this assertion based on human reason but on the principle found in the apostle Paul's discussion on sacred days and foods:

> One man considers one day more sacred than another; another man considers every day alike. Each one should be fully convinced in his own mind . . . As one who is in the Lord Jesus, I am fully convinced that no food is unclean in itself. But if anyone regards something as unclean, then for him it is unclean . . . For the kingdom of God is not a matter of eating and drinking, but of righteousness, peace and joy in the Holy Spirit. (Rom 14:5, 14, 17)

Another characteristic of non-essentials is that these views were speculated and fully developed centuries after the Apostles and early Church Fathers. This is because theology is often progressive and influenced by its surrounding historical context. The Bible would be filled with anachronisms if, for example, we were to read the Apostles debating whether believers only or infants should be baptized, whether a believer must be dunked or spring-cleaned with water! Like so many other doctrinal differences, it simply was not an issue during first-century Christianity.

THE FOURTH STEP TOWARD UNITY: ENGAGING IN FRUITFUL DISCUSSIONS

Discussions over our theological differences can turn into quite a draining and disheartening experience if the aforementioned three steps toward our unity are not properly administered or simply ignored. Fruitful and edifying discussions can blossom only if we first begin by "sorting out our terminology" and avoid misrepresenting each other's views; second, if we avoid the temptation that we can know everything; and third, if we distinguish between the essentials and non-essentials. If these steps are ignored, we will return to full-blown sectarianism:

> Matters of conviction in interpretation must be held open to discussion with others who have alternate matters of conviction. Otherwise, parochialism develops. Sectarianism attempts to persuade me that the others are entirely wrong and I am entirely right; or worse, I and mine alone constitute the true church since we have more of the truth. A healthy denominationalism means that I must discuss with my fellow pilgrims from other denominations issues we disagree on, without ridicule and with full respect to them as brothers and sisters.[41]

CONCLUSION

Sectarianism/fundamentalism is the cause of disunity within the body of Christ, while our diverse views on the non-essentials have resulted in denominationalism. Disunity is detrimental to the body of Christ, while diversity is healthy to the church. Realizing that we belong to one body and believing in the same gospel and essentials of the Christian faith, we can engage in fruitful discussions with believers who belong to different denominations or who hold to different non-essential doctrines than our own. This will be a testimony to the world that God loves us and has sent his Son into the world (John 17:23). This is what *Preserving Evangelical Unity* is all about.

41. Koivisto, *One Lord, One Faith*, 100.

3

Unity and Purity in the Church

CRAIG BRANCH

MICHAEL MEIRING HAS ASKED me to critique his contributions to this book and to share an apologetics perspective on the topic. Michael has a very important goal: to identify the issues that promote, cause, and exacerbate disunity among fellow Christians, and to chart a course to enhance unity amidst the current diversity. I agree that this needs to be a high priority for Christians individually and the church collectively.

In contrast to the historical controversies and necessary corrective actions taken by the early church councils responding to heresies like Marcionism, Montanism, Arianism, Gnosticism, and later, the Reformation response to Roman Catholicism, there have also been unhealthy schisms resulting in church splits, factions, and hundreds of denominations. But in addition to the various denominational leaders and their institutions, Michael points the finger at "especially those in the discernment ministries" (p. xiii). So let me begin by putting forth the positive and negative aspects of apologetics, especially in its application to the visible church.

THE POSITIVE AND NEGATIVE ASPECTS OF APOLOGETICS

Apologetics can be a difficult and controversial task. Having been in the apologetics ministry for thirty years, I can relate to a sad but too-often-true quip, "If you have two apologists in the same church, you'll have a church split."

There should be no doubt, though, that the application of apologetics has an important and necessary function in God's kingdom. Apologetics is a biblical imperative and has significant historical relevance. Evangelism and apologetics, though distinct, are normally joined. Apologetics is valuable for personal and corporate discernment, correction and protection, and is a helpful tool in defending and advancing the truth claims of the gospel and the Christian worldview in the face of skepticism, doubt, and alien philosophies of men (2 Cor 10:3–5; 1 Pet 3:15). Indeed, there are repeated exhortations to church leaders and Christians to beware of false teachers, to point out their errors, and to defend the faith.[1] The legitimacy of apologetics has to do with the necessity and centrality of knowing, defending, and advancing the life-giving truths in Scripture (John 8:31–32).

Indeed, Paul makes a rather curious statement regarding an apparent positive purpose that divisions can produce. He writes that, "there must be factions among you in order that those who are genuine among you may be recognized" (1 Cor 11:19).[2] So these "factions" also can serve as a divine sifting process, distinguishing and clarifying truth from error. Error may include wrong and divisive attitudes and actions amidst conflict.

But this process can be both constructive and divisive because it is administered through fallible Christians. Certainly pointing out the difference between truth and error is constructive, especially if the error produces a harmful or spiritually fatal result. Close attention and stern warnings are to be given about false teachers who "twist [the Scriptures] to their own destruction" (2 Pet 3:16), and who will exploit people, even leading them to hell (2 Pet 2:1–4). Paul even uses harsh words, calling those who pervert the gospel, "dogs" and "evildoers" (Phil 3:2). Paul calls their teachings "doctrines of demons" (1 Tim 4:1 NASB). Jesus calls them "whitewashed tombs," and "You serpents, you brood of vipers," and "ravenous wolves in sheep's clothing" (Matt 23:27, 33; 7:15). Yet Paul also tells us, when personally engaging an unbeliever or heretic, that we must be kind, patient, gentle, gracious, and respectful, not quarrelsome, and our "speech seasoned with salt" (Col 4:6 cf. 2 Tim 2:23–26; 1 Pet 3:15; Titus 3:2).

So how are these harsh words reconciled with having a gentle, gracious manner? I have come to the conclusion that when speaking or teaching in the church, notably to the body of Christ, it is important to issue a strong warning about false teachers as the level of the believers' maturity

---

1. See Matthew 7:15; 24:23–24; Ephesians 5:11–13; 1 Timothy 4:1–3, 6–11, 16; 6:2–5; 2 Timothy 2:14–15, 23–26; 4:2–4; Titus 1:9–11; 2:1; Jude 3–4.

2. Unless otherwise indicated, all Scripture quotations are taken from the *English Standard Version*.

and discernment is typically so low and the consequences so dire. But when interacting with a deceived individual, our approach should reflect the latter. Yet even then, there is a point of disengaging from a contentious unbeliever after several admonitions (Titus 3:10).

DISCERNMENT AND DOCTRINAL DIVERSITY

What about differences in doctrine among fellow Christians? More specifically, what about errors and false teaching among fellow Christians who are not trying to deceive but are just in error?

Many apologists have seen first hand the devastation and results of spiritually harmed followers of deception and error. But while we do not have an "exclusive corner on the truth," I do agree with Scripture that tells us that we can and should know the truth.[3] At the same time, we must also be people of faith, believing that God is the One who sovereignly begins that good work in us and will complete it (Phil 1:6). But God uses means to bring about that completion, and sometimes those means involve warnings and rebukes (Prov 9:8; Rom 15:14; 2 Thess 3:14–15; 2 Tim 4:2; Titus 1:13). As noted earlier, he even instructs the church to reject a factious or heretical person after a second warning (Titus 3:10). Apologists are aware that most cults did not immediately begin with fatal heresies. They began with error on contingent doctrines that later emerged into fatal error.

There *is* a place for bringing correction. Exercising discernment is necessary. Some things *are* wrong. Correction brings life and improvement, and discernment can produce growth and progress. Both are motivated by love for the Lord, for his people, and for those in error.

As evangelical Christians we claim that the inspired, infallible, and inerrant Bible reveals God's truth (Deut 29:29; Ps 119:97–105; John 17:17; 2 Tim 3:16). Yet Bible scholars, Bible teachers, and students from many different denominations and traditions (sometimes even within the same denomination) differ on some doctrines. The doctrines range from significant to peripheral. Yet they all claim to be based on the Bible. For example, there are differing views on: the end times (i.e., premillennialism, dispensationalism, amillennialism, and postmillennialism, futurism vs. preterism); forms of church government; the mode, purpose, or effect of baptism; the purpose of the sacraments; cessation or continuation of the

---

3. See John 8:31–32; Acts 20:20, 27; Ephesians 4:17–24; 1 Timothy 4:1, 6–10; 2 Timothy 2:15; 4:1–4.

miraculous spiritual gifts; the place of tithing today; women's role in the church; old earth/young earth creationism; predestination and free will; eternal security or loss of salvation; Calvinism vs. Arminianism; Christian mysticism; quietism or pietism in sanctification; the New Perspective on Paul; the Christian's or church's role in politics; Christian environmentalism; just war or pacifism; apologetic methodology; worship styles; seeker sensitive churches or traditional— and all of these differing views are among evangelicals! Although the implications of some of these doctrines are more important than others, they are not essential doctrines of saving faith.

Whereas it can be useful to truly listen to one another and to study and weigh the Scripture, to "test everything [and to] hold fast [to] what is good [or true]" (1 Thess 5:21), Christians can err in two ways: As Michael points out, we can exaggerate the importance of a particular doctrine, making acceptance a criteria for fellowship, and to respond with a condemning, critical, even arrogant attitude when addressing the issues.

THE DISCERNMENT DILEMMA

So Christians, and especially apologists, are left with a dilemma. On the one hand we are repeatedly commanded to love one another: "By this all people will know that you are my disciples, if you have love for one another" (John 13:34–35; see also 1 John 3:11, 23; 4:7–8). One of the ways this love is manifested is described by Paul who says, "I appeal to you, brothers, by the name of our Lord Jesus Christ, that all of you agree and that there be no divisions among you, but that you be united in the same mind" (1 Cor 1:10). A good example of this corrective approach is seen in Priscilla and Aquila as they heard the fervent Apollos teaching some error. They gently took him aside and taught him "more accurately" (Acts 18:24–28). They then encouraged him and his work.

But on the other hand, Paul goes on to describe and rebuke the factions that existed in the church composed of those who claimed to follow specific teachers such as Paul, Apollos, Cephas, or Christ (1 Cor 1:12). This sounds to me like the way doctrinal differences foster today's denominations. We are also commanded to "be ready in season and out of season; reprove, rebuke, exhort with great patience and instruction. For the time will come when they will not endure sound doctrine; but . . . will accumulate for themselves teachers in accordance to their own desires, and will turn away their ears from the truth and will turn aside to myths" (2 Tim 4:2–4 NASB).

Similarly, Paul believed Mark had not obeyed the Lord in an area provoking a "sharp disagreement" between him and Mark and Barnabus (who sided with Mark) and caused them to split up (Acts 15:37–39). But Paul later reconciled as he calls for him and commends his ministry (Col 4:10; 2 Tim 4:11). I believe Paul had Mark in mind when he wrote Colossians 2:12–14. Indeed, this is the crux of the matter. Two of the vital callings of the church have historically been to seek both unity and purity. How do we hold those two callings in balance (or in tension)?

The Scripture gives us analogous encounters that reinforce our concern and response. In addition to Priscilla and Aquila's encounter with Apollos, and Paul's separation from Mark and Barnabus mentioned earlier, we are given the confrontation between Paul and Peter. The books of Galatians and Romans thoroughly set forth the essential doctrine of justification on the basis of Christ's righteousness imputed to us by faith and not by or of our works. And in the context of defending that truth, Paul relates how he confronted the apostle Peter (Gal 2:11–16).

Peter had been an apostle for at least 15 years before his encounter with Paul in Antioch. He was known as one of the "pillars" of the church (2:9). He had already received the vision/revelation that God was directing him to go to the Gentiles with the gospel. He was chosen to lead Cornelius and his family to Christ, and he baptized them (Acts 10). Peter then strongly defended this action to the other apostles and brethren in Jerusalem, and even to the "circumcision party" who were critical (Acts 11:1–18). The latter were Jewish "believers" who claimed to accept Christ as the Messiah yet still insisted that believers must receive the sign of the covenant, circumcision (now baptism), and be obedient to the Law as necessary for salvation (Acts 11:2; 15:1–5).

The inclusion of Gentiles had also become a controversial issue in Antioch where Paul and Barnabus had seen many Gentile conversions to Christ (Acts 11:19–26; 13:42–49). It was at Antioch where Paul noticed that Peter was compromising the gospel message by caving in to the pressure of the "circumcision party" as he withdrew from table fellowship with Gentile Christians and remained aloof from them (Gal 2:11–12).

When Paul saw how this act influenced the other Jewish believers, and even his close friend and co-laborer Barnabus, he "opposed him [Peter] to his face, because he stood condemned." Peter's actions compromised "the truth of the gospel," in that his behavior and example compromised the fact that our justification is not based in any measure by our obedience to the Law but is through faith in Christ (Gal 2:11–21). Peter obviously received the reproval of Paul as he stood up to and corrected the Judaizers, or circumcision party, along with Paul and Barnabus at the council of Jerusalem (Acts 15:1–29).

REALIZING TWO OF CHRIST'S PRIMARY GOALS

This brings us back to the goal of this book. How can we be part of realizing two of Christ's primary goals—to bring both unity and purity to the body of Christ? What can be done to minimize divisions among Christians and foster biblical unity?

Michael begins by identifying some key factors that contribute to schism and division. He correctly points to the "sectarian" mindset that insists on requiring a broader spectrum of doctrinal beliefs beyond biblical boundaries for fellowship. Thus, for spiritual unity and fellowship, sectarianism requires uniformity on a broader range of doctrines than the biblical essentials.

Michael recommends the adoption of three levels of orthodoxy— saving, sustaining, and secondary non-essentials (p. 16). The only problem will be to get everyone to agree on the three levels. For example, I would submit that the doctrine of the Trinity and deity of Christ does sustain the "core" level doctrine of the gospel, but it is also a core or a level one essential. If one denies or adds to the gospel, or if one denies or substitutes a different Jesus or God, he is lost. The Person and work of Christ are the essentials (Exod 20:3; 2 Cor 11:3–4, 13–15; Gal 1:6–9; 4:8). That does not mean that one must thoroughly understand the deity of Christ or even the doctrine of imputational righteousness and substitutionary atonement in order to be saved, as Michael explained elsewhere.[4]

Michael also points to the problem of laying too much emphasis on the Spirit's illumination as a basis for the correctness of one's doctrinal view over all others (pp. 7–8). The issue then becomes hermeneutics or rules of biblical interpretation, which is also not without some problems.

I agree with Michael that John 16:13–15 and 14:26 are specifically directed toward the disciples and apostles who would be led by the Spirit to recall, speak, and write infallible Scripture. But I believe the exegesis

---

4. See Introduction, footnote 13.

of 1 Corinthians 2 does not restrict the Holy Spirit's teaching of truth to the gospel message only. The Spirit illumines our minds to the truth of Scripture (Eph 4:20–24), but Michael is correct that no fallible human always gets it right (1 Cor 13:12).

In my remaining space, I want to weigh in on three elements that could help to achieve more biblical unity in the church. These three elements are (1) sound hermeneutics (standards of biblical interpretation), (2) perspectivalism, and (3) tolerance, love, and unity being adopted as a high priority or command to be obeyed.

Sound Hermeneutics

Prior to the Reformation, common folk were not expected (or allowed) to be able to understand or interpret the Bible on their own. One of the changes wrought by the Reformation was the concept of "the priesthood of believers." But without a central ecclesiastical authority, individual leaders and movements developed into denominations based on their interpretations. Nevertheless, Christians *are* called to study the Scriptures as a "worker" who is "rightly handling the word of truth," for the purpose of "training in righteousness," and therefore, "equipped for every good work" (2 Tim 2:15; 3:16–17 cf. Heb 5:12–14). We are called to personally study and correctly interpret the Bible.

Michael correctly notes that many theologians and teachers use basic hermeneutical principles but can still arrive at different doctrinal conclusions. The explanation is that "our theological and denominational traditions and cultural backgrounds" lead to our diversities (p. 9). So does this mean that no one can claim any certainty of interpretation on any doctrine, or even most doctrine? Are we to accept those leaders on the theologically liberal side, and those on the postmodern side of the Emerging Church Movement who *dogmatically* affirm that one cannot make any *dogmatic* assertions of truth?

The fact of some differing interpretations—from even Bible scholars—does not negate the general perspicuity of Scripture. And difference does not affect the objective certainty of God's revelation, since the truth of Scripture is independent on anyone's ability to fully comprehend or apprehend it. But it has been my experience that when one consistently applies multiple rules of interpretation (meaning of original languages, cultural context, eternal principles, the immediate context, chapter and book context, Scripture interpreting Scripture, taking in all the passages dealing with that subject), the differences in interpretation are significantly reduced. Yes, theological and denominational backgrounds will affect interpretation, so it helps to understand those biases and therefore be better able to keep those commitments from distorting the text.

Perspectivalism

One of my life's adages ironically was written by an agnostic, John Stuart Mill, who stated, "He who knows only his own side of the case knows little of that."

God's truth is like a sphere and man passes through that sphere in linear planes. Dr. Vern Poythress wrote a book, *Symphonic Theology*, in which he affirms the absoluteness of God's revelation, while acknowledging that "our knowledge of the truth is partial. We know truth but not all of the truth" in many cases. Poythress compares God's truth to a precious jewel with several facets: "The facets are all present objectively . . . but not all facets of the jewel [truth] may be seen equally through one facet [perspective]."[5]

We must listen carefully to what other theologians are saying and examine their claims. I'm not saying that one or both parties couldn't simply be in error. I am saying that there may be perspectival differences that may contain some truth that could somewhat alter the other's conclusions. For example, we humans do not like logical tensions. In the debate between Calvinism and Arminianism, each side typically caricatures the other's position and clings to his own position tenaciously. Instead, the Calvinist and Arminian should listen to and carefully weigh the many passages presented by the other side. Inevitably, there are no real contradictions in the Bible, "a" cannot be "non-a," but there are such things as paradoxes and antinomies.[6] The Calvinist should seek to show that his

---

5. Poythress, *Symphonic Theology*, 46.

6. "Paradox: a seemingly absurd or contradictory statement, even if actually well-founded; antinomy: a contradiction between two beliefs or conclusions that are themselves reasonable." *Oxford American Dictionary and Thessaurus* (New York, NY: Oxford University Press, 2003). *Webster's New Twentieth Century Dictionary* defines an antinomy as "the unavoidable contradiction to pure reasoning which human limitations produce" (The World Publishing Company, 1970). As J. I. Packer articulates in his classic work, *Evangelism and the Sovereignty of God*, an antinomy is "an appearance of contradiction . . . seemingly irreconcilable, yet both undeniable . . . put down the semblance of contradiction to the deficiency of [our] own understanding" (Packer, *Evangelism*, 18, 21). See also Isaiah

view does better justice to human freedom and responsibility, and the Arminian should seek to show that his view results in a credible biblical exposition of divine sovereignty.

There are other tensions or paradoxes we accept. For example, the commands of Scripture are imperatives or absolutes, but historical contexts appear to relativize certain imperatives (e.g., 1 Cor 11—women's head coverings; 1 Cor 7:1—"it is good for a man not to marry"). And we are responsible to personally interpret (Acts 17:11). Yet we should give great weight to time honored historical creeds and councils. Another tension is that the Bible is both divine and human. Evangelicals believe the Bible was totally superintended by God so that it is preserved, inspired, and infallible. Yet it was not written by robots but by fallible humans with real choices, different personalities, and life experiences (which is an example of the paradox-antimony of divine responsibility and human responsibility).

Unity as a High Priority

Finally, we must intentionally raise the priority of biblical unity to be a higher biblical imperative than to "get it exactly right" on non-essential doctrines. If it is indeed the Holy Spirit who guides us to truth, then let us minimize the quenching of the Spirit by being led by the Spirit and his fruits (Gal 5:16–25). In so doing we can advance both unity and purity to the body of Christ.

55:9 and Romans 11:33–36.

4

Spiritual AIDS and Unity

L. L. (DON) VEINOT JR.

Watch out for false prophets. They come to you in sheep's clothing, but inwardly they are ferocious wolves.

MATT 7:15 NIV

JESUS, WHO, AS WAS pointed out in the introduction, prayed for the unity of his disciples, was the same person who also warned his followers to be on the look out for false prophets. In the Jewish culture of the first century, the group Jesus was addressing had memorized definitions of false prophets and false teachers. According to Deuteronomy 13:1–5, a false prophet was one who may make true predictions but who leads others to worship false gods. And according to Deuteronomy 18:20–22, a false prophet was one who had just one prophecy fail. The mandate to guard ourselves and the flock (Acts 20:28–30) is a theme in the Old and New Testament. In fact, much of the New Testament was written to correct false teaching and direct church leadership, as well as to urge individuals to stand against and expose false teachers.

As is the case with a number of aspects of the Christian life, Scripture seems to hold unity and defense of the faith in tension. Both are clearly taught and mandated for believers. Part of the dilemma for redeemed humans is the problem of balance. Being involved in apologetics and discernment, I can understand how we can become so fixated on minute aspects of doctrine that we can miss the bigger picture. It has been said that apologists will fight at the drop of a hat, and they are more than willing to drop the hat. The result is that many pastors view apologists as mean-spirited, divisive, and more concerned about winning an argument than about the soul of the individual they are debating.

On the other hand, there are pastors and leaders who are seemingly more concerned about peace at any cost and appear to embrace and promote fraternity over orthodoxy in many cases. This causes some apologists to wonder if the pastor who is tolerating serious heresy on the "altar of getting along" is concerned about the souls of those in their charge. In these settings Christianity appears to have been redefined to say that niceness is the closest thing to godliness, and saying that someone is wrong is not nice and therefore ungodly. This tends to ramp up the rhetoric on both sides without offering much hope in the way of reconciling the two focuses. The strong draw for unity, coupled with the desire to not be seen as divisive, has also had some disastrous effects.

SPIRITUAL AIDS

As I approach this subject, it is important to know that I really believe that most pastors and elders want to serve their churches well. Pastoring is a very difficult task. Pastors are often viewed as the paid professional Christian whose job it is to grow the church and expand its "market base." They often labor for long hours doing individual counseling of various types. Moreover, they often have to "separate the children" who are often times fighting over silly issues, and attempt to bring about some sense of unity within the body. They rarely go into the ministry with visions of national notoriety or aspirations of making a lot of money. I suspect that the majority of pastors are faithful believers who are under-paid, over-worked, and under-appreciated. Very often they are expected to measure up to the celebrity pastors on radio, television, and bookstores. Of course, the congregation can see their pastor's weaknesses and strengths, but they cannot see any of the weaknesses of the celebrity pastor. They have a sort of "air brushed" appearance that few, including themselves, can actually live up to.

If it is true that most pastors desire to serve the church well, and again I believe that is so, why is doctrinal anorexia flourishing virtually unchecked in the church? According to George Barna, only nine percent of "born-again Christians" have a biblical worldview.[1] Why is biblical lit-

---

1. *Church Doesn't Think Like Jesus: Survey shows only 9% of Christians have biblical worldview*; WorldNetDaily.com, December 3, 2003, online at http://www.worldnetdaily

eracy at such low ebb? It may be because, according to Barna, nearly fifty percent of pastors do not have a biblical worldview.[2] I would suggest there is a spiritual AIDS in the church: *Acquired Ignorance of the Doctrines of Scripture*. This developed largely as a result of ecumenism, which began taking root in the 1960s and 1970s in an effort to diminish denominational differences and bring about a better sense of unity within the body of Christ. The intentions were good. Prior to that movement, it was rare for denominations to find common ground. They were not only denominationally different but acted in sectarian ways as was defined in chapter one. Each denomination viewed all of their doctrinal positions as the essential doctrines of the faith. But with the shift toward ecumenism, there was also a gradual move away from sound theology, perhaps unwittingly, which gave way to a more experiential faith. As false teaching and false teachers rose up in the church, the ability to expose them diminished for fear of forsaking unity and reverting to sectarianism. The more or less standard response became "God will take care of them," or "I just eat the meat and spit out the bone." The assumptions were that there was meat, it wasn't rancid, and they could tell which portion was bone. As we look at the current statistics we can see where this has taken us.

The church of Martin Luther's day wasn't very different in this regard, although for different reasons. The church was largely biblically illiterate, and the lay-people were simply following the leadership. The Reformers challenged false teachings with the Scriptures in areas of fundamental, essential doctrines. What began as an important battle and turning point in the church over time, degenerated as various reformers began holding that their particular views on less clear doctrine was God's final word on the matter. We see this in areas such as the mode and time of baptism:

> In Early January 1525 a Baptismal disputation was held with Zwingli. The Radicals were no match in debate with the eloquent Zwingli, and the Council (having already made up its mind to support Zwingli), condemned the Radical's bible meetings and antipaedobaptist views. In defiance, on the 25 January, the Radicals formed the first congregation of believers through baptism (by pouring).

.com/news/article.asp?ARTICLE_ID=35926

2. *Only Half of Protestant Pastors Have A Biblical Worldview*; The Barna Group, Ltd., 2004, online at http://www.barna.org/FlexPage.aspx?Page=BarnaUpdate&BarnaUpdate ID=156.

Following this, in response to the rapid spread of baptist beliefs and practice through the canton, the Zurich authorities forbade the teaching, or even association of anyone with the Anabaptists on pain of imprisonment or banishment. By 1526 the Council decreed the death penalty by drowning for persistent Anabaptists. On the 5th January 1527, Felix Manz was the first of many Anabaptists to be drowned.[3]

"IN ESSENTIALS, UNITY; IN DOUBTFUL MATTERS, LIBERTY; IN ALL THINGS, CHARITY"

These words, which are often attributed to Augustine, most likely originated with Rupertus Meldenius in AD 1627 in response to this sort of behavior:

He condemns the pharisaical hypocrisy, the philodoxia, philargia, and philoneikia of the theologians, and exhorts them first of all to humility and love. By too much controversy about the truth, we are in danger of losing the truth itself. Nimium altercando amittitur Veritas. "Many," he says, "contend for the corporal presence of Christ who have not Christ in their hearts." He sees no other way to concord than by rallying around the living Christ as the source of spiritual life. He dwells on the nature of God as love, and the prime duty of Christians to love one another, and comments on the seraphic chapter of Paul on charity (1 Cor. 13). He discusses the difference between necessaria and nonnecessaria. Necessary dogmas are (1) articles of faith necessary to salvation; (2) articles derived from clear testimonies of the Bible; (3) articles decided by the whole church in a synod or symbol; (4) articles held by all orthodox divines as necessary. Not necessary, are dogmas (1) not contained in the Bible; (2) not belonging to the common inheritance of faith; (3) not unanimously taught by theologians; (4) left doubtful by grave divines; (5) not tending to piety, charity, and edification. He concludes with a defense of John Arnd (1555–1621), the famous author of "True Christianity," against the attacks of orthodox fanatics, and with a fervent and touching prayer to Christ to come to the rescue of his troubled church (Rev. 22:17).[4]

Rupertus, like so many before and after him, desired a peaceful unity among believers. What he saw was that at a little over 100 years since

---

3. Good, "The Anabaptists and the Reformation," 29–34.

4. O'Donnell, "A common quotation from 'Augustine'?" 32–40.

the beginning of the Reformation, the doctrinal battles still raged on and seemed to invade every aspect of church life and thinking. To be sure, some battles needed to be fought while others, although important, should have been viewed as "nonnecessaria." Things haven't changed from then until now, and in fact these issues have been with us since the beginning of the church. Much of the New Testament was written to correct false teaching, bad behavior, *and* disunity. Many times the disunity and bad behavior were the result of bad teaching and arrogance. First Corinthians 12:4–6, 14 and 27, which were cited in chapter one of this book, came on the heels of chapter one through eleven where the Apostle had taken the church to task for their infighting over unbiblical things (1:10–17). He went on to demonstrate that the division was the result of a lack of understanding God's message about the cross (1:18–2:5). They misunderstood the Holy Spirit's ministry (2:6–16). The result was a lack of spiritual growth (chapters 3 and 4). Although they were sharply divided in areas that were not in Scripture or were of secondary importance, they were united in looking the other way about sin and behavior, which is clearly addressed in Scripture (chapters 5 and 6).

As Paul addressed these and other issues, he stated in chapter 11, "For there must be also heresies among you, that they which are approved may be made manifest among you" (v. 19 KJV). False teachers and false prophets will continually attempt to infiltrate the church or will rise up from within, and those who are grounded in the essential doctrines will "be made manifest" and are to guard the flock (Acts 20:28–30). In making his case, Paul sometimes used satire (2 Cor 11:8); other times he demonstrated his righteous anger (Gal 5:12). In these instances, Paul's language was clearly divisive and as such was used to divide the truth from falsehood in order to bring about repentance and correction to the church.

ALL IN THE FAMILY

Michael Meiring is correct in chapter one in pointing out that there is decidedly a difference between unity and uniformity. All too often the divisions within the church are not over essential doctrines but over secondary, yet important, ones. Michael attempts to delineate between "essentials" and "non-essentials" in chapter two, but perhaps we might think about these as two different categories. Category one I will call "essentials," and are the things God did and does. This would include creation of the universe from nothing, creating Adam from the dust of the ground, causing the Red Sea to part and the water to stand up, incarnating as fully human and yet remaining fully God, dying for the sins of the world and yet resurrecting himself to secure and offer salvation to all who call upon his name.

Category two would be the "mechanics of the faith." How does God work in his creation? How did he create everything from nothing? He doesn't tell us. How did he make water stand up? He doesn't tell us. How does predestination and free will work? The infinite God doesn't give a comprehensive answer, and in many cases he provides no details to finite humans of how it all works. Category one is main, plain, and clear. For category two we may have some hints or even our own ideas, but the answers are a bit murky and in some cases dependent on other things that are less clear. For example, one's view of the end times question (the mechanics of how God will or has fulfilled the book of Revelation) is largely dependent on one's view of ecclesiology (how and when God began the church or whether the church has replaced Israel). So the answer to the mechanics of the end times is dependent on the answer to the mechanics of the church.

Michael is correct in chapter one that "moderate" fundamentalists may project an attitude of "*We* are right, and *they* are wrong" (p. 4). However, that isn't necessarily a bad thing, nor does it have to lead to "a rejection of involvement with other believers who do not accept their views." This is where tolerance comes in. Tolerating someone else's view assumes we think they are wrong and we are right, but that is how it actually is in family relationships. We love our family members in spite of our disagreements. Perhaps we may even snicker at something they believe but will defend them to an outsider because they are family.

As children grow up, marry, and begin their families, they may modify or even begin a new set of practices. In terms of the church we call that "Orthopraxy" (right practice), which is different than "Orthodoxy" (right belief). Orthopraxy is the mechanics of the faith rather than the essential beliefs of the faith. One segment of God's family has different practices and understandings of living out the faith than another. An example from my family may help.

My daughter Jennifer married her husband Jason. They have three children, Nathan David, Zachary Lee, and Sarah Diane. Nathan, when he was five, called me one day and during the course of the short conversation he asked me if I take showers in the morning or night. To his surprise, I told him that I take baths, not showers. He was positively horrified, and in his most concerned voice told me, "Men take showers and women take baths. Bappa (grandpa), you must start taking showers." The practices in his home are different than the practices in our home. The practices or mechanics are not what makes us family. The family is the result of our birth and lineage. We are connected, for better or worse, through things that are beyond our control. The sectarianism that was outlined in chapter one would demand that, in order to be viewed a man by my grandson, I must change my cleanliness mechanics to showering rather than bathing.

Another helpful part of holding to a view that we believe is correct, while regarding someone else's as perhaps wrong, is the realization that we are talking about things that are less than clear in Scripture, or perhaps not there at all and are arrived at through implication and conjecture rather than explicit statements from God. We can hold on to these beliefs but should do so a bit loosely so that God doesn't have to break our fingers to shake those beliefs loose from us if we are wrong.

CONCLUSION

Living in unity is a relational statement. It denotes that we have a common bond at the core, but it doesn't demand that we believe all things identically as we move out from the core. Unlike Zwingli, paedobaptists do not and should not drown immersionists over this disagreement. We are inextricably connected through the blood of Christ and are therefore family. The differing views on the mechanics of the faith add richness to the faith that would otherwise not be there. Some years ago Pastor Chuck Swindoll spoke about his exasperation with his wife who saw things differently than he did, which led to her doing things differently than he did. No matter how much he tried to correct her, she continued seeing and doing things differently. One day God brought him to the realization that if they both saw everything the same, one of them was unnecessary.

PART TWO

Diversity in Non-Essentials

5

Divine Sovereignty and Human Freedom:
A Calvinist View

COLIN MAXWELL

INTRODUCTION

WHAT DO WE MEAN *by Calvinism?* Many *de facto* Calvinists care little for the name of Calvinism. I have no hang-ups over titles and only use them here for convenience sake. Calvinism consists of much more than its teachings on salvation, which usually come packaged under the five-point TULIP acrostic.[1] Calvinism embraces *all* the fundamental doctrines of the evangelical faith. Theological controversy casts us into the position of giving special (although balanced) emphasis to the doctrine of the sovereignty of God. Calvinism simply lets God be God. It sets forth God as he reveals himself in his word. It puts God on the throne and sinful man into the dust. Perhaps more than any other school in Christianity, Calvinism refuses to let any flesh glory in God's presence. B. B. Warfield simply defined Calvinism like this: "We should begin, I think, by recalling precisely what Calvinism is. It may be fairly summed up in these three propositions. Calvinism is (1) Theism come to its rights. Calvinism is (2) Religion at the height of its conception. Calvinism is (3) Evangelicalism in its purest and most stable expression."[2] The latter point echoes a thought by A. A. Hodge that "The last issue must be between Atheism and its

---

1. Total Depravity, Unconditional Election, Limited Atonement, Irresistible Grace, Perseverance of the Saints.

2. Warfield, "Calvinism Today," 32–34.

45

countless forms and Calvinism. The other systems will be crushed as half rotten ice between the two great bergs."[3]

What do we mean by human responsibility? The Bible teaches that people are in bondage to their sin (John 8:34; Rom 6:16) and that only the gospel truth can make them free (John 8:32). Calvinists differ with other Christians over the extent of this bondage. We hold that it extends even to the human will. A person will always follow the dictate of his heart (Prov 23:7). And since his heart is in bondage to sin (Jer 17:9), his will cannot be considered to be free. It cannot be in bondage and have freedom at the same time. If the will is to be considered free, then it is only free *from* righteousness (Rom 6:20). Curtis Hutson sums up the shallow non-Calvinist position on depravity when he writes, "The Bible teaches total depravity, and I believe in total depravity. But that simply means that there is nothing good in man to earn or deserve salvation."[4] Calvinists believe that people are responsible for their sin and the actions that flow from it. People cannot blame God's sovereignty nor avoid giving an account for what their sinful heart leads them to think, do, or say.

SOVEREIGNTY AND RESPONSIBILITY: THE PROBLEM OF RECONCILIATION

Here we run into a problem. How can God hold people responsible for something they cannot do? Or if they need grace to do it, why does God give such grace only to some people and not to "all without exception"? How can God ordain certain events and make them certain, including sinful events, and yet punish those sinful participants for their actions? Where does divine sovereignty end and human responsibility begin? Can such a distinction be made? When do we sit back and attribute something to God? When do we keep going and feel responsible ourselves?

Calvinists admit the problem of reconciliation. John Calvin certainly viewed the tension between the two as a potential problem. In his comments on the Son of Man going to die as it was written of him, and yet it being better for his betrayer (Judas) had he never been born, Calvin admitted, "Those two principles, no doubt, appear to human reason to be inconsistent with each other, that God regulates the affairs of men by his Providence in such a manner, that nothing is done but by his will and

---

3. Quoted by an unnamed writer in Hodge, *Princeton Sermons*, xv.

4. Hutson, *Why I Disagree*, 11.

command, and yet he damns the reprobate, by whom he has carried into execution what he intended."[5] In the same place, he refers to those commentators who "sought to avoid this rock." Calvinistic theologian, Louis Berkhof, urged restraint from "assuming a contradiction here, even if we cannot reconcile both truths."[6]

Unfortunately, some Calvinists—and here they really become hyper-Calvinists—have cut through the knot and simply denied the doctrine of human responsibility. They deny that the non-elect have any duty to repent or believe the gospel and that it is unsafe to draw any absolute and universal rules from the examples of Apostolic preaching as set forth in the brief records possessed.

The various Reformed confessions of faith practically admit to the problem of reconciliation. Although they set forth the glory of the doctrine of God's absolute sovereignty, they do (to quote the *Westminster Confession of Faith*) warn of the need of handling it with "special prudence and care."[7]

Non-Reformed apologists have also pointed out the difficulties of reconciling the two principles. This is of course a natural thing to do on their part. John Wesley published his infamous sermon entitled "Free Grace" against Calvinism and pointed out:

> In either case, your advice, reproof, or exhortation is as needless and useless as our preaching. It is needless to them that are elected; for they will infallibly be saved without it. It is useless to them that are not elected; for with or without it they will infallibly be damned; therefore you cannot consistently with your principles take any pains about their salvation. Consequently, those principles directly tend to destroy your zeal for good works; for all good works; but particularly for the greatest of all, the saving of souls from death.[8]

According to Wesley, it is inconsistent to urge sinners to repent and believe the gospel if you believe that all the elect will be infallibly saved in the end. In other words, you cannot reconcile God's sovereignty and human responsibility. "Needless" and "useless" are both strong indictments. Significantly, when George Whitefield made a spirited reply to

5. Ibid. John Calvin's comments on Matthew 26:24.

6. Berkhof, *Systematic Theology*, 106.

7. *Westminster Confession of Faith*, ch 3, no 8.

8. Wesley, *Wesley's Works*, 7:418.

Wesley's sermon, he tackled this point, making it a priority to denounce this "sophistry."[9]

Other non-Reformed writers have constantly sought to build upon the point to oppose Calvinism. Among the moderns, John R. Rice wrote, "I believe hyper-Calvinism is not a Bible doctrine but is a perversion by proud intellectuals who thus may try to excuse themselves from any spiritual accountability for winning souls."[10] (Rice defined hyper-Calvinists as those who believe in the TULIP doctrines.) Laurence Vance, upon whom Dave Hunt and others have relied heavily, seeks to expose those whom he brands as "closet Calvinists." Why does he call them such?

> . . . they keep their Calvinism, like the proverbial skeleton, in the closet, lest their church members take to heart what their pastor believes and stop visitation and giving to missions. This is not to imply that these men disdain visitation and missions—quite to the contrary—they might be ardent about visiting and support many missionaries. They are woefully inconsistent; they never resolutely employ their theology.[11]

There's the charge. It is "woefully inconsistent" for a man whose theology magnifies the sovereignty of God to engage in door-to-door evangelism or support missionaries.

So there is a difficulty in reconciling the absolute sovereignty of God and the absolute responsibility of man. However, this is different from saying that it is an impossibility. We may make some kind of an attempt by looking at both doctrines in a little more depth.

DIVINE SOVEREIGNTY

The Bible states positively that God is absolutely sovereign. The very designation "God," along with the meaning of his personal name (Jehovah, i.e., the Self-Existent One), will not allow us to admit anything less than absolute sovereignty. God cannot share or limit his sovereignty with any other, for he will not give or share his glory with another (Isa 42:8). God works only within the confines of his own attributes. To do otherwise would be to deny himself (2 Tim 2:13). He positively declares himself to be King.

---

9. Letter from George Whitefield to John Wesley, available online at http://www.spurgeon.org/~phil/wesley.htm.

10. Rice, *Hyper Calvinism*, 5.

11. Vance, *The Other Side of Calvinism*, 52.

He is King of glory, of saints, of Israel, of all the earth, and ultimately King of kings and Lord of lords.[12] Whatsoever he has pleased, that he has done (Ps 115:3). He says that his counsel shall stand and that he will do *all* his will (Isa 46:10). Surely as he has thought, so shall it come to pass, and as he has purposed, so shall it stand (Isa 14:24).

The same truths are also expressed negatively. There is *no* wisdom nor understanding nor counsel against the LORD (Prov 21:30). It is not that none take counsel against God's will (Ps 2:2)—such rebellion simply does not succeed because none can stay God's hand nor query what he is doing (Dan 4:35). If any issue is of God, then it is useless to fight against it, for fighting against God is evidently a non-starter (Acts 5:39). When Paul dealt at length with the doctrine of God's sovereignty, he simply answered the jibe "Who hath resisted his will" with the rebuke: "Nay but, O man, who art thou that repliest against God?" (Rom 9:19–20).[13]

The sovereignty of God extends to the doctrine of creation. It is God who, in the beginning, created the heavens and the earth in the space of six days, and all was "very good." He created all things out of nothing by the sheer power of his word (Heb 11:3). It is he that decided to make man in his own image and yet a little lower than the angels (Gen 1:26–27; Ps 8:5). Every last difference in the various things created came about because God exercised his sovereign control. Nothing was left to chance. Why were all things thus created? To bring glory, honor, and power to a worthy God who created all things for his own pleasure (Rev 4:11).

The sovereignty of God extends to the doctrine of providence. Every last event has the stamp of God's sovereignty upon it. God works all things after the counsel of his own will (Eph 1:11). There is not an event, no matter how big or small, that takes place without either his knowledge or command. Kings reign through him because the powers that be are ordained of God (Prov 8:15; Rom 13:1). The king's heart is in God's hand, and God turns it whichever way he pleases (Prov 21:1). The weather is in God's hand. To the natural eye the wind blows where it wills (John 3:8), but the eye of faith in God's sovereignty discerns that even the stormy wind fulfills his word (Ps 147:8). How could it not when it is God who commands and raises this wind (Ps 107:25)? It would be amiss of him to

12. See Psalm 24:7–10; Revelation 15:3; Isaiah 44:6; Psalm 47:7; 1 Timothy 6:15 respectively.

13. Unless otherwise indicated, all Scripture quotations are taken from the *King James Version.*

promise continuity of the seasons if it were not infallibly in his hand to deliver (Gen 8:22).

It is not merely generals or politicians who draw and redraw borders, but ultimately it is God who has determined the times before appointed and the bounds of men's habitation (Acts 17:26). Although people may not know the day of their death (Gen 27:2), such is known and appointed by God (Heb 9:27). This knowledge gives rise to the popular saying that "we are immortal until our work on earth is done." Until that day arrives, a thousand may fall at our side and ten thousand at our right hand, but death cannot touch us (Ps 91:7). It was this blessed thought that steeled Peter on the night before his supposed execution and Paul during his awful shipwreck (Acts 12:6 cf. John 21:18; Acts 27:22–25). Even though they were staring death in the face, they knew their appointed hour had not arrived.

As for small matters, the result of the lot being cast into the lap—or in modern parlance, the roll of the dice or the flipping of a coin—is ordained of God (Prov 16:33). No cheaply bought sparrow can fall to the ground without the Father's permission, while all the hairs of our head are numbered (Matt 10:29–30). Spurgeon certainly believed that God's sovereignty extended to the very small and almost insignificant things:

> I believe in predestination, yea even in its very jot and tittles. I believe that the path of a single grain of dust in the March wind is ordained and settled by a decree which cannot be violated; that every word and thought of man, every flittering of a sparrow's wing, every flight of a fly, the crawling of a beetle, the gliding of a fish in the sea, that everything, in fact is foreknown and foreordained.[14]

Both good and evil things are ordained of God. We need not wonder at (nor supply examples of) good things being ordained of God. However, that evil deeds are equally ordained will certainly raise some eyebrows. Yet any serious Bible student knows that this ought not to be the case. God makes the evil man for the day of evil (Prov 16:4). He makes the wrath of man to praise him and restrains the rest so that their plans do not come to pass (Ps 76:10). Joseph was not denying the historical fact that his brethren wickedly sold him into the sorrows of Egypt, but ultimately it was God who planned their course of action (Gen 50:20). Obviously

---

14. Spurgeon, *Metropolitan Tabernacle Pulpit*, vol. 15.

both parties operated on a different wavelength—a point that must be emphasized to avoid confusion, but the wording is clear.

It makes little difference whether God is said to positively ordain or allow. He has power to do both. He withheld Abimelech from sinning (Gen 20:6), and we may safely assume that he withholds us from sinning when we pray, "Lead us not into temptation, but deliver us from evil" (Matt 6:13). But we also read: "Now therefore, behold, the LORD hath put a lying spirit in the mouth of these thy prophets, and the LORD hath spoken evil against thee" (2 Chr 18:22). Whatever God does he had always planned to do, and the event then was never uncertain but sure. This does not make God the author of sin because God cannot be tempted himself with evil nor does he so tempt any man (Jas 1:13). But he does ordain sinful events to take place right down to the very last details. His sovereignty extends even to the wicked deeds that take place.

God's sovereignty extends to the realm of salvation. Here is the real battleground and the place where Calvinism often becomes a stumbling block to many. Yet it ought not be, and will not be if we carry the same principles acknowledged elsewhere into this most vital of all domains.

God's sovereignty extends to the provision of salvation, that is, the provision of the cross and all the events that surround it. Jesus Christ did not die by chance. Neither was his death some kind of dispensational afterthought with God, avoidable by Israel receiving her King. Jesus Christ came specifically to give his life a ransom for many (Matt 20:28). No man, including Pilate, had power to take Christ's life from him, but he would lay it down of himself (John 10:18). There was a determination to put Christ upon the cross (Luke 22:22), yet this determination did not belong to Pilate because we read that the Roman Governor was determined to let him go (Acts 3:13). Rather, this determination belonged to God: "For of a truth against thy holy child Jesus, whom thou hast anointed, both Herod, and Pontius Pilate, with the Gentiles, and the people of Israel, were gathered together, For to do whatsoever thy hand and thy counsel determined before to be done" (Acts 4:27–28). It was this truth that Peter preached so effectively at Pentecost: "Him, being delivered by the determinate counsel and foreknowledge of God, ye have taken, and by wicked hands have crucified and slain" (Acts 2:23). The words could not be clearer. Who delivered Christ up to the cross? We may argue that it was Judas Iscariot and the Israelite people along with Pilate and the Romans. They are all indicted with the crime. Yet Romans 8:32 says that God did not spare his own Son but delivered him up for us all.[15] The question here is not, "Are these things palatable?" but when searching the Scriptures, "Are they so?" (Acts 17:11)

God's sovereignty extends to the application of salvation, that is, the bringing of lost sinners into pardon. Again the battle rages hottest in this part of the battleground, and yet why should it? No person, unless they believe either in a frustrated God or in the universalist gospel,[16] can believe that God purposed to save every last human being. There were people in hell when Christ died. No amount of blood would ever bring them out again (Luke 16:26). Although others of us wade knee deep in gospel tracts (I exaggerate) and can easily and freely access gospel services, Christian bookshops, and church websites, and talk at length to loving, enthusiastic, dedicated, and extremely gifted Christians, some people will live and die in heathen darkness without hearing the gospel or even the name of Jesus once. Is this not so? Why is it so? Although we may attribute some of the opposition to evangelistic activity to Satan (1 Thess 2:18) and can rightly mourn the failure of lazy, self-seeking, professing Christians, we do read of the Spirit forbidding some evangelistic work (Acts 16:7). Ultimately, we must answer the question as to why some get the opportunity to repent (which they promptly reject) and others don't (and would have repented had they gotten the opportunity) with the words of the Lord Jesus, "Even so, Father: for so it seemeth good in thy sight" (Matt 11:26). Such an answer excuses no one but recognizes God's sovereignty in the application of salvation.

Jesus tells us that, although many are called, few are chosen (Matt 22:14). These chosen ones are they whom God foreknew and predestined and will infallibly call, justify, and glorify (Rom 8:29–30). They were not chosen because they were any better than those who were passed by. They were not chosen because God foresaw a positive response to the gospel. This is putting the proverbial cart before the horse. If God was going to save certain individual sinners, then he was *always* going to save them. We cannot impose a time-centered event upon an eternal decision. It is illogical to say that God foresaw an event and then ordained it to happen. If it were foreseen then it was certain, whether God ordained it or not.

God saves the sinner purely on the basis of his grace. This grace extends not only to desiring to save the sinner (election) and providing

15. The Greek word for "delivered" is the same word translated as "betrayed" so often in relation to Judas Iscariot.

16. Universalism teaches that everyone will eventually be saved at the end of the age.

salvation (Calvary) but also the application of it. Not everyone has saving faith (2 Thess 3:2). On the one hand, they do not want it, loving darkness rather than light (John 3:18–19). On the other hand, they were not given it, and this withholding of faith is the sovereign prerogative of God.

Let those who cry "Unfair!" remember that God is not obliged to save *anyone*, and therefore, he is not obliged to save *everyone*. I have never heard anyone question God's refusal to save the angels who sinned and who will be tormented forever in the lake of fire (Matt 8:29). Is this fair? Must those poor sinful creatures be left without a fighting chance of being saved? Why should God only purpose to save sinful humanity and not fallen angels? The same argument applies to those who will live and die without Christ. Although they (like the angels that sinned) will righteously suffer for their wicked deeds, God has also chosen to pass them by. There were many widows in Israel, all with great needs, yet to none of them was Elijah sent but to the Gentile woman in Serepta. There were many lepers in Israel, all with great needs, yet Elisha was sent to none of them but to Naaman the Syrian (Luke 4:25–27). This is the sovereign choice of God and is consistent with every last attribute he has, including his holiness, justice, goodness, and truth. It is in the context of his sovereignty that "they sing the song of Moses the servant of God, and the song of the Lamb, saying, Great and marvellous are thy works, Lord God Almighty; just and true are thy ways, thou King of saints" (Rev 15:3).

HUMAN RESPONSIBILITY

The Bible states that people are also absolutely responsible for their deeds. Here is the other side of the coin. As a Calvinist, with my belief in the absolute sovereignty of God, I have no qualms about what I must write in the following paragraphs. I am totally at ease with both great truths.

The exhortations of Scripture show man to be absolutely responsible. The Ten Commandments clearly instruct everyone as to what is acceptable and unacceptable before God. It is by these commandments that sin is defined (1 John 3:4). The book of Proverbs is also a rich source of valuable exhortations, as are the parables of Jesus and also the practical passages in the epistles. The wording of Micah 6:8—"What doth the LORD require of thee?" followed by the answer, "but to do justly, and to love mercy, and to walk humbly with thy God"—clearly shows responsibility.[17] God is not

---

17. Similar words appear again in Deuteronomy 10:12.

exhorting us to do something without expecting us to do it. This shows that we are responsible.

The rewards set before man to induce him to obey show him to be absolutely responsible. What blessings follow the one who obeys God! Their provision recognizes that humans are not blocks of wood or puppets but people who are capable of weighing the advantages of obeying God. David's willingness to fight Goliath was preceded by an inquiry into what reward was promised (1 Sam 17:26). John Gill observes that David was not interested in the reward for its own sake, but to observe the necessity (i.e., the *obligation*) of someone taking up the challenge.[18] When people do God's will, he subsequently awards them accordingly, with some receiving greater rewards than others, but all hearing him say, "Well done thou good and faithful servant" (Matt 25:14–23).

The warning of Scripture likewise shows man to be absolutely responsible. Not only are we exhorted and actively encouraged to obey God, but we are also warned of the consequences of not obeying. The words "Take heed" appear again and again. The illustration of the watchman refers to those who do not heed to his warnings: "Then whosoever heareth the sound of the trumpet, and taketh not warning; if the sword come, and take him away, his blood shall be upon his own head" (Ezek 33:4). In such a case, the watchman is specifically relieved of any responsibilities, and the responsibility belongs solely to the citizen (Ezek 33:7–9).

The indictments of Scripture likewise show man to be absolutely responsible. Those who do not obey God, ignoring both the rewards and the warnings, are treated as being guilty. They are stigmatized by many and varied names. They are called "sinners against their own souls" (Num 16:38)—a term that oozes with the thought of responsibility. They are indicted as "rebels" (Num 17:10)—again the thought of responsibility to keep the law. The charge of "fool" is sometimes laid against people who evidently should have known better (Ps 14:1; Luke 12:20). Charges are laid against the children of Israel whom God "rose up early and sent them prophets," and yet they did not obey (Jer 7:13). Perhaps the most harrowing reading is in Proverbs 1:23–30 where God lists a whole series of indictments against the people. He called, he stretched out his hand, he counseled, he reproved, and yet they would not listen but mocked and refused. Every action of God showed how responsible the people were,

18. Gill, *Gill's Commentary*, 179–80.

and each act of disobedience being listed and written in the Bible shows that these indictments carry great force. This could not be if people were but puppets or blocks of wood.

The punishments of Scripture likewise show man to be absolutely responsible. That there is a day of judgment and a Judge appointed—none other than Jesus Christ himself (Acts 17:31)—with witnesses for the prosecution and the angels of God to round up the guilty (Heb 11:7; 1 Cor 6:2; Matt 13:41–42), all show that humans are responsible for their sins. If they perish, they do so in their own corruption (2 Pet 2:12). People who are lost will bear the stigma of their sins for all eternity. Thus, it is the fearful and unbelieving, the abominable and murderers, the whoremongers and sorcerers, the idolaters, and all liars that shall have their part in the lake of fire (Rev 21:8). Of course, there are often (although not always) punishments here on earth for sin. The wicked do not always prosper and some reap what they sow here on earth (Gal 6:7–9). The book of Proverbs gives us useful insights into the temporary harvests that adulterers (5:1–13), drunkards (23:29–35), and sluggards (6:6–11), among others, are left to reap.

Both saints and sinners alike confess to being responsible before God. Even the heathen with no Bible has a conscience that condemns sufficiently, leaving them without excuse (Rom 2:15). How much more, then, the person who has a Bible? The saints of God have often expressed their deep feelings of guilt and responsibility.

We have all come into God's presence rejoicing in that great fountain opened up for sin and uncleanness because we are conscious that we have failed in our responsibility to walk with God (Zech 13:1). With all their belief in God's sovereignty, David, Isaiah, Job, and Paul still saw themselves as sinful beings.[19] Even though it was determined by God that Jesus Christ should be both denied and betrayed, Peter still "wept bitterly" (Matt 26:75) and Judas still confessed, "I have sinned in that I have betrayed the innocent blood" (Matt 27:4)—a fact seized upon by the Apostles when they said, "Judas by transgression fell" (Acts 1:25).

The unconverted who confessed freely that they had sinned included Pharaoh, Balaam, Achan, and King Saul, whose full confession includes these words: "I have sinned . . . I have played the fool, and have erred exceedingly."[20] It is also significant that the rich man in hell never once

---

19. See Psalm 51; Isaiah 6:5; Job 42:6; Romans 7:24 respectively.

20. See Exodus 9:27; Numbers 22:34; Joshua 7:20; 1 Samuel 26:21 respectively.

complained of any injustice (Luke 16:19–31). Again, the shutting of every mouth in the day of Judgment shows that the whole world perceives its responsibility and is indeed guilty before God (Rom 3:19).

QUESTIONS AND OBJECTIONS

Establishing both doctrines from the Scriptures is not hard to do. However, it does open several questions for debate.

If man is responsible, is he able to perform what God requires of him? People were originally able to perform what God required of them, but now they lack the ability because of sin. However, such loss of ability does not relieve them of responsibility before a holy God. A murderer, who cannot stop murdering, will always face the full brunt of any human law. God commands everyone everywhere to repent, even though the natural man can only produce a worldly sorrow unto death (Acts 17:30; 2 Cor 7:10). A true, saving repentance is only produced when the goodness of the Lord actually leads people into it (Rom 2:4). Such repentance is evidently not given to everyone, and no one, because of sin, has any right to it. A similar scenario arises when we remember that God requires us to keep his law perfectly, even though there is no one upon the earth capable of doing so. Such failure constitutes sin and is the immediate cause of damnation (1 John 3:4; Ezek 18:4).

What then can a man, who can do nothing, do? Although sinners cannot save themselves nor naturally produce true repentance and saving faith, experience shows us that they can give attention to the means of grace. This is why we conduct gospel meetings where we sing hymns, exhorting them to come to Christ, and where we read the Bible publicly and preach persuasive and evangelistic messages. Every time a sinner cares to attend these meetings, he stands in judgment of those who never care to darken the door. The man with the withered hand couldn't raise it in his own strength, but he responded to the call of Christ to do it (Matt 12:10–13). Let sinners get to the places where Christ is known to be—among the Bible preaching people of God—and it may be that God will grant them repentance (2 Tim 2:25). The Christian ought to impress upon the sinner his responsibility to repent and believe the gospel (Mark 1:15) and to encourage him with the many sweet gospel promises to do so. Sow the seed and water it, even though it is God alone who gives the increase (1 Cor 3:7).

Why evangelize if God is going to save his elect anyhow. God isn't going to save his elect "anyhow." He has not only ordained the end but the means thereto. These means are evangelism. If we don't evangelize, someone else will or God will make the very stones of the street cry out (Luke 19:40).

Does Calvinism stunt or encourage evangelism? Has Calvinism a history of evangelism? There is no reason why a strong belief in the sovereignty of God should hinder evangelism. That God has ordained a great number of sinners who will be infallibly saved through evangelism is surely the spur we need to get out, knock on doors, and pass out tracts. Many years ago a Calvinist preacher, Bennett Tyler, preached from Acts 18:9–10 where God told Paul that he had many people in Corinth. The main lesson from the sermon was this: "The doctrine of election: the only ground of encouragement to preach the gospel to sinners."[21]

Many of the greatest soul winners in the history of the church were solid Calvinists (e.g., Whitefield, Spurgeon, McCheyne, etc.), while the man known as the "Father of Modern Missions," William Carey, was a solid Calvinist. The Calvinistic churches from the time of the Reformation have always been missionary minded. Calvin sent out young men (later martyred) for missionary work in Brazil.[22] If a missionary is someone who leaves his own country to preach the gospel in another, then Calvin himself may be considered a missionary. The mind of the Calvinist evangelist is perhaps summed up in the words of one of Horatio Bonar's hymns. Bonar himself was a noted soul winner, especially among the young. As well as penning a very penetrating book called *Words to Winners of Souls*, he wrote these words in his famous hymn: "Go labour on while it is day/ The world's dark night is hastening on/Speed, speed thy work, cast sloth away/It is not thus that souls are won."

Is the concept of the free offer of the gospel consistent with Calvinism? Yes. God commands that the gospel be preached to every creature (Mark 16:15). Most Calvinists believe with Calvin, "The gospel is to be preached indiscriminately to the elect and to the reprobate: but the elect alone come to Christ, because they have been taught of God."[23] George Whitefield sought to explain the reason for this to a rather belligerent John Wesley:

> And since we know not who are elect and who reprobate, we are to preach promiscuously to all. For the Word may be useful, even

21. See Tyler, *The Doctrine of Election*.
22. See Simmons, *John Calvin and Missions*.
23. Calvin, *Commentary on Isaiah*, 2:413.

to the non-elect, in restraining them from much wickedness and sin. However, it is enough to excite to the utmost diligence in preaching and hearing, when we consider that by these means, some, even as many as the Lord hath ordained to eternal life, shall certainly be quickened and enabled to believe. And who that attends, especially with reverence and care, can tell but he may be found of that happy number?[24]

Along with all the rest, Calvinistic preachers are happy to proclaim, "whosoever will may come," and they are content to leave the results of such preaching to the sovereign purposes of God.

Doesn't the Calvinist concept of the sovereignty of God negate prayer? Why should it? God ordinarily accomplishes all his purposes through various means, and he often brings things to pass through Christians praying to that end. Even though he knows what we need before we ask, he still wants us to ask; and even then, he is answering before we call (Matt 6:8ff; Isa 65:24). In E. M. Bounds's book, *Power through Prayer*, many of those named as great examples of praying saints were also noted Calvinists. Why should I pray to God if he is limited, one way or another, in his sovereignty and cannot deliver?

If Calvinism is indeed evangelicalism come to its own, as claimed above by Warfield, what are its aberrations? With apologies to those who hate being saddled with labels, especially when we are being somewhat general, we may divide the aberrations into two main camps:

The first camp is *Arminianism*. The error of Arminianism is that it tends to elevate humankind, especially their ability beyond what is written, and to limit the sovereignty of God. It seems that the sinner has more power in this matter of salvation than God. God appears to wait, relatively helplessly in the wings, while the sinner decides to have him or not. Although I don't view Arminianism as *another gospel,* as some tend to, it is certainly a weakening of the gospel. Thankfully, when Arminians pray that God will graciously intervene and save the lost, they are being more consistent with Calvinism than their Arminianism.

The second camp is *hyper-Calvinism*. These folk may hold high views of God's sovereignty, but they effectively deny human responsibility. They disallow the free offer of the gospel and deny that the non-elect sinner has any duty to repent or believe the gospel. People may only hope that the gospel is for them if they can discern evidence of being one of the elect.

24. Letter from George Whitefield to John Wesley.

This leads sinners to look within rather than look away to Christ. The obvious danger is that people will linger on the very doorstep of heaven and not enter in. At least the Arminian with the true Calvinist, on the basis of the free and indiscriminate offer of the gospel, will exhort the sinner to enter in and be saved.

We may summarize the three positions like this: Arminians believe that God has ordained the means of salvation but not the end. Hyper-Calvinists believe that God has ordained the end but not the means. The true, biblical Calvinist believes that God has ordained both the means and the end. And so he evangelizes with full faith that God's word will not return to him void but *will* accomplish that which he pleases and *will* prosper in the things whereto he sends it (Isa 55:11).

CONCLUSION

If you were looking for an attempt to reconcile God's sovereignty and human responsibility, then you will doubtless be disappointed. *I never even tried* to reconcile them. Such attempts are usually self-defeating. It is best to state both doctrines as they stand. If we attempt to reconcile them, then the likelihood is that we will dilute them, and that serves no cause. If we stand by the old maxim that salvation is all of grace and damnation is all of sin, then we will be kept on the theological straight and narrow.

The writer has trawled through many anti-Calvinistic books and websites. Some are well written and fair in their criticisms, while others display the greatest ignorance of the subject they are purporting to expose and correct. Such caricature happened in Calvin's own day, causing the great Reformer to say, "If you will attack my doctrine, why not at least show candor enough to quote my own language."[25] The main caricature of Calvinism, in its relationship to human responsibility, tells us that Calvinists believe that men are mere puppets whose strings are pulled by a sovereign God and there is nothing they can do about it. The "Fundamental Baptist World Wide Mission Position on 5 point Calvinism" actually employs the term "robot" three times in their page long criticisms.[26] Hopefully, my essay will serve to help debunk this caricature once and for all.

25. Calvin, "Secret Providence of God," 29.

26. "Five Point Calvinism: The Position of Fundamental Baptist World-Wide Mission," available online at http://www.biblebelievers.net/Calvinism/kjcalvn1.htm.

An Arminian Response

Michael J. Meiring

WHAT A SPLENDID ESSAY on Calvinism! Pastor Colin Maxwell portrays an exalted view of God's sovereignty while attempting not to diminish human responsibility. As a "Classical Arminian," I agree with much of what he has written. For example, I agree that sin's bondage "extends even to the human will." As I state in my essay, James Arminius believed in total depravity when he wrote, "In this state, the free will of man towards the true good is not only wounded, maimed, infirm, bent, and weakened; but it is also imprisoned, destroyed, and lost."[27] Thus, I agree with Colin that Hutson's non-Reformed definition of total depravity is "shallow."

Having said that, I can't help but feel that Colin's opening paragraph on the definition of Calvinism is equally shallow. He quotes a definition from B. B. Warfield that says much but reveals little. I could equally define Arminianism into those three propositions as listed by Warfield. Rather, as a former Calvinist, I would have simply defined Calvinism as a theological system that is built on the premise that God "from all eternity did, by the most wise and holy counsel of His own will, freely, and unchangeably ordain whatsoever comes to pass."[28] And according to the Calvinist systematic theologian, Louis Berkhof, God's decree to foreordain "whatsoever comes to pass" is eternal, efficacious, and unconditional; it is not based upon

---

27. Arminius, *The Writings of Arminius*, 1:526.

28. *Westminster Confession of Faith*, chap. 3, no. 1. Elsewhere, Colin writes that this "is in many ways the root doctrine of Calvinism" ("Some of the hard things of Calvinism explained to those who wish to learn more," available online at http://www.corkfpc.com /hardthings.html).

God's foreknowledge of future events.[29] It is at this point, as I will now show, where the whole system of Calvinism collapses, proving to be inconsistent and detrimental to the character of God's goodness and justice.

THE CALVINISTS' PROBLEM OF RECONCILIATION

Aware that there is a problem to reconcile the Calvinian view of God's sovereignty with human responsibility, Colin lists some of the concerns that have been raised. For example, he asks, "How can God ordain certain events and make them certain, including sinful events, and yet punish those sinful participants for their actions?" (p. 46) To answer this question, Colin says that he will make "*some kind of an attempt* by looking at both doctrines in a little more depth" (p. 48).[30] However, toward the end of his article he unapologetically admits, "If you were looking for an attempt to reconcile God's sovereignty and human responsibility, then you will doubtless be disappointed. *I never even tried* to reconcile them" (p. 59). What is going on here? Why does Colin say that he would make an attempt to reconcile them, only to later acknowledge that he never even tried to?

I too hold to the "old maxim" that salvation is all of grace and damnation is all of sin, but that doesn't make me a Calvinist. The "old maxim" in fact has nothing to do with the Calvinists' "problem of reconciliation." The problem has rather to do with their view that God unconditionally foreordains our actions, even sinful ones, and yet holds us responsible for them. One way to approach this dilemma is to simply claim that it is an antinomy. In other words, both statements are true, although they may *seem* contradictory. J. I. Packer advocates this approach when he wrote:

> What should one do, then, with an antinomy? Accept it for what it is, and learn to live with it. Refuse to regard the apparent inconsistency as real; put down the semblance of contradiction to the deficiency of your own understanding; think of the two principles as, not rival alternatives, but, in some way that at present you do not grasp, complementary to each other.[31]

Colin also seems to advocate this approach when he says, "It is best to state both doctrines as they stand. If we attempt to reconcile them, then the likelihood is that we will dilute them, and that serves no cause" (p. 59).

29. Berkhof, *Systematic Theology*, 104–7.

30. Emphasis mine in *italics*.

31. Packer, *Evangelism*, 21.

Yet if we state both doctrines as they stand, from the example provided by Colin in 2 Chronicles 18:22, his argument may look like this:

(A)   God foreordains sinful actions, including the sin of lying.

(B)   The prophets of Ahab lied.

(C)   The prophets are responsible for lying.

As one can see, premises B and C are not contradictory and are thus compatible, but not A and B, or A and C. Ahab can only be held responsible for his choice of action *if he could have chosen otherwise*. But he could not have chosen otherwise because of A.[32]

To be honest, I don't blame Colin for not attempting to reconcile the two doctrines because the issue here is not whether God has sovereign control over everything that happens, but whether God positively ordains (not merely allows) a sinful action to take place so that a person could not have done otherwise, even though he will still be held accountable for that sinful action.

CALVINISM'S INCONSISTENT CASE FOR GOD'S SOVEREIGNTY

In dealing with the issue of God's foreordination of evil events and actions, Colin states, "It makes little difference whether God is said to positively ordain or allow" (p. 51). Actually, it makes all the difference in the world; otherwise I would still be a Calvinist today! The reason I left Calvinism was because of its view that God doesn't merely *allow* evil to take place, but that he actually *positively* ordains it.[33] This, in my view, makes God

---

32. A few details of 2 Chronicles 18:22 and its surrounding context must be noted in order to disprove the Calvinian notion that God ordained, or causally determined, the prophets to sin by lying. First, it was a spirit (probably a demon) that enticed the prophets to lie (v. 20). Secondly, it is true that God decreed the day of Ahab's death by allowing the lying spirit to entice Ahab, through his prophets, to attack Ramoth Gilead. But at the same time, we cannot ignore the fact that God sent the prophet Micaiah to warn Ahab of what he had seen, viz. the conversation between God and the lying spirit (v. 18). This no doubt implies a gracious act of God in allowing Ahab to make the choice: Either to trust the word of the Lord and not attack Ramoth Gilead, or to believe the lying prophets who will lead him to his certain death. And finally, while God "decreed disaster" for Ahab (v. 22b NIV), this decree was no more efficacious than the decree to bring disaster upon the city of Nineveh—which was later overturned (Jonah 3:4 cf. 3:10).

33. Or to put it into philosophical terms, God *causally determines* sinful actions.

out to be the author of sin even though I am fully aware that Calvinists do not believe this.

Yet by using the language of "allowance," Colin (along with other Calvinists such as R. C. Sproul) seems to suggest that sinful actions are foreordained only in the sense that God *permits* them to take place.[34] But if God permits or allows evil to take place, then it must logically follow that God *foreknew* that it would take place. Is Colin then saying that God's foreordination of evil is based on his foreknowledge? He seems to deny this when he says, "It is illogical to say that God foresaw an event and then ordained it to happen" (p. 52). Of course he would have to say this; otherwise, he would be contradicting the main premise of Calvinism, viz., God's foreordination of "whatsoever comes to pass" is unconditional and not based on his foreknowledge. The Calvinist, G. K. Beale, wrote, "God's actions would be unjust if they were responses conditioned by the creature."[35] In other words, Calvinism argues that what God decrees (and that is everything) is not dependent on human actions. God does not *react* to human actions, but rather, he *causes* them.

To state it positively, Calvinists believe that God's foreknowledge is based on his foreordination, or as William Lane Craig said, "God knows what will happen *because he makes it happen*."[36] Loraine Boettner said that God foreknows what will occur because he has, according to his good pleasure, "freely and unchangeably foreordain[ed] whatever comes to pass."[37] In other words, God foresees all events and actions *because* they have been fixed and rendered certain according to his good pleasure—"the great first cause," to quote Boettner.[38]

So when Colin states that God *allows* sin, but at the same time agrees with his tradition that human actions are fixed and set—not according to God's foreknowledge of them but according to his good pleasure—then for all intent purposes Colin's usage of terms such as "allow" is misleading and inconsistent.

34. R. C. Sproul wrote, "God must have foreordained the entrance of sin into the world. That is not to say that God forced it to happen or that he imposed evil upon his creation. All that means is that God must have decided to *allow* it to happen" (Sproul, *Chosen by God*, 31). Emphasis mine in italics.

35. Beale, "An Exegetical and Theological Consideration," 152, quoted in Cottrell, "The Nature of the Divine Sovereignty," 103.

36. Craig, "Middle Knowledge," 135. Emphasis mine in italics.

37. Boettner, *The Reformed Doctrine of Predestination*, 46.

38. Ibid.

CALVINISM'S INCONSISTENT CASE FOR HUMAN RESPONSIBILITY

In building a biblical case for human responsibility and accountability, Colin states, "God is not exhorting us to do something without expecting us to do it. This shows that we are responsible" (p. 53–54). Colin thus speaks of God raising up prophets to call and counsel sinners to listen and obey him. However, another inconsistency then appears within his tradition if Calvinism states, on the one hand, that God "expects" us to repent and believe in Christ, and yet on the other hand, states that God is "withholding" saving faith from those whom he did not elect to salvation before the creation of the world. It appears, in the words of I. Howard Marshall, that in the Calvinian scheme of things:

> [God] gives a man the precept "believe in Jesus," and at the same time by his decretive will he resolves that this man is not one of the elect and therefore cannot obey his preceptive will . . . it makes God out to be hypocritical, offering freely to all men a salvation that he does not intend them all to receive. Certainly, on the human level, all who wish to respond to the gospel can respond; nobody who wants to respond is excluded. But on the divine level, when we look "behind the scenes" at what God is doing, he is doing one thing with his right hand and another with his left.[39]

Perhaps seeing the inconsistency here, and in answer to those who cry "unfair," Colin responds, "God is not obliged to save *anyone* and therefore he is not obliged to save *everyone*" (p. 53).[40] I agree that God is not obliged to save anyone, but I do know that God is "not willing that any should perish, but that *all* should come to repentance" (2 Pet 3:9) and that he "will have *all* men to be saved, and to come unto the

---

39. Marshall, "Predestination in the New Testament," 137.

40. Colin also answers the "unfair" objections to unconditional election by the following challenge: "I have never yet heard anyone question God's refusal to save the angels who sinned and who will be tormented forever in the lake of fire (Mt. 8:29). Is this fair?" Yes it is. The difference is that the celestial beings who chose to follow Lucifer did so *consciously*, whereas in the case of human beings, we are born as infants (albeit with a sinful nature) not consciously knowing the difference between right and wrong until an age of accountability. As Walls and Dongell point out, in Aquinas' view "angels, as purely spiritual beings, have an immediate grasp of truth. As such, an angel has such clarity of understanding that when he makes a choice, it is unchangeable" (Walls and Dongell, *Why I am not a Calvinist*, 180). In light of this clear difference, God provides fallen human beings, which is everyone, the chance to receive salvation, but not the fallen angels who were never created as infants.

knowledge of the truth" (1 Tim 2:4).[41] These verses are problematic for Calvinists because if God wills the salvation of all—and we know that all will not be saved—then God's will can be thwarted.[42] So Calvinists solve this "problem" in one of two ways: Either (1) God truly desires, out of his benevolence, that all should be saved (i.e., his *preceptive* will), even though it is not his elective purpose to save all (i.e., his *decretive* will). Or (2) "all" does not refer to every individual person but rather to classes or groups of people. However, (2) does not hold water because groups are made up of all individuals. And (1) is extremely puzzling and illogical because God desires that all should be saved, and yet he withholds his saving grace from them.

Here is an illustration to show the inconsistency between the Calvinian view of unconditional election and their view of people's responsibility to repent and believe in Christ: Imagine there are five deaf children who are unable to hear their father's call to get out of the sea as there are sharks approaching them. So the father shoots into two of his children a dart containing a solution that enables them to heed his call to come. However, for some unknown "secret" will of the father, he decides to withhold the solution from his other three children. But at the same time, he still desires *and even expects* them to come when he calls! According to Calvinists, God beckons all people, desiring and expecting them to come, while knowing full well that they cannot unless he enables them. Then why does God bother to call them?[43]

---

41. Unless otherwise indicated, all Scripture quotations are taken from the *King James Version*.

42. Fortunately, as an Arminian I do not have to believe in a "frustrated God" or in universalism, as Colin supposes, in order to believe that God wills the salvation of all men. In my essay on Arminianism, I answer the Calvinists' argument that Arminians portray a frustrated God when we say that God's will can be thwarted.

43. Here I do not dispute Colin's argument that the "free offer of the gospel [is] consistent with Calvinism." I do believe that Calvinists offer the gospel freely to everyone because, as he points out, they do not know who the elect are. However, I strongly reject Colin's label of Arminianism as an "aberration" of evangelicalism. An "aberration" has been defined as an "error in some important way, such that the doctrine or practice should be rejected and those who accept it held to be sinning" (Bowman Jr., *Orthodoxy and Heresy*, 115). Who in their right mind would accuse John Wesley, C. S. Lewis, D. L. Moody, and Billy Graham of sinning because they held to Arminianism? The evangelical faith is grounded in the gospel of Jesus Christ, and not on the doctrine of predestination.

AGREEMENTS WITH CALVINISM

I would like to close my rebuttal on a positive note by listing two major agreements Classical Arminians have with Calvinists. The first, as I've mentioned above and included in a quote from Arminius, is that we *do* believe in total depravity—in that man's will is in bondage to sin; they are "dead in trespasses and sins" (Eph 2:1).

Second, as an Arminian I would agree with Colin that God "saves the sinner purely on the basis of his grace" (p. 52) and that sinners "cannot save themselves" (p. 56). A sinner is justified (declared right) before God by faith, not by works. Yet Colin believes that the Arminian view of conditional election—that God predestines to eternal life those whom he foreknows will have faith in Christ—makes faith a meritorious work. In one of his other articles, Colin wrote, "To make faith the *condition* of election to eternal life is to effectively make it meritorious."[44] But how can faith be regarded as meritorious when Paul clearly states, "to him that worketh not, but believeth on him that justifieth the ungodly, his faith is counted for righteousness" (Rom 4:5)?[45] In fact, one Calvinist writer has said, "We are not to think that since we are saved by faith, therefore faith is something meritorious. Faith is like the act of a beggar in stretching out the hand to receive my gift."[46] This sounds very much like James Arminus who said, "A rich man bestows, on a poor and famishing beggar, alms by which he may be able to maintain himself and his family. Does it cease to be a pure gift, because the beggar extends his hand to receive it?"[47] It is a rhetorical question. According to Arminius, faith is bestowed by "Divine grace"; the act of faith is thus not meritorious.

Discussions like this will hopefully bridge the gap between Calvinists and Arminians who are believers in the same Christ and trust solely in the grace of God for our eventual glorification. And so I extend the right hand of fellowship to all Calvinists, including my brother in Christ, Colin Maxwell.

---

44. Maxwell, "Some of the hard things of Calvinism."

45. I have also explained in my essay on Arminianism that we believe that faith is a gift from God.

46. Pieters, *Facts and Mysteries of the Christian Faith*, 167, quoted in Fisk, *Election and Predestination*, 29.

47. Arminius, *The Writings of Arminius*, 1:365–66.

Counter Response

Colin Maxwell

Michael's graciousness in all my dealings with him, both privately and in this book, is greatly appreciated and extends to my short reply to his criticisms of my essay on Calvinism.

Michael's keen eye spots a contradiction on my part when I first declare my attempt to reconcile divine sovereignty and human responsibility, but only to confess later that I failed to even try. I will resist the temptation to exploit the opportunity for a sophist's answer. Suffice it to say that ultimately I believe that *both* doctrines should stand as stated and not be diluted in any way. One doctrine should not be preached at the expense of the other.

I made the charge of aberration in the sense of *"deviation from a straight line."* By the same definition, I would expect Michael, as an Arminian, to view my Calvinism in the same way. No offense was intended and none taken on my part if applied to me, although, naturally, I would dispute it.

Calvinists charge Arminians of making faith a work because *their theology* makes faith the *cause* of God's salvation as opposed to the *channel* that brings it. The Arminian gives himself grounds to boast that his faith, coupled with God's grace, has ultimately made the difference between him and the lost. The Calvinist is happily robbed of such boasting and can only marvel at the electing love of God, which granted him faith in the first place. I am not suggesting that Arminians spend their days praising themselves, but their theology certainly allows them room to do so. We are thankful that the vast majority of Arminians who don't engage in such a thing are better than their doctrine.

It is regrettable that the whole concept of the sovereignty of God in relation to the cross has not been discussed more in this debate. There is no mention of it at all in Michael's response, and hardly more than a footnote in his essay, yet I gave a whole section to it in my essay. It is still a logical absurdity to say that God foresaw a response and then ordained it to happen. If God saw it happen beforehand, then it was going to happen, whether God foreordained it or not. If God merely used the outcome that he knew would come to pass, then the cross is reduced to being an adaptation on God's part. I grant that the water here is deep for everyone, but to my mind the Calvinist position gives more satisfactory answers.

In his response, Michael uses the illustration of a father saving only some of his five deaf children from sharks in the sea. Although he calls, desires, and expects them all to come, he only sends a dart with a solution enabling two out of the five to hear him. The illustration explains that the reason for this decision to withhold the solution from the other three lies in the "secret will" of the father. Michael then makes the application that this is effectively what Calvinism teaches, and he asks the question, "Why does God bother to call them?" (p. 65)

The illustration, however, is fatally flawed because it takes no account of the fact that human beings are sinfully responsible for their own deafness. They are not innocent swimmers in a shark-inhabited ocean. To legitimize the illustration, you would have to say that the law forbade swimming in this particular ocean on the pain of death and that large notices and vigilant lifeguards warned faithfully of the danger. Yet the three children who were left to perish deliberately went into the water and did not want to come out. They perished solely because they were stubborn lawbreakers who ignored all the warnings and reaped what they sowed. The two were saved, not because they were any better than the other three, but because the father chose to save them from their rebellious ways. Yes, it's true that the reasons why God saves some, enabling them to come while leaving others in their sins, lies within himself. The Lord Jesus dealt with this issue in Matthew 11:20–27 and happily resigned any unanswered questions to the sovereign purposes of God. "Why bother to call them?" Because such reveals the love of God, which admittedly stops short of salvation but is nevertheless much more than they deserve. It also renders them without excuse and magnifies his grace in the salvation of those he does save.

Calvinists and Arminians must agree to disagree on these matters. We are usually willing to tolerate in others what we would not tolerate among ourselves. Obviously I cannot recommend that Arminian churches cleave to their Arminianism, but I would recommend Calvinist churches to hold fast to their doctrine, provided it is balanced, and resist any attempts to water down their perceptions of the gospel. Even though Michael rightly points out that Warfield's statement—Calvinism is the purest and most stable expression of evangelicalism—is not an argument, it is true, as I trust I have sufficiently proved in these exercises.

6

Divine Sovereignty and Human Freedom:
An Arminian View

MICHAEL J. MEIRING

INTRODUCTION

"**W**HAT AM I AGAIN?" asked my friend. "*An Arminian!*" I replied with a grin.

I suspect that many Christians have never heard of "Arminianism," although they would hold to the very doctrines as taught by James Arminius on predestination, grace, and free will.

James Arminius (1560–1609) was a Protestant theologian and pastor in Holland. During his studies, he once attended the university in Geneva and "sat under the feet" of John Calvin's successor, Theodore Beza. Upon his return to Amsterdam, a Calvinistic professor requested Arminius to "expose and refute the errors of Coornhert," who had attacked Beza's view of predestination.[1] Ironically, Arminius refuted Beza's *supralapsarian* view and favored *infralapsarianism*![2] However, Arminius later rejected the lat-

---

1. Arminius, *The Writings of Arminius*, 1:12.

2. *Supralapsarianism* is the view that God first decreed to elect some men to salvation, followed by his decree to create the world and the fall of man. *Infralapsarianism* teaches that God first decreed to create the world, and after permitting the fall, to elect some men to salvation. The problem in holding to Supralapsarianism becomes apparent, for it inevitably leads to the conclusion that the fall of man into sin was necessary, being a consequent of God's elective decree. This makes God the author of sin. Infralapsarianism doesn't fair any better. All Calvinists, *if they were consistent*, should reject it. Because if God decreed to first permit the fall and then determined to predestine an elect people, election would be based on God's foreknowledge of the fall. However, this contradicts another Calvinistic tenet, namely, that God's eternal decree is not based on his foreknowledge.

ter view as well and summarized his own sentiments on predestination, which I paraphrase:

1. Before the creation of the world, God first decreed to elect his Son to be the Savior of the World.

2. God then decreed to receive into favor everyone who would believe in Christ and remain faithful to him but to punish those who refuse him.

3. God then decreed to administer the means that were necessary for repentance and faith.

4. Finally, God decreed to save and damn particular individuals. "This decree has its foundation in the foreknowledge of God, by which he knew from all eternity those individuals who *would*, through his preventing grace, *believe*, and, through his subsequent grace *would persevere* . . . and, by which foreknowledge, he likewise knew those who *would not believe and persevere*."[3]

On the other hand, John Calvin (1509–1564) refuted the idea that election was based on God's foreknowledge.[4] Calvinists believe that, before the creation of the world, God unconditionally elected to save a certain number of individuals. God determined, by his secret will, who should receive his mercy and who should not.[5] God the Son was then chosen to die for the elect only.

---

3. Arminius, *Writings of Arminius*, 1:248.

4. Calvin wrote, "For generally these persons consider that God distinguishes among men according as he foresees what the merits of each will be" (Calvin, *Institutes of the Christian Religion*, 932). Calvin then referred to this foreknowledge of "works" view as a Pelagian error (p. 941). However, it is not clear from his *Institutes* whether Calvin ever dealt with a pre-Arminius view that election depends on foreseen faith, for Arminius would have agreed with Calvin that believers are not elected according to their merits or works, because faith is not a work, and faith is bestowed through God's preventing or prevenient grace.

5. D. Steele and C. Thomas wrote, "[God's] eternal choice of particular sinners unto salvation was not based upon any foreseen act or response on the part of those selected, but was based solely on His own good pleasure and sovereign will. Thus election was not determined by, or conditioned upon, anything that men would do, but resulted entirely from God's self-determined purpose. Those who were not chosen to salvation were passed by and left to their own evil devices and choices" (Steele and Thomas, *The Five Points of Calvinism*, 30–31).

From Calvin to Arminius

Shortly after I was converted to Christ, I became a member of a Reformed Baptist church and was taught the "Doctrines of Grace" (which is really the "Five points of Calvinism" formulated by Calvinists in 1618). However, ten years later I began to question the Calvinian doctrine of God's exhaustive divine sovereignty, which stated that God, by his divine decree, had determined and foreordained whatsoever comes to pass. The *1689 Baptist Confession of Faith* says, "God has decreed in Himself from all eternity, by the most wise and holy counsel of His own will, freely and unchangeably, all things which shall ever come to pass."[6] This decree of God also includes the foreordination of human decisions and even human sinfulness.[7]

In questioning the Calvinian view of God's exhaustive divine sovereignty, I saw huge flaws in the doctrine of unconditional election (which I hadn't seen before), especially as it related to the justice and mercy of God and the responsibility and accountability of moral agents.

Charting the Course

I wholeheartedly agree with Robert Picirilli's assessment that his "Arminian friends often do not understand what Calvinism really is, and that Calvinists often misunderstand Arminianism. The resulting arguments are often emotional rather than based on careful understanding of each other."[8]

Many fundamentalist Calvinists have grossly misrepresented the beliefs of Arminian Christians and have done so with vigor and recklessness. For example, Arminians have been accused of believing in an impotent God because we do not believe that God foreordains "whatsoever comes to pass." Some Calvinists have accused us of not believing that salvation is all of grace because we deny unconditional election. And so they dream up fanciful notions that Arminians deny the depravity of the sinner (Eph 2:1) or that our free will regenerates us! Some Calvinists have said that

---

6. Masters, *Baptist Confession of Faith*, 3.

7. Reformed theologian, John Frame, wrote, "[I]t is important to see that God does in fact bring about the sinful behavior of human beings, whatever problems that may create in our understanding. However we address the problem of evil, our response must be in accord with the great number of Scripture passages that affirm God's foreordination of everything, even including sin" (Frame, *No Other God*, 68).

8. Picirilli, *Grace, Faith, Free Will*, iii.

Arminians preach a *diluted* gospel, while others have been downright malicious by saying that we preach a *different* gospel![9]

It is therefore the aim of this essay to dispel such false notions by accurately presenting the Arminian view of God's sovereignty and human freedom in general and in the context of salvation.

FREE WILL IN THE IMAGE OF GOD

In the beginning the sovereign and omnipotent God determined to create human beings in his image: "Let us make man in our image, in our like-ness" (Gen 1:26). Man was created in the *natural*, as well as, *moral* like-ness of God. The former likeness entails the personality, which "possesses certain powers, faculties, and characteristics . . . spirituality, knowledge and immortality."[10] And concerning the moral likeness, man was created in righteousness and holiness (cf. Eph 4:24; Col 3:10).

Being created in the natural likeness of God presupposes that Adam was created with a relative amount of autonomy to rule over the lower order of creation (Gen 1:28). And being created in the moral likeness of God presupposes that he was created with the faculty or ability to either obey or disobey God. Indeed, the intellectual and moral responsibility of man is indispensable to the existence of free will.[11] Adam was intellectu-ally responsible for naming the animals; so he was free to decide what names to give them (Gen 2:19). He was also morally responsible to the LORD's command: "You are *free* to eat from any tree in the garden; but you must not eat from the tree of the knowledge of good and evil" (Gen 2:16–17).[12] So Adam was free to either obey or disobey God.

> [Human beings] are like God in the fact that they reflect his own creative agency in being able to make plans and carry them out. They have the ability to transform the creation and themselves and to act self-consciously to the glory of God . . . Human beings are able to respond (or refuse to) in love to their Creator and enter into a partnership with God . . . In the light of this possibility we must conclude that human freedom is significant and real.[13]

9. I feel it's prudent not to mention the names of these Calvinists!

10. Culbertson and Wiley, *Introduction to Christian Theology*, 156–57.

11. See Pinnock, "Responsible Freedom," 95.

12. Emphasis mine in *italics*.

13. Clark Pinnock, "God Limits his Knowledge," 147–48.

Although the image of God in all of us is corrupted and distorted because of the Fall, we nevertheless continue to reflect the natural and moral image of God (Gen 9:6; Jas 3:9). So even with an inherited sinful nature, Cain was a free moral agent who had the ability to master sin by not murdering Abel: "[sin] desires to have you, but you must master it" (Gen 4:7).

SELF-DETERMINISM AND LIBERTARIAN FREEDOM

Arminian theologians believe that humans created in the image of God are self-determining. Clark Pinnock says, "[man] has been made to reflect the personhood of God and made capable like him of self-awareness, of self-determination and of responsible conduct."[14] Culbertson and Wiley agree: "Man by his constitution is a self-conscious, self-determining being."[15]

Self-determination does not mean that our choices are made without the presence of influences. Rather, it means that our choices are made without being causally determined by those influences so that in the end we could have chosen otherwise. Jack Cottrell notes, "sometimes the will [of man] opts for a certain choice against overwhelming influences in the opposite direction (see Amos 4:6–11; Hag 1:1–11)."[16]

Likewise, libertarian freedom has been defined as a free action "that does not have a sufficient condition or cause prior to its occurrence."[17] In other words, if people are truly free, "causal conditions are not sufficient to cause them to choose or act."[18] For example, in Genesis 3 Satan had tricked Eve into disobeying God. Adam found himself surrounded by conditions that were sufficient in *influencing* him to listen to Eve; they

14. Pinnock, "Responsible Freedom," 98. Pinnock wrote this *before* he embraced Open Theism. Even so, both Open Theists and Arminians would agree that man is a self-determining being.

15. Culbertson and Wiley, *Introduction to Christian Theology*, 162.

16. Cottrell, "The Classical Arminian View of Election," 101.

17. Walls and Dongell, *Why I am not a Calvinist*, 103.

18. Reichenbach, "God Limits his Power," 102. Calvinists would disagree here as most of them hold to "soft determinism." In theological terms, this view states that nonconstraining causes influence or persuade the human's desire to freely act in the way which God has determined. John Feinberg wrote, "God can guarantee that his goals will be accomplished freely even when someone does not want to do the act, because the decree includes not only God's chosen ends but also the means to such ends. Such means include whatever circumstances and factors are necessary to convince an individual (without constraint) that the act God has decreed is the act she or he wants to do. And, given the sufficient conditions, the person will do the act" (Feinberg, "God Ordains all Things," 26).

were not, however, sufficient in *causing* him to disobey God. Satan and Eve's influence did not determine Adam's choice. Adam had the power or ability to choose otherwise (cf. 1 Tim 2:14a). Bruce Reichenbach says, "To say that a person is free means that, given a set of circumstances, the person . . . could have done otherwise than he did . . . The individual is the sufficient condition for the course of action chosen."[19]

Consider also Joseph's brothers who plotted to kill him because they were jealous of him (Gen 37:11, 18). All the causal conditions were present to influence them to kill Joseph: Jacob had sent Joseph to Shechem (v. 14); Joseph met a man there who told him that he had overheard his brothers say that they were on their way to Dothan (v. 17); the brothers saw Joseph in the distance (v. 18). None of these conditions, however, were sufficient to cause them to kill Joseph. The brothers were free to perform the murderous plot or to refrain from it. Reuben chose the latter (v. 21).

The main premise of libertarian freedom is that humans can be free only if they *could have chosen otherwise*. Yet Calvinists adamantly maintain that the concept of libertarian freedom is not taught in the Bible. John Frame says, "Scripture does not explicitly teach the existence of libertarian freedom."[20] Perhaps it isn't *explicit*, but it is *implicit*. Here are three biblical examples:

> Then the LORD said, "If they do not believe you or pay attention to
> the first miraculous sign, they may believe the second." (Exod 4:8)

Moses was concerned that the Israelites may not believe that the LORD had appeared to him (4:1). So the LORD endowed Moses with the ability to perform miraculous signs in order to convince the people. Now notice in God's response the usage of "if" and "may," which naturally indicates the possibility that the Israelites may or may not decide to believe Moses. In other words, there would be true contingencies in the Israelites' decision-making process.

> And the LORD was grieved that he had made Saul king over Israel.
> (1 Sam 15:35)

Saul had disobeyed the word of the LORD by not destroying all the Amalekites (15:1–3). The prophet Samuel confronted Saul with his disobedience, and although the latter repented, God grieved that he had

---

19. Reichenbach, "God Limits his Power," 102.

20. Frame, *No Other God*, 124.

made Saul king (15:11). So why would the LORD grieve if, as the Calvinist says, he had causally determined Saul's actions? Moreover, Saul's response to Samuel indicates that the king could have obeyed the LORD: "*I* was afraid of the people and so *I* gave in to them" (15:24). Saul didn't say, "*God* caused me to give in to them."

> I thought that after she had done all this she would return to me
> but she did not, and her unfaithful sister Judah saw it. (Jer 3:7)

The LORD lamented that Israel would not return to him and repent of her spiritual adulteries. Again, God's words indicate there was the possibility that Israel, as a nation, could have repented. God didn't say, "I knew that she would return to me," but "I thought."[21] In other words, God expected them to choose the right way but they didn't. This verse can only make sense if the Israelites were free in a libertarian sense.

Calvinists may argue from the above passages that God was the first cause of all these choices, including the sinful ones. But if they do, then we cannot even trust our own basic moral intuitions.[22] For example, we

21. Open Theists, such as Gregory Boyd, have used this verse to mean that God "perfectly expected (but was not certain) that Israel would turn to him" (Boyd, "The Open Theism View," 25). I agree with Boyd that God expected Israel, under the circumstances, to repent. However, I disagree with him that God was uncertain of their future decision. God can still express feelings of expectancy even if he knows what the outcome will be. For example, let's say that on Day 1 God reveals to me the fact that on Day 2 a certain Christian X will not repent of his sins even when I confront him about it. On Day 3 I could say, "Even though I had foreknown that X would not repent, I thought that he would repent given the fact that I confronted him about his sin." Expectancy doesn't negate foreknowledge, and my foreknowledge didn't cause X to be disobedient.

22. Loraine Boettner wrote that God is the "great first cause" of everything that happens (Boettner, *The Reformed Doctrine of Predestination*, 46). But does God cause sinful actions? Calvinist theologian, Arthur Pink, has argued that God cannot be the author of sin because his "decrees are not the *necessitating cause* of the sins of men, but the foredetermined and prescribed *boundings* and *directings* of men's sinful acts" (Pink, *The Sovereignty of God*, 156–7). Whilst I admire Pink's determination to point out that Calvinists do not believe that God causes men to sin, his statement flatly contradicts Martin Luther who wrote, "Some people may want to know how God *produces* evil effects in us, hardening us, giving us up to our desires and *causing* us to go wrong. We ought to be content with what the Bible tells us" (Luther, *Born Slaves*, 67—emphasis mine in *italics*). And John Frame wrote that God hardened Pharaoh's heart by creating the "unwillingness" in him (Frame, *No Other God*, 69). He then explains that God can do this because men are already sinful. In fact, God deals with sinners "by causing them to become more sinful" (p. 70). I do not believe that God created the unwillingness in Pharaoh or caused him to become more sinful, for when God hardens a man's heart he gives them over to *their* sinful desires (Rom. 1:24ff).

instinctively know that when injustices take place the perpetrators were free to refrain from such immoral acts. To agree with Calvinists that everything that occurs is the result of "God's will"—what God purposed to happen—would be to strip all moral responsibility from human beings. The legal system demonstrates that moral responsibility requires free will:

> The common-sense view of freedom is libertarian freedom and . . . this view is foundational to our [American] legal system. One indication of this is that lawyers sometimes defend clients on the grounds that the accused could not have avoided his or her actions due to factors such as upbringing, emotional state and the like. Even if the defendants performed the actions willingly, they are sometimes considered less culpable if it is apparent that they could not have done otherwise. By contrast, when we are convinced that criminals could indeed have acted otherwise (the assumption of libertarian freedom), we have a clear sense of their moral responsibility and legal liability.[23]

SOVEREIGNTY OF GOD AND LIMITED FREEDOM

Arminians believe that God is sovereign and is in perfect control of everything that happens. An Arminian pastor in Zimbabwe wrote, "God is ultimately in control of all actions and events."[24] However, when we say that God is *ultimately* in control of everything, we do not mean that his control is *absolute* in the sense that he determines "whatsoever comes to pass," which would include all sinful human actions like murder, rape, and so on.

To use again the example of Joseph in Egypt: God was ultimately in control in spite of the sinful actions of the brothers. It was not God's will for them to plot a murder or to sell Joseph into slavery, but God used their sinful actions to bring about his ultimate purpose: "the saving of many lives." However, in order to accomplish his purpose, God did not bring about the evil thoughts or actions of Joseph's brothers for this would make God the author of sin (Jas 1:13). *Therefore, control does not equal causation.* Jack Cottrell says, "Rather, God controls all things in the sense that he is 'in complete control of' every situation: he monitors, supervises, plans, permits, intervenes, and prevents as he pleases through his infinite knowledge and power."[25]

23. Walls and Dongell, *Why I am not a Calvinist*, 106.

24. Roser, *God's Sovereignty*, 35.

25. Cottrell, "Classical Arminian," 103.

On the other hand, Calvinists believe that God is in *absolute* control, meaning he is the first cause of everything that happens. They make a distinction between the *preceptive* and *decretive* aspects of God's will whereby God does not will or desire that man should sin (*preceptive*), and yet in eternity past he had actually willed or purposed it to occur (*decretive*) so that "God's will is indeed the ultimate explanation of everything."[26] These two distinctions are diametrically opposed to each other.[27] Rather, the will of God can be spoken of in at least four different senses.[28]

God's Purposive Will

God is self-existent. He is not dependent on anything or anyone. On the other hand, humans depend on God for breath and life (Acts 17:25). Yet at the same time, some of God's actions—his decrees and works—are conditioned by the actions of people. In determining to create a world of free will beings, God's relationship and dealings with people would be conditioned upon their free choices.

Contrary to James White, a Reformed Baptist, this does not mean that God is impotent or that "God tries, but in the final analysis, men dispose."[29] Instead, as Nathan E. Wood, an Arminian Baptist, explained:

> It is not derogatory to His infinite sovereignty to say that [God] is conditioned in His relations with men, by the will of man. It is a condition which He chose to put upon Himself when He created men free moral beings... God acts omnipotently but always within limits which preserve man's moral freedom and responsibility.[30]

The fact that God's actions are conditioned by the free choices of his creatures is exemplified in the first eleven chapters of the book of Genesis.[31] Adam freely chose to disobey the LORD, and God responded in judgment (3:16–19). Cain freely decided to murder his brother, and

---

26. Frame, *No Other God*, 57.

27. To understand how these two distinctions are inconsistent with each other, see my quotation of I. Howard Marshall in response to Colin Maxwell's essay on Calvinism.

28. Although it is difficult to deal with each aspect of God's will separately, because they are so closely linked together, I've nevertheless tried to do so.

29. Hunt and White, *Debating Calvinism*, 39.

30. Wood, *The Person and Work of Jesus Christ*, 130–1, 157, quoted in Fisk, *Election and Predestination*, 53.

31. See Clines, "Predestination in the Old Testament," 112.

God reacted by placing him under a curse (4:10–12). The LORD saw how great man's wickedness had become, and he responded by sending a flood (6:5–7). When the people exalted themselves by building a high tower, God reacted by tearing it down and confusing their language (11:5–7). Therefore, God's purposes are a reaction or response to our free will.

Although I've only highlighted God's negative responses to men's free decisions in Genesis 1–11, the LORD's positive responses are also clearly expressed. For example, he showed mercy to Adam and Eve by clothing them and promising a Messiah (3:15, 21). In the context of redemption, God foreknew that Adam would fall, and thus in eternity past he purposed or determined to send his Son into the world he loved in order to save the world (John 3:16; Acts 2:23). Yes, God could have left us in our sin, but he loved us and by his good pleasure he purposed, in the beginning of time, to save for himself a people—both Jew and Gentile—by grace through faith (2 Tim 1:9) and to include them under the headship of Jesus Christ, receiving all the blessings of salvation (Eph 1:9–11).

A number of Calvinists have objected to the fact that God responds to human decisions. They seem to think that this somehow demotes God's sovereignty and control over everything. Boettner, for example, believes that it pictures God "as an idle, inactive spectator sitting in doubt while Adam fell, and as quite surprised and thwarted by the creature of His hands."[32] This is a clear misrepresentation of Classical Arminianism. First of all, God's reactions to human choices do not demote his sovereignty because he responds in his own way and for his own purpose (Isa 55:8).

> To suppose that any of this catches God by surprise, or even that all of these human decisions are merely human decisions which God has to make the best of now that they have happened would doubtless be contrary to the spirit of the Old Testament. But the story does not stop to point to decrees established in the dark counsels of eternity. What is important in the story of mankind, Genesis 1–11 might well be saying, is not what God has already decided to do, but with what freedom he can respond, in mercy or judgment, to man's decisions, creating good from evil and swallowing up wrath with mercy.[33]

Second, Arminians believe that God has exhaustive foreknowledge of all events. James Arminius wrote, "God foreknows future things

---

32. Boettner, *Reformed Doctrine*, 235.

33. Clines, "Predestination in the Old Testament," 113.

through the infinity of his essence, and through the pre-eminent perfection of his understanding and prescience . . ."[34] This is clearly a biblical idea (Ps 139:1–4). More important, the foreknowledge of God is crucial in understanding the relationship between God's ultimate control and his purposive will over the free actions of people. If God has exhaustive foreknowledge of all things (which he does), then he has, as Jack Cottrell says, "genuine option" to control human plans through prevention or permission (cf. Jas 4:13–15).[35] In this way, God is certainly "working out everything according to the purpose of his will" (Eph 1:11). At the same time, people are truly exercising their freedom.

God's Preventive Will

Closely related to the idea of God's *purposive* will is God's *preventive* will. In other words, in order for God to accomplish his purposes, he sometimes prevents or restrains his creatures from fulfilling their plans. At this point Calvinists may argue that we are being hugely inconsistent with our view of libertarian freedom. I don't believe this is the case because we can still make self-deterministic choices toward a plan, even if God prevents it from coming to fruition. A good example of this would be Jonah.

The LORD commanded Jonah to preach against the wickedness of the people of Nineveh (1:1). But knowing that God was gracious, compassionate, and slow to anger, Jonah didn't want to (4:2). So he tried to flee to Tarshish by boat, but the LORD caused a violent storm to arise that threatened to damage the ship (1:4). The sailors, knowing that Jonah was to blame for the storm, reluctantly threw him overboard (at Jonah's request).[36] In the end, the LORD prevented Jonah from running away, and the prophet eventually preached to the Ninevites. This story is the clearest example of divine control and human free will. In order for God to accomplish his purpose, viz., that the Ninevites receive a message of judgment, God prevented Jonah from fulfilling his plan to head to Tarshish (through the storm) and from drowning in the sea (through the fish). Yet in all of this, God did not cause Jonah's decisions and actions (and certainly not his depression).

---

34. Picirilli, *Grace,* 40.

35. Cottrell, "Classical Arminian," 103.

36. Jonah suffered from depression and suicidal tendencies (4:3).

God's Perfect Will

The term "perfect will" appears in Romans 12:2 where Paul wrote, "Do not conform any longer to the pattern of this world, but be transformed by the renewing of your mind. Then you will be able to test and approve what God's will is—his good, pleasing and perfect will."

If we have to seek God's perfect will for our lives, then it is obvious that God's will is not always done in our lives. Although we can say that God is definitely working in us, "to will and to act according to his good pleasure" (Phil 2:13), sometimes we "grieve the Holy Spirit" when we do not will and act in accordance with God's will (Eph 4:30). So we are to ask God to "fill [us] with the knowledge of his will through all spiritual wisdom and understanding . . . in order that [we] may live a life worthy of the Lord" (Col 1:9–10).

God's Permissive Will

Because of sin, people often rebel against God, resisting his will and rejecting his purpose for their lives (Luke 7:30; Acts 7:51). Their rebellious actions are outside of God's will. God doesn't cause or foreordain their disobedience, but he does permit them to reject his purposes because they are free-will beings. This inevitably leads us to the difficult issue of the "problem of evil," which is: If God is good and all-powerful, then why does he permit evil that causes suffering? Why, for example, would a good God permit a man to rape a young girl if it was in his power to prevent the tragedy?

Some have suggested that God's power is limited in order to allow humans to have free will.[37] I would argue that God has purposely chosen not to exercise his power in every situation (though he sometimes does); for we know that God could wipe out the devil and all the evil in the world in a split of a second. God could have sent his angels to destroy the rapist, so why didn't he? I will conclude this section with an extensive quote from C. S. Lewis who expressed the answer clearly:

> God created things which had free will . . . And free will is what has made evil possible. Why, then, did God give them free will? Because free will, though it makes evil possible, is also the only thing that makes possible any love or goodness or joy worth having. A world of automata—of creatures that worked like machines—would hardly be worth creating. The happiness which God designs for His higher

37. Reichenbach, "God Limits his Power," 118.

creatures is the happiness of being freely, voluntarily united to Him and to each other in an ecstasy of love and delight . . . And for that they must be free. Of course God knew what would happen if they used their freedom the wrong way: apparently He thought it worth the risk. Perhaps we feel inclined to disagree with Him. But there is a difficulty about disagreeing with God. He is the source from which all your reasoning power comes . . . If God thinks this state of war in the universe a price worth paying for free will—that is, for making a live world in which creatures can do real good or harm and something of real importance can happen, instead of a toy world which only moves when He pulls the strings—then we may take it, it is worth paying.[38]

ELECTION OF CHRIST AND BELIEVERS

Arminians believe that God the Son, before the creation of the world, was foreordained to be the redeemer of sinful humanity, chosen to become the sacrificial Lamb of God who would remove the sins of the world (1 Pet 1:18–20 cf. Luke 9:35; John 1:29). Jack Cottrell says, "This election of Jesus is the central and primary act of election. All other aspects of election are subordinate to it and dependent upon it. It is the very heart of the redemptive plan."[39]

The death of Christ on the cross was according to God's plan. Peter said to the Jews, "This man was handed over to you by God's set purpose and foreknowledge; and you, with the help of wicked men, put him to death by nailing him to the cross" (Acts 2:23).[40]

The Bible also speaks of believers being elected before the creation of the world:

> For he chose us in him before the creation of the world to be holy and blameless in his sight. In love he predestined us to be adopted as his sons through Jesus Christ. (Eph 1:4–5)

38. Lewis, *Mere Christianity*, 39–40.

39. Cottrell, "Conditional Election," 52.

40. Calvinists have taken this verse to mean that God foreordained the sinful actions of the Jews to bring about Christ's crucifixion (see Frame, *No Other God*, 73). However, there is nothing in the text which suggests that God caused the Jews to act sinfully. It says that it was God's "purpose" that Jesus was handed over to be crucified. The key word in understanding God's sovereignty and people's free actions in relation to the death of Christ is *foreknowledge*. God foreknew that in sending his Son the Jews would crucify the Messiah. In other words, God first foreknew the free acts of his creatures, and then he purposed that their wicked hands should crucify his Son, because through it, Christ's blood would atone for our sins.

The elect constitute those individuals who are "in" (Gk. *en*) Christ. They are *not* predestined to believe. Instead, they are elected to be holy and adopted as his children (which involves sanctification and glorification, not conversion). Likewise, Romans 8:29 does not say that God predestined certain individuals to exercise faith in Christ. It says that he predestined those whom he foreknew to be "conformed to the likeness of his Son" (i.e., sanctification, not conversion).[41]

The essence of God's predestining decree does not involve an arbitrary choice of causing some individuals to be saved, while leaving the majority of humankind to be damned, refusing them his enabling grace. John Wesley probably best expressed the nature of God's decree when he said, "I believe the eternal decree concerning both [the elect and the reprobate] is expressed in the words: 'He that believeth shall be saved; he that believeth not shall be damned.'"[42]

UNLIMITED GRACE

Although people have free will to choose what they will do and where they will go, they are *not* free in and of themselves to accept the offer of salvation by believing in the Lord Jesus Christ. Their will is bound in sin, and they are unable to do any good before God (Rom 3:9ff). We cannot save ourselves; we are *unable* to save ourselves. This is exactly what Jesus meant when he said, "No one can come to me unless the Father who sent me draws him . . . unless the Father has enabled him" (John 6:44, 65).

But God enables sinners to believe in Christ through his prevenient grace when the gospel is proclaimed. The gospel is known as the "message of God's grace" (Acts 14:3). Through the word and Spirit, people are convicted of their sins and commanded to repent and believe in Christ (John 16:8; Acts 17:30). Jesus died on the cross for everyone,[43] and he draws everyone to himself:

---

41. Calvinists usually appeal to Acts 13:48 which says, ". . . and all who were appointed for eternal life believed." But again, it doesn't say that God ordained the Gentiles to believe; rather, he ordained them to eternal life.

42. Picirilli, *Grace*, 54.

43. Loraine Boettner argued against the Arminian view of universal atonement because "when the atonement is made universal its inherent value is destroyed. If it is applied to all men, and if some are lost, the conclusion is that it makes salvation objectively possible for all but that it does not actually save anybody" (Boettner, *Reformed Doctrine*, 152). He further protested, "If the suffering and death of Christ was a ransom for all men

> But I, when I am lifted up from the earth, will draw all men to myself (Jn. 12:32); For there is one God and one mediator between God and men, the man Christ Jesus, who gave himself as a ransom for all men (1 Tim 2:5–6).

Indeed, the grace of God that brings salvation has appeared to all (Titus 2:11). This enabling grace is initiated by God and "He calls faith forth ... [and] when God's call awakens him, he can respond in faith, or he can resist the Spirit and go back to sleep in death [Eph 5:14]."[44] Therefore, it is by grace that people believe in the gospel (Acts 18:27).

God's grace makes faith possible for every person—"elect" and "non-elect" alike. We know, however, that not all accept the gift of salvation. Not everyone, whom the Father, Son, and Holy Spirit calls, draws, and enables, accepts the gospel. The Israelites had rejected the gospel "because those who heard did not combine it with faith" (Heb 4:2). And in Jesus and Paul's day they continued to willingly reject God's grace (Matt 23:37; Rom 11:23). Today, whenever people reject Christ, they are rejecting God's grace because Jesus is the embodiment of "grace and truth" (John 1:17). Those who have rejected Jesus have chosen to do so out of their own free will, which is why they will be held accountable for their actions in the future (2 Thess 1:8). But until then ...

> The Spirit and the bride say, "Come!" And let him who hears say, "Come." Whoever is thirsty, let him come; and whoever wishes, let him take the free gift of the water of life. (Rev 22:17)

AVOIDING MISREPRESENTATIONS

Misrepresentations of Classical Arminianism abound when Calvinists attempt to portray our views of human sinfulness and faith in Christ. Due to limited space, I will only identify three:

---

rather than for the elect only, then the merits of His work must be communicated to alike and the penalty of eternal punishment cannot be justly inflicted on any. God would be unjust if He demanded this extreme penalty twice over, first from the substitute and then from the persons themselves" (p. 155). However, Boettner has misrepresented the Arminian view, for we do not believe that the atonement is applied to all men. While Christ has certainly made atonement for the sins of the whole world (1 John 2:2), dying for all men (2 Cor 5:15), propitiation is only made effective "*through faith in his blood*" (Rom 3:25, emphasis mine in *italics*).

44. MacDonald, "The Spirit of Grace," 84, 87.

First, Calvinists state that Arminians hold to "semi-Pelagianism,"[45] the view that humans are born with a sinful nature, although they have the ability to choose Christ with some help by God's grace.[46] And so, when describing the "first point of Arminianism," our Reformed brethren postulate that, in contrast to Calvinism's first point, *Total Depravity*, we hold to *Human Ability*:

> This taught that man, although affected by the Fall, was not totally incapable of choosing spiritual good, and was able to exercise faith in God;[47] . . . his will is not enslaved to his sinful nature;[48] . . . Man therefore merely needs divine grace to assist his personal efforts. Or, to put it another way, he is sick, but not dead.[49]

Even during Arminius's lifetime Calvinists misrepresented his teachings, as he protested, "If they suppose, that I hold some opinions from which these assertions may be good consequence be deduced, why do they not quote my words?"[50] So why don't Calvinists quote his own words? I suspect that if they do, they will place their hands over their mouths as they read Arminius:

> In this state, the free will of man towards the true good is not only wounded, maimed, infirm, bent, and weakened; but it is also imprisoned, destroyed, and lost. And its powers are not only debilitated and useless unless they be assisted by grace, but it has no powers whatever except such as are excited by Divine grace. For Christ has said, "Without me ye can do nothing."[51]

Therefore, Arminians do believe in total depravity.[52] What we reject is that unconditional election is a necessary consequence of total deprav-

45. Pelagius denied original sin, believing that every person is unaffected by Adam's sin.

46. See Berkhof, *Systematic Theology*, 245.

47. Seaton, *The Five Points of Calvinism*, 7.

48. Steele and Thomas, *Five Points*, 16.

49. Boettner, *Reformed Doctrine*, 48.

50. Arminius, *Writings*, 1:365.

51. Ibid., 526.

52. Granted, there are some Arminian Christians who *say* they deny total depravity, but either they misunderstand what the doctrine is because it is so closely associated with the Five Points of Calvinism, or what they are *really* denying is the Calvinian tenet that if a sinner is not one of the elect, he is unable to believe in Christ even if he hears the gospel of grace and the Holy Spirit graciously calls him to repentance. That is why Dave Hunt, an

ity. For example, the Calvinist reasons, "If man is unable to save himself on account of the Fall in Adam being a total fall, and if God alone can save, and if all are not saved, then the conclusion must be that God has not chosen to save all."[53] Arminians reject that conclusion because we believe that every fallen person who hears the gospel can exercise faith in Christ, *but only through God's enabling grace.*

James White's following statement is thus the second misrepresentation of Arminiansism: "Why should we give thanks to God upon hearing of the faith of fellow believers [Col 1:3–4], if in fact having faith in Christ is something that every person is capable of having without any gracious enablement by God?"[54] The fact is we *do* believe that every person is incapable of having faith in Christ without any gracious enablement by God. The fundamental difference between Calvinism and Arminianism is that the former believes that God only bestows his enabling grace on those whom he unconditionally elected to salvation, whereas we believe that his grace is given to all who hear the gospel: "For the grace of God that brings salvation has appeared to all men." (Titus 2:11)

The third misrepresentation is the misconception that Arminian Christians "think that faith and repentance are in a man's power to produce."[55] Now, it is true that some Arminians reject the Calvinist interpretation that the word "gift" in Ephesians 2:8 is referring to "faith."[56] Nevertheless, James Arminius saw in the Scriptures that faith is clearly a divine gift from God. He wrote, "That act of faith is not in the power of a natural, carnal, sensual, and sinful man . . . no one can perform this act except through the grace of God."[57]

Arminian author, says he denies "human inability", and argues, "That men serve sin does not prove that they cannot repent and turn to Christ when convicted by the Holy Spirit" (Hunt and White, *Debating Calvinism*, 80). So Hunt isn't denying that everyone is born with a sinful nature (i.e., original sin), and neither is he denying that without the conviction of the Holy Spirit man is unable to repent and turn to Christ (i.e. total depravity). Unfortunately, there are scholars, like Jack Cottrell, who claim to be "Arminian", and yet they really do deny total depravity and original sin. These men however belong to 'the Churches of Christ' (a.k.a. Campbellism)—a modern-day Pelagius church (see footnote # 45).

53. Seaton, *Five Points*, 12.

54. Hunt and White, *Debating Calvinism*, 202.

55. Storms, "Prayer and Evangelism under God's Sovereignty," 316.

56. MacDonald, "Spirit of Grace," 87ff.

57. Picirilli, *Grace*, 58.

If Calvinian Christians would only avoid stating these misrepresentations of our view, then I believe that progress can be made toward our "unity in the faith" (Eph 4:13).

A Calvinist Response

Colin Maxwell

CALVINISTS CONSISTENTLY SEE ARMINIANISM as proclaiming a *diluted* gospel, although it is "downright malicious," as Michael rightly puts it, to say that they preach "another gospel." Calvinists and Arminians who accuse each other of "preaching another gospel" need to sit down and seriously think through what they are saying. Is heaven only populated by Calvinists *or* Arminians? What about two- or three-point Calvinists/ Arminians? What if the diehards are wrong in their allegations? How can they curse what God has not cursed (Num 23:8)? Although I do not want to overplay the differences between Calvinists and Arminians, we should not underestimate them either.

FREE WILL

Michael informs us that the "main premise of libertarian freedom is that humans can be free only if they *could have chosen otherwise*" (p. 75). Earlier on, he bases man's free will on the basis of God's free will: "And being created in the moral likeness of God presupposes that he was created with the faculty or the ability to either obey or disobey God" (p. 73). This is an interesting comparison, and it is here where I can show that the main premise is in fact a false one. If the will is not free unless it has the power of a contrary choice, then we must conclude that God (who is supremely free) can freely choose to sin. This view would mean that God *can* lie (contrary to Titus 1:2) and deny himself (contrary to 2 Tim 2:13).

When Calvinists talk about human free will, we mean that they are free to follow the dictates of their own heart. Although the term "free to follow the dictates" may sound like an oxymoron, it is no more so than when James talks about the "royal law" of liberty (2:8) or when David said, "And I will walk at liberty: for I seek thy precepts" (Ps 119:45).[58] Human hearts are desperately wicked, chronically biased against God, and this is reflected in everything they think or do. It is only the restraining, or better yet, the regenerating, hand of God that prevents humans from manifesting their full wickedness. Even this thought limits human freedom. The Jews were no less murderous in John 7:30 when they sought to lay hands on Christ than in John 18 when they eventually did. The only difference was the permissive hand of God, working according to his eternal plan. Christ's decreed hour had come in John 18, and the wicked Jews were *then* allowed to freely take Christ and crucify him.

I always feel that Arminians become a little vague when they speak about God being in overall control. They agree with Calvinists that nothing happens outside his divine control. This of course limits people to doing at least what God is prepared to allow them to do. However, the Bible goes even further by saying that God himself works all things according to his own will, that is, God is not merely reactionary. To me, the ultimate proof of this is the Cross of Calvary. Was this central act in our redemption a mere reaction on God's part? Did God merely foreknow that wicked men would crucify his Son and "adopted" their wicked ways to suit his overall plan? God works all things according to his own will (Eph 1:11). The natural order of the grammar suggests that God has willed what will be, and into this plan falls the free actions of people. So decided is this order of events that *God* is said to have sent Joseph into Egypt and not his brethren (Gen 45:8). Of course, this is not denying that they sent him to Egypt—the earlier narrative says they did (37:25–28)—but it does underline the fact that ultimately the plan was God's and that they were the willing players, still guilty as their consciences later proved.

Conclusion on free will: Although there is evidently some disagreement here, the *average* Christian in the pew—be they Calvinist or Arminian—will not concern himself with the *details*, which are largely philosophical in nature. They both agree in making people responsible for their actions. Even though the Calvinist is laying a stronger emphasis on God's sovereignty in the matter, he does not argue that the sinner is a pawn who is relieved of any responsibility or punishment. Calvinist evangelists readily press upon sinners the horror and responsibility of their

---

58. Unless otherwise indicated, all Scripture quotations are taken from the *King James Version.*

actions and freely urge them to flee to Jesus Christ as the only One who can wipe away their guilt.

ELECTION OF CHRIST AND BELIEVERS

John Wesley's observation, "I believe the eternal decree concerning both [the elect and the reprobate] is expressed in the words: 'He that believeth shall be saved; he that believeth not shall be damned'" is true as far as it is the *outcome* of election. The elect believe, the non-elect perish, being left without any complaint in their chosen unbelief.

I must confess surprise at Michael's statement that no one is elected to faith or to evangelical conversion (p. 83). Acts 13:48 states, "As many as were ordained to eternal life believed." God ordains not only the end but also the means thereto, which naturally covers faith. Romans 8:28–30 goes further than Michael's somewhat limited application, that it is only unto holiness. Romans 8:28–30 is a golden chain of which holiness is but a link. On the one side of the link of holiness lies glorification; on the other side lies a number of links and, working backward, these are justification, [effectual] calling, predestination, and foreknowledge. Only the foreknown are predestined, and only the predestined are effectually called, and only the effectually called are justified, and only the justified are conformed to Christ's image, and only the holy are glorified. This whole chain is given to substantiate, or at least illustrate, Paul's contention that all things work together for the good of those who love God and are called according to his purpose.[59]

It was God's purpose to have a redeemed people in heaven with himself. This has not been left to chance or man. God has ordained every last detail necessary for its fulfillment. This may be followed through in the Scriptures, for example, with the specific directions for Philip to go out to the desert to meet with the Ethiopian eunuch who "just happened" to be reading Isaiah 53 when Philip finally caught up with him (Acts 8:26–40). Again, doors for evangelistic preaching were opened while some were closed according to the divine will (1 Cor 16:9; Acts 16:7). As every saint looks back, he will readily cry out that even the preparations of his heart were of the Lord who worked in him both to will and do of his good pleasure (Prov 16:1; Phil 2:13).

---

59. Verse 28 is connected to verse 29 by the word "for."

Again, it is unlikely that the vast majority of believers will study these things in any great depth. A somewhat imperfect illustration—and aren't they all somewhat imperfect—is like driving a car. The vast majority of drivers just get in and get on with the journey. Only a relatively few take time to know the *ins and outs* of the workings of the engine. The car still goes whether we can explain its workings or not, although we are more likely to admire and appreciate the car if we understand something of the brains that have invented and improved upon it. Likewise, the great advantage in studying these doctrines, and in particular coming to the Calvinistic interpretation, is a greater appreciation of God's grace in salvation.

UNLIMITED GRACE AND ATONEMENT

Every Arminian (self-confessed or otherwise) with whom I have discussed these things has automatically assumed that the universal terms in God's word, such as "all," "world," or "every man," automatically refers to *every last sinner ever born without exception*. Michael makes the same assumption here. Yet use of any concordance shows that the Scripture does not. The same phrase may also mean "every sinner without distinction" and still be grammatically and doctrinally correct. A good example of this is found in Luke 16:16: "The kingdom of God is preached, and every man presseth into it." If "every man" presses into the kingdom of God, then "every man" is saved because those who so press in gain an entrance. It is evidently "every man" without *distinction* rather than without *exception*. The phrase "the world" carries several connotations in Scripture, meaning in certain places "all men without exception" (Mark 16:15), while in others it is a limited reference to either the unsaved wicked (John 14:17) or the elect Gentiles as opposed to the elect Jews (1 John 2:2 cf. John 11:51–52).

We know that all men (without exception) have enough light to condemn them for their sins (Rom 1:19–20; 2:15), but not all are dealt with equally in regards to the gospel. The Arminian needs to tackle the great issue of why, for thousands of years, the Gentile heathen were left without any saving light at all and why, even today, there are millions of people still enveloped in benighted countries where the religions of Islam, Hinduism, and Buddhism still abound and where true missionaries are very few. Of course, I am not arguing against missionary work. But it is a fact that God will allow many to die without hearing the simple gospel message. Are we allowed to ask "Why?" and, if so, what answer does Arminianism give?

The Calvinist is not burdened with trying to defend the thought that God must treat all men equally. And so with the Lord Jesus who spoke in similar circumstances, we take cover in the fact that it seemed good in God's sight (Matt 11:20–27). Isaac Watts even puts it into one of his hymns:

> Mortals, be dumb; what creature dares+
>
> > Dispute His awful will?+
> > Ask no account of His affairs,+
> > But tremble, and be still.+
> > Just like His nature is His grace,+
> > All sovereign and all free,+
> > Great God, how searchless are Thy ways,+
> > How deep Thy judgements be!+

There are a lot of unanswered and unanswerable questions to be asked if Christ truly died for all men without exception. For example, he must have suffered and died for those who were already in hell and would never leave that dreaded place. Did he take away their sins as he did the sins of the rest of the world (John 1:29)? If so, where did he take them and when did they come back? Did he cast all their sins into the depths of the sea (Mic 7:19)? Did he blot them out as a thick cloud (Isa 44:22)? Did he actually make propitiation for their sins (1 John 2:2)? If so, why are they in hell? Surely the same blood that has been said to cover their every other sin covers their sin of unbelief? Did Christ die for the unpardonable sin? If so, why is it unpardonable? If not, then it cannot be said that he died for all the sins of all men!

Another objection to unlimited or universal atonement is that the Arminian scheme effectively reduces the definite atonement that Christ made for definite believers to a hypothetical atonement for hypothetical believers. Christ did not merely die to make salvation possible but to *actually* save. To avoid the damnable heresy of universalism, Arminianism must dilute many of those plain statements that relate to what Christ has actually done as opposed to what he merely offers or has tried to do. For example, Romans 5:18 declares: "Therefore as by the offence of one judgment came upon all men to condemnation; even so by the righteousness of one the free gift came upon all men unto justification of life." If we insist on interpreting both the "alls" in this verse the exact same way (i.e., "all without exception"), then we end up insisting that Adam's offense led to "all without exception" being actually condemned, which is scriptural.

However, it also means that Christ's obedience and free gift also comes upon "all without exception" and actually justifies them unto life. We know that this cannot be unless we embrace universalism, which both Calvinists and Arminians reject. The Calvinist therefore insists that the second "all" is "all without distinction" (i.e., the elect) and so maintains the definite language that they shall be justified unto life. The Arminian, being tied into maintaining the "all without exception" interpretation, tampers with and weakens the definite language. In the words of a leading Arminian interpreter, "The mercy of God, in Christ Jesus, shall have its due also; and therefore all shall be put into a salvable state here . . ."[60] We move from "being saved" to merely "being found in a salvable state." The Calvinist thus monitors and reflects the fluctuating meaning of the "all" of Scripture and produces a more accurate interpretation.

Furthermore, Christ will yet achieve *all* that he set out to do—to save his people from their sins (Matt 1:21). If it was the *intention* of Christ to save the world (i.e., all without exception), then we must admit that he has failed. Although Calvinists will readily admit that there is unlimited worth and merit in the atonement to save a thousand worlds if God so decreed, we limit the *intention* to the end result, that is, to the 100 percent successful ingathering of the elect.

This great truth does not in any way infringe upon the "whosoever will" invitation in Revelation 22:17. Many of the greatest preachers and evangelists were Calvinistic in their doctrine. Belief in particular redemption never hindered Whitefield or Spurgeon or a host of others in their soul winning. Calvinists invite sinners to an atonement that knows no failure either in accomplishment or application. Should any sinner inquire sincerely or otherwise, as to whether Christ has died specifically for them, we may answer that he has died for sinners and invites all to embrace the work of the cross. Let them take God at his word, and, if they do, they will not have any future worries as to whether their sins are under the blood or not.

CONCLUSION

I have been emphasizing the fact that although these things are important to a proper and fuller understanding of the gospel, belief one way

---

60. Adam Clarke's comments on Romans 5:18 in his Bible commentary is freely available from the E-Sword edition at http://www.e-sword.net/.

or the other is not fatal to the soul. It may however affect our assurance, joy, and peace.

Another thought may be that folks on both sides, though inconsistent with their creed, are consistent with their Bible! Calvinists are really pleased to hear Arminians pray that "God will save so and so" even though they have often assured us that "God has done all that he can," and "it's up to you." I suspect Arminians quietly smile too when Calvinist evangelists go that extra mile as if everything depended on them.

Counter Response

Michael J. Meiring

I WAS RATHER DISAPPOINTED that Colin took little consideration of my philosophical and theological arguments concerning self-determination, libertarian freedom, and the Arminian view of God's sovereignty, which had constituted two thirds of my essay. In my opinion, he practically swept them away with one argument—which supposedly demonstrated a flaw in my main premise for libertarian freedom—and then focused mainly on defending the Calvinian views of unconditional election and limited atonement. Nevertheless, here are a few comments in response:

1. I am saddened that Colin believes that Arminians proclaim a "diluted gospel." Is it not obvious that the content of the gospel has absolutely nothing to do with one's view of election?[61]

2. I seriously challenge Colin's claim that "coming to the Calvinistic interpretation" of election and predestination will bring about a "greater appreciation of God's grace in salvation" (p. 91). Colin is asking us to believe that God's grace will be greatly appreciated if we believe that God unconditionally elected certain people to salvation while denying the majority of humankind access to salvation. He wants us to believe that Christ died only for the elect and we cannot confidently say to a person that Christ died specifically for him or her—only that "he has died for sinners." In all sincerity, I ask how can God's universal grace be appreciated when Colin's tradition says that a loving and merciful God withholds his saving grace from the majority of humankind whom he did not elect to salvation?

3. Colin says, "The Arminian needs to tackle the great issue of why, for thousands of years, the Gentile heathen were left without any saving

61. See chapter 2, "Toward a Biblical Unity," for a biblical definition of the gospel.

light at all" (p. 91). Holding to an "exclusivist" view of salvation, I'm not surprised that Colin would say this. The exclusivist believes that everyone who dies without hearing the gospel will burn in hell forever, as they constitute the great majority of the non-elect. Instead, I hold to an "inclusivist" view, which states that God by his grace will accept some people who never had the opportunity to hear the gospel because the Holy Spirit, through their consciences, convicted them of their sins and led them to cry out to God for forgiveness.[62]

4. Colin refers to the "golden chain" in Romans 8:30 to argue against my view that God elects believers to holiness even though the preceding verse clearly expresses this idea: "God . . . predestined [us] to be conformed to the likeness of his Son" (v. 29). In verse 30 Paul uses the past tense to express God's redemptive acts (". . . those he justified, he also glorified"). It seems that Paul is viewing the divine actions and salvific purposes of God from a perspective as seen *at the end of history*, when all believers will be glorified.[63] This explains why Paul does not highlight the human actions that are necessary for justification (i.e., faith) and glorification (i.e., faithfulness) as he has done elsewhere (Rom 5:1; 8:12–13, 17).

5. Colin either fails to understand or appreciate the distinction Arminians make between the *provision* and the *possession* of the benefits of the atonement, and so he asks regarding those who were in hell when Christ died, "Did he actually make propitiation for their sins (1 John 2:2)?" (p. 87). To answer this question, I must first emphasize our belief that the benefits of the atonement were *provided* for at the cross but is only *possessed* "through faith in his blood" (Rom 3:25). Therefore, Christ did actually make propitiation for the sins of the whole world. Second, those who were in hell while Christ died obviously had not exercised faith in God as opposed to those who did even though they lived before the incarnation (cf. Heb 11). Colin is surely not saying that pre-messianic believers did not benefit from Christ's atoning death simply because they happened to live before the incarnation!

6. Failing to see the above distinction leads Colin to assume that Arminians must embrace universalism if we interpret "all" in Romans 5:18b to mean "all without exception." In other words, the

62. For a biblical interpretation and defense of inclusivism see Sanders, "Inclusivism," 21–61.

63. For a further explanation, see James Dunn quotation in Walls and Dongell, *Why I am not a Calvinist*, 81.

one act of righteousness (by the second Adam, Christ) led to life for "all without exception." Actually, Paul writes, "the result of one act of righteousness was justification *that brings life* for all men." He does not say that it brings life *to* all men. And in the preceding verse, Paul makes a condition for one to receive this life when he writes, "how much more will *those* [not "*all without exception*"] who receive God's abundant provision of grace and the gift of righteousness" (v. 17).[64] Therefore, I actually agree with Colin that the second "all" in verse 18 means "all without distinction" or "all those who receive God's provision of grace."

7. I conclude with Colin's concluding statement: "belief one way or the other is not fatal to the soul. It may however affect our assurance, joy, and peace" (p. 89). Here I totally agree.

---

64. Emphasis mine in *italics*.

7

Infant Baptism

Eric Severson

INTRODUCTION

THE BAPTISMAL RITUAL, AS it is taken up in contemporary Christianity, overflows with rich and abundant meanings and symbolic interpretations. Like most of the religious rituals, baptism has its origins behind the mists of early human civilization. Humans are, and always have been, creatures fascinated with water; it has power to heal, to nourish, to clean, to drown, and to destroy. When Christians pause to consider the meaning of Christian baptism, they contemplate an issue that is in one sense prehistoric. People have been undergoing ritualized baptismal and water-cleansing ceremonies since long before such rituals were recorded.[1] Archaeology of the earliest civilizations in India, China, Mesopotamia, and Egypt all testify to a strong inclination of the ancients to connect water with the sacred. Ritual immersions in streams, rivers, and seas are among the first known religious practices of both nomadic peoples and early human settlements.[2] Biblical texts themselves contain a marvelous array of terrible and wonderful water-imagery. Scripture begins by testifying to the Spirit of God hovering over the chaotic "waters of the deep" (Gen 1:2), then moves through narratives of an epic flood (Gen 6–7),

---

1. Gabriel, *God of our Fathers*, 186.

2. "Although the Jews were the first to record their spiritual bathing traditions, they were not the first Semitic people to practice ritual ablutions and immersions. Their traditions are particularly indebted to other Semitic peoples, such as the Sumerians, who roamed the crossroads of Asia, Europe and Africa" (Avrigo, *Spiritual Bathing*, 33).

the crossing of the Red Sea (Exod 14), and the miraculous damming of the Jordan. In the New Testament, Jesus turns water into wine (John 2), calms the tempestuous sea, and walks on the Sea of Galilee (John 6). Paul compares the experience of the Israelites as they walked through the Red Sea with Christian baptism (1 Cor. 10:1–2). Clearly to be human, let alone a religious one, is to stand in an intriguing relationship with H_2O.

Baptism is cherished by most worshipping Christian communities as a sacrament because of an intersection of this ancient reverence for water with the particular history of Jesus Christ of Nazareth. The ritual, instituted by Jesus and resoundingly endorsed in Matthew's "Great Commission," is transformed and reconstituted through Christianity. Like most religious practices and their implications, we are not offered any scriptural treatise on baptism to simplify our theological reflections. What part of first century Jewish baptism should be retained in Christian baptismal practice? What aspects of ancient water rituals are active in the Christian sacrament? The New Testament has a few examples of Christian baptism, but how can we allow these texts to guide us to best understand this ritual without overestimating the accuracy of our own interpretative moves? As we turn to the issue of *who qualifies for baptism* we immediately encounter these and a host of other relevant questions. Determining whether infants ought to participate in the Christian sacrament of baptism will require a delicate treatment of important divergences of opinion that are mostly based on theological commitments external to the ritual of baptism.

My essay on baptism will in no manner attempt to answer all of these questions. The modest goal here is to review the well-worn arguments for and against infant baptism and present a particular theology of Christian baptism that appears to make the baptism of infants an acceptable sacramental practice. Because sincere Christians have drawn deeply entrenched lines in the sand over this issue, it seems important to think creatively about alternative ways to approach the meaning of Christian baptism. To explore the relationship between baptism and children, it is important that we reopen the complex set of biblical images that weave together our contemporary understanding of baptism. A comprehensive examination of these rich symbols would exceed the parameters of this essay, but we must at least review some of the scriptural images. The multifaceted nature of baptism becomes readily apparent as the biblical authors emphasize initiation, remembrance, mark, cleansing, rebirth, covenant, identity, and other rich concepts.

Theologian Karl Barth leads an impressive list of theologians and Biblicists with reservations about infant baptism, and their concerns must be addressed. Though these issues have been well rehearsed from both sides of the infant baptism debate, they remain the fundamental groundwork for any discussion on whether it is permissible to extend the sacrament of baptism to our youngest children.

BAPTISM AS CLEANSING

Symbolic cleansing is among the earliest and most clear images of baptism. Jewish baptism, or *mikvah,* is historically linked with the ritual cleansings that were prescribed for childbirth, healings, preparations for temple rites, and other bodily purifications. It is notoriously difficult to discuss the issue of cleansing with respect to Christian baptism. Though most Christian communities that practice baptism embrace some of the cleansing symbolism, there is little agreement on how this cleansing takes place, what the baptized person is cleansed from, and whether this cleansing is necessary for salvation. It is more than a little tricky to try to discuss how or if a person is "cleansed" in baptism without a thorough and exhaustive discussion of the various theological commitments that influence a particular understanding of baptism. We quickly discover a rather cataclysmic clash in vocabulary as we attempt to understand the nature of Christian baptism. There is simply no clear consensus in Christianity about the meaning of cleansing, grace, salvation, covenant, and so on. It really should come as no surprise that Christianity is so deeply divided over the criteria for Christian baptism.

Ritual water cleansings are frequent in both Hebrew Scripture and the New Testament. In Ezekiel we read, "I will sprinkle clean water upon you, and you shall be clean from all your uncleannesses, and from all your idols I will cleanse you" (Ezek 36:25).[3] The concept of "sprinkling" almost certainly carries with it imagery from the sacrificial process, which included the process of sprinkling blood. This language is echoed in Hebrews with clear baptismal connotations: "let us approach with a true heart in full assurance of faith, with our hearts sprinkled clean from an evil conscience and our bodies washed with pure water" (Heb 10:22). In 1 Peter

---

3. A famous and important verse follows this one: "A new heart I will give you, and a new spirit I will put within you; and I will remove from your body the heart of stone and give you a heart of flesh" (v. 26). Unless otherwise indicated, all Scripture quotations are taken from the *New Revised Standard Version.*

we learn that "baptism . . . now saves you—not as a removal of dirt from the body, but as an appeal to God for a good conscience, through the resurrection of Jesus Christ . . ." (3:21). The New Testament is far from theologically univocal on the topic of baptism; each author offers a unique vocabulary with which to understand this central ritual. Still, it seems incontrovertible that there is a consistent emphasis on baptism as *cleansing*.

Pivotal to questions about baptismal cleansing is the concept of "original sin," another concept that rings quite differently in the diverse theological atmospheres of Christian theology. Because the term "original sin" does not appear until Tertullian, we can expect a wide divergence in Christian understandings of this doctrine.[4] Pope Benedict XVI, then Cardinal Ratzinger, wrote in 1985: "The inability to understand 'original sin' and to make it understandable is really one of the most difficult problems of present-day theology and pastoral ministry."[5] We might precariously generalize that "original sin" refers to some form of guilt associated with an ancient and contemporary disposition of humans. Christians differ regarding the source of this guiltiness. Some claim it is hereditary, some that it is to be blamed on a historical Adam; others believe that the story of Adam and Eve represents a mythological explanation for human sinfulness. One relatively recent movement in Christian theology connects original sin to the evolution impulse to promote self-survival, a sort of "original selfishness."[6] At least it can be said that few deny that evidence of "original sin" can be seen in the universal human disposition to act out of self-interest.

We reach a nearly impossible theological impasse as we attempt to explore how baptism relates to this universal human disposition. Somehow baptism applies to this primeval human problem. Baptismal cleansing addresses and corrects this issue that has plagued humanity from the very beginning.[7] Rather than get hung up on the variety of ways that original sin can be understood, we can say with reasonably theological consensus that baptism applies to this original human orientation. Whatever theological content is loaded into the event of baptism, this ritual is regularly described as a cleansing or purification.

4. Tertullian, *On Baptism*, 26.

5. Ratzinger, *The Ratzinger Report*, 79.

6. See Daryl P. Domning, "Original Selfishness."

7. Wiley, *Original Sin*, 236. Augustine considered original sin to be transmitted sexually.

It is important to note a number of consistent aspects to the cleansing of baptism. Any argument regarding the allowance and efficacy of infant baptism must be conversant with the symbolic language of cleansing. A number of problems arise when one attempts to determine whether baptism is primarily a corporal event or a personal one. Sensible theologians across the spectrum agree that baptism includes both of these dimensions. It cannot be denied that baptism occurs in the context of a community and that those being baptized are undertaking a sacrament that focuses on the baptizee. In other words, few ministers advocate private bathtub baptisms, nor do entire liturgical communities join the one being baptized in the water. Some rich blend must be made of the corporate and the personal elements of baptism.

Here, the question of emphasis again rears its head. For if baptism *primarily* represents the cleansing of a particular individual, the question of infant baptism takes on very different connotations. The more one emphasizes the individual cognitive process by which a person qualifies for baptism the less likely one is to condone the baptism of an infant, who is certainly not capable of making statements of faith. If baptism *primarily* represents entrance into the cleansed community, it would seem far more likely that infants would be incorporated into the sacrament. But it should be clear that cleansing is but one part of the complex set of symbols that contribute to our understanding of baptism. We are left to wonder: *Who is capable of such cleansing?*

BAPTISM AS INITIATION

The rich tapestry of baptismal imagery also bears the common thread of *initiation*. At its heart, baptism is Christianity's ritual of beginnings. The aquatic imagery of baptism recalls important initiations and covenants throughout biblical history. From the waters God brought forth life in Genesis 1, and from the watery flood God brought forth a new beginning in Genesis 8.[8] The Hebrew people have yet another beginning in their journey through the heart of the Red Sea in Exodus. As it has in many religious cultures, Hebrew Scripture depicts water as a site of birth and

---

8. It is on the authority of 1 Peter 3 that we draw a parallel between the story of the flood and Christian baptism: ". . . God waited patiently in the days of Noah while the ark was being built. In it only a few people, eight in all, were saved through water, and this water symbolizes baptism that now saves you also . . ." (vv. 20–21)

death, a source of dissolution and regeneration.[9] Water gives life and takes it away. In the beginning and at the end, there is water.

These images inform Christian baptism a variety of manners. The baptism of Jesus by John marks the beginning of Jesus's ministry, a watery beginning that anticipates Jesus' descent into the baptism of death.[10] Apparently, Jesus's own Jewish baptism was important enough to be mentioned in all four Gospels, though, Christians have resisted any insinuation that Jesus had any sin, original or otherwise, for which he needed cleansing. Each telling of Jesus's baptism includes some dove-like form of divine approval and in each Gospel this moment appears to be an important initiation of the public ministry of Jesus. So perhaps it is helpful to see Jesus's baptism as invoking the imagery of watery beginnings; out of the baptismal waters comes a new and different chapter in Jesus's life and in history itself. The life of Jesus, until now relatively benign, now becomes anything but commonplace. Something new is beginning, and it begins with a baptism.

A number of theologians, including John Calvin, have made much of the parallel between baptism and circumcision. Such a comparison has been particularly important for those interested in supporting the viability of infant baptism in Christian communities.[11] The parallel has some merit based on the way both rituals function as a sort of community initiation. In both infant baptism and circumcision the infant is incorporated into a religious community that clearly precedes the baby's awareness or cognitive acceptance. Colossians 2:11–12 may lend significant support to this parallel:

> In him also you were circumcised with a spiritual circumcision, by putting off the body of the flesh in the circumcision of Christ; when you were buried with him in baptism, you were also raised with him through faith in the power of God, who raised him from the dead."[12]

9. Eliade, *The Sacred and the Profane*, 130.

10. Romans 6:4, "we have been buried with him by baptism into death . . ."

11. Calvin, *Genesis*, 168.

12. Note that this connection is generally accepted by exegetical scholars but some, including Ladd, disagree (Ladd, *A Theology of the New Testament*, 548). Opponents of infant baptism often take great pains to avoid the connection between infant baptism and circumcision.

For reasons we need not trace here, this parallel becomes problematic at a number of levels, but it can scarcely be denied that baptism carries forward the initiatory role of circumcision. Infant baptism sheds the male-centeredness of circumcision but retains the profound sense of initiation; one is not the same after one has been baptized.

Jewish baptism, depicted in the New Testament through John the Baptist, placed considerable emphasis on both cleansing and initiation. During the first century, baptism was critical, along with circumcision and a temple sacrifice, for any proselyte converting to Judaism. Christianity shed both circumcision and animal sacrifice, which left only baptism as a transitional ritual for converts. In the Christian ritual, bodies are left without a physical mark to illustrate the conversion, but baptism continues to carry the connotation of a seal, which confirms that a person is a member of the redeemed community.

The tension between those who espouse "believer-only baptism" and those who embrace "infant baptism" begins here, with the question of initiation.[13] What are the qualifications for initiation into this covenant, this community? Like other initiatory rituals, baptism marks the transition between life *inside* and life *outside* the church. If a cognitive, mature religious decision were required to be inside this ecclesial community, then one would certainly have to deny the validity of infant baptism. But these criteria would indefinitely suspend the initiation of a number of humans into the Christian community. Many people with autism, Downs Syndrome, brain injuries, and other disabilities never reach the point when they can achieve such mental maturity. Opponents of infant baptism often dismiss this situation, but it points to an important question about this transition into the church. Is the criterion for admittance into this "body" a certain IQ quotient? Must one be capable of a certain level of emotional and logical maturity? The concept of "initiation" is clearly an important element of Christian baptism, but we are again pushed to wonder: *Who is capable of such initiation?*

---

13. I use the title "believer-only" baptism in differentiation from "infant baptism" to avoid the insinuation that those who embrace infant baptism do not also support the baptism of converted believers. "Believer-only" baptism denies the validity of any baptism not performed on someone who has personally professed some form of Christian faith. For this reason I am intentionally avoiding the terms "pedobaptism" and "credobaptism."

BAPTISM AND EXEGESIS

The great victim of the infant baptism conflict has almost certainly been Scripture itself, contorted and twisted on a regular basis to provide either support for infant baptism or evidence against it. The lack of direct scriptural reference to the baptism of infants has driven the search for scriptural verification to frightening heights. Almost all discussions of infant baptism make reference to the story when Jesus tells the disciples to "let the little children come to me, and do not stop them; for it is to such as these that the kingdom of God belongs. Truly I tell you, whoever does not receive the kingdom of God as a little child will never enter it" (Luke 18:16–17).[14] Proponents of infant baptism point to the way that Jesus elevates, accepts, and includes children in this passage. Certainly this story, mentioned in each of the synoptic Gospels, is an important indication of the profound value of children. Still, it comes as no surprise that this passage, no matter how forcefully offered, changes almost no minds about the issue of infant baptism and, as will be obvious below, the general situation concerning the exegesis of passages with a supposed relationship to infant baptism. As is too frequently the case with other theological issues, readers of Scripture tend to discover answers in the Bible that look remarkably like their original position.

In several places in the New Testament, we are told of baptisms that are household events. Paul baptizes the whole "household of Stephanus" (1 Cor 1:16), and Lydia and "her household" were baptized together in Acts 16, among other instances. It seems unlikely that these households happened to have no children. Proponents of infant baptism rest rather heavily on these household baptisms and the implication that infants were probably baptized by Paul, Peter, and other leaders of the early Church. The argument that household baptisms probably included children at least forces us to ask important questions of what *happens* in a baptism. Even if infants were *not* included in these events, the idea of a household-wide conversion and baptism has unsettling implications for those who wish to associate baptism primarily with a personal event of conversion.

On the other hand, Scripture provides an abundance of baptismal events and references that appear to show a strong connection between baptism and adult decisions of faith. Peter's Pentecost sermon appears to call adults to "repent and be baptized" (Acts 2:38). Similarly, Philip

---

14. Parallel passages are found in Matthew 19:13–15 and Mark 10:13–16.

baptizes the Ethiopian eunuch in response to his conversion to the nascent Christian faith (Acts 8:36–38). Adults are the primary targets of New Testament preaching, and the majority of references to baptism follow this pattern. In addition, a specifically *Christian* understanding of baptism is still under development in Scripture. Like the doctrine of original sin, or the doctrine of the Trinity, a mature understanding of baptism required some significant time to develop. At the level of logistics, the church depicted in the New Testament is young enough and dealing with enough persecution that the issue of infant baptism is hardly a pressing concern.

Adding to the difficulty is the odd fact that Jesus baptized nobody, adult or child; at least we have no convincing evidence of this sort from either Christian Scripture of early church history. So Jesus does not baptize but commands that we baptize. Would Jesus have baptized infants? The passages in Acts that make reference to household baptisms seem to indicate that some apostles, particular Paul, considered it appropriate. This argument has merit but is still too thin to provide conclusive evidence from the Bible that infant baptism should be accepted and practiced. Opponents of infant baptism have claimed as much, anyway.[15]

We must conclude that there is nothing conclusive in Scripture that would make this question easy to answer. One is almost certain to find in Scripture some sound support for whatever position on infant baptism one brings to the text. Adult baptism appears to be the dominant way that baptism is manifested in Scripture, but there are a number of ways that one could see incidents of, and openness to, the baptism of children as well. Ultimately, the Bible both muddies and clears the baptismal waters. And we should always be leery when sincere and exegetically minded Christians find opposing answers in the pages of Scripture. We are wise to place at least a mild caveat on our arguments when believers with equal commitment to these texts read them so very differently.

Because exegesis fails to yield a definitive answer to this question, the subject of infant baptism becomes a theological and practical one. And Christian theology has had much to say about the subject across Christian history.

---

15. J. Rodman Williams said, "The attempt to relate Jesus' blessing of children to infant baptism is quite misguided." (Williams, *Renewal Theology*, 233).

INFANT BAPTISM AND CHRISTIAN HISTORY

Contemporary Christians attribute varying degrees of respect and import to the theology and practices of the church after the close of the New Testament. Though some hold the early church and her liturgy in high regard, others consider it of minor importance for determining the way baptism should be practiced today. This lack of consensus on the value of Christian history somewhat clouds the clearer picture of infant baptism that develops as we read the work of our earliest theologians and church leaders.

We know from the work *Apostolic Tradition*, written by Hippolytus of Rome around AD 215, that baptism was acceptable and recommended for children:

> At dawn a prayer shall be offered over the water . . . baptize the children first, and if they can speak for themselves, let them do so. Otherwise let their parents or other relatives speak for them. Next baptize the men, and last of all the women.[16]

Origen (AD 185–254) claimed in AD 244, "the Church received from the apostles the tradition of giving baptism, even to infants."[17] This sentiment is confirmed and reinforced by the bishops at the Council of Carthage, by Cyprian, and from numerous other sources. The baptism of infants was an assumed practice early enough in Christian history for us to safely state that Christians have *always* baptized infants, probably from the first century until today.

It was necessary almost immediately for this pervasive early practice to be defended. Tertullian (AD 160–215) questioned the validity of infant baptism based on the inability of infants to "know Christ" for themselves. His objection is doubly interesting because he offers the first direct and explicit debate over the validity of infant baptism, and his statements clearly imply that the baptism of infants is an established practice by AD 200. Tertullian offers some articulate objections to infant baptism, recommending that baptism should be reserved for people who are old enough to understand what they are doing.[18] It does appear that Tertullian is the

---

16. Dix, *The Treatise on the Apostolic Tradition*, 33.

17. Origen, *Commentary on Romans*, 5:9.

18. Lutzer, *The Doctrines that Divide*, 119.

exception to the rule; most of the evidence surrounding infant baptism from early Christian history reveals a general acceptance of this practice.

Whatever objections to infant baptism may have existed before the Reformation, they hardly compare to the movement called "Anabaptism." Until this era, Christians generally had an inclusive policy on baptism, allowing anyone who requested the rite for themselves or their children to be baptized.[19] The Anabaptist movement pushed for a specific requirement for baptism: *faith*. For the Anabaptists, humans who could not testify to having faith in salvation through Christ were not qualified for baptism. This excludes from the sacrament adults suffering from senility or dementia, people of all ages with mental handicaps, and of course children. The Anabaptist movement, which began in the sixteenth century, has a number of theological descendants that actively embrace this criterion for baptism. Anabaptism appears in Christian history as a distinct product of the Enlightenment, which re-centered the identity of the human person in the individual. The baptism of infants rubbed some enlightenment Christians the wrong way for its deep reliance on the community that imparts the ritual on behalf of the pre-cognitive child.

Predictably sympathetic with the emphasis on faith, Martin Luther argued that faith is different from *reason*. Luther wished to show that faith was not a product of intellectual capacity but that infants and children are actually the model of faith. He claimed that children are "more fitted for faith than older and more rational people who always trip over their reason."[20] Perhaps Luther has a point here; who could doubt that an infant has faith in the gift of the next breath, the next meal, and the next parental embrace? Are these faiths so different from faith in God's grace? It is not enough, insist Anabaptists, for children to be capable of generic "faith," they must be able to articulate a particular faith in the tenants of Christianity.

Some important theologians have embraced the theological rationale for infant baptism but rejected the practice for practical and sociological reasons. It is painfully common for parents to bring children to the church only for baptism and never even remember to tell their children that they are baptized. Karl Barth and Jurgen Moltmann, perhaps influenced by a European culture in which such treatment of baptism is rampant,

19. Stookey, *Baptism: Christ's Act in the Church*, 41.

20. Staples, *Outward Sign and Inward Grace*, 165.

argued against infant baptism because it is so rarely connected with the ecclesial environment in which baptism is nourished.[21] This concern is noteworthy, but it seems hasty to discard a practice with such deep roots in Christianity because of the way it is being abused in parts of the world today. From Barth and Moltmann we are made mindful of the danger of cheapening baptismal grace in this way. But what of parents, ministers, and churches whose understanding of grace and baptism is richer and more faithful to the ancient Christian practice of following baptism with intimate nourishment, education, and confirmation? Practical concerns about the "abuse" of infant baptism serve as an important reminder, but they do not serve as theological rationale against baptizing infants correctly.

The pervasiveness of infant baptism throughout Christian history might turn the tide in favor of baptizing infants in the church today. But Anabaptists and their modern day descendants *knowingly* reject the dominant historical practice of infant baptism. To move beyond this impasse it seems compelling to look for new ways to articulate the symbolism of baptism and how it might relate to the baptism of infants.

BAPTISM: CHRISTIAN IDENTITY AND RENAMING

Daniel Migliore calls baptism the sign of our membership as "citizens of a new society."[22] Baptism marks the transition between life outside and a life inside the covenant of God's salvation through Christ. In an attempt to argue past the usual deadlock with regard to infant baptism, I will now direct attention toward the peculiar part of the baptismal formula where we are baptized "in the name" of the Father, Son, and Holy Spirit. The stalemate that Christians reach with regard to infant baptism usually results from a fixation on the importance of cognitive conversion. By focusing attention on the "naming" aspect of the baptismal formula, perhaps our discussion of infant baptism can bypass the theological deadlock evident in the preceding pages.

Last year my daughter began kindergarten, with all the joys and traumas that come with this transition. It becomes clear at a frighteningly young age that children are capable of treating each other with deep respect or severe disrespect. The transition into public schooling presented

21. Moltmann, *The Church in the Power of the Spirit*, 226–42.
22. Migliore, *Faith Seeking Understanding*, 215.

her with an opportunity to encounter a host of strange experiences, exposing her to a world much more complicated and diverse than the simple and protected world of her first five years. Dropped off for three hours in an alien environment, she experienced both the thrills and terrors of such novelty. Her world expanded, and into that small world were folded a set of classmates, a teacher, a crossing-guard, and so on.

At first she was genuinely afraid that some of these new people might cause her harm, but before long my daughter assimilated these people into the intimate world, which she found comfortable. Upset by these transitions into kindergarten, her world reached equilibrium again just in time for a "new girl" to arrive. The arrival of the "new kid" presented an interesting problem for her gaggle of kindergarten girlfriends. They were slow to accept this outsider, who might potentially disrupt their stable worlds. For months the poor newcomer was referred to as "the new Sarah" because the comfortable class already had a perfectly good Sarah. Over dinner I told her, "You know, honey, Seversons sit with new kids." This soon became a family mantra, and we often talk about the way "Seversons" talk, treat their neighbors, eat their vegetables, and so on. Her identity is something chosen for her, though it is an identity that she will some day be free to reject. We do not raise her with the constant refrain, "If you are going to be a Severson someday, you had better sit by the new kid." Instead, she is given the identity without any prerequisite. The primary presumption is that she is *included* by the identities that we associate with our name. Her rearing is precisely the process of nurturing her to make such identifications on her own.

Christian "identity" does not work in exactly the same way. Being baptized is in fact being *renamed* (Christened) and identified with something outside of our grasp. When Christians are baptized we are in fact given over into the Triune name, baptized in (and into) *the name* of the Father, Son, and Holy Spirit. This movement into the name of God is a movement outside of our own identity and into the identity of the Triune God. In this sense, we are never qualified to receive a Christian identity. We are never, of ourselves, capable of becoming Christian. The fundamental question of baptism is a question of *naming*, of being willing to accept a new name, or more appropriately, a willingness to be un-named by the baptismal waters. Such an un-naming casts our identity into the eschatological future. The person who has been baptized, if truly living in the splendor of baptism, is to live a life that constantly relinquishes the right to self-identity. She always insists on being identified with Christ, and with the ecclesial body of Christ. Her surname is always "Christian" and this name is itself an active un-naming. As long as we claim our baptism, we disclaim the other forms that our identity might take. To be baptized is to be first and foremost identified with the crucified, buried, and resurrected Christ.

The key, then, to understanding Christian baptism is bound up in the question of what it means to be baptized *in the name* of this Trinitarian God. The issue of divine "naming" is a particularly intriguing one in both scriptural texts and Christian history. Jacob wrestles with the stranger in the night at Peniel and begs, to no avail, that the man reveal his name to Jacob (Gen 32).[23] Moses begs for God's name and is given instead the elusive moniker "YHWH," an elusive name if ever there was one (Exod 3:14). Recently, exegetes have become increasingly aware of the richly eschatological nature of this "name." The common translation of "I am" circumvents a richly futurist element to the Hebrew word YHWH, which probably means something closer to "I will be who I will be" or even "I will be there."[24] God's name does not bring God into our possession but instead casts us into a future that is beyond our control and imagination. The God in whose name we are baptized is a God who beckons us to a rich, eschatological future. To be baptized is to receive a new name, a new identity that shapes and forms the way we live, worship, and especially *hope*.

Gregory of Nyssa, commenting on the baptismal formula, claims that we grasp at the world around us through the "signification of their names."[25] But, notes Gregory, the name of God is unusual in the fact that it is an "un-nameable name," a name that defies our attempt at grasping. This elusive character of God calls Jacob, Moses, and the church into an unidentified future that is characterized by this un-nameable God. To be baptized is to be given this new name, to be un-named by the God who provides a new identity through the death and resurrection of Jesus Christ. So we are unnamed by God in baptism, given a new identity that is the *name* of the Father, Son, and Holy Spirit. This identity shapes and forms the character of the Christian community.

23. Jacob later supposes that his opponent was in fact God.

24. For a dynamic exploration of such eschatological readings of Exodus 3, see Kearney, *The God Who May Be*, 20–38.

25. Jean-Luc Marion quotes this passage from Gregory of Nyssa (Caputo and Scanlon, *God the Gift and Postmodernism*, 38).

The baptismal moment is a moment of "Christening" in the richest of senses, for the baptized person is renamed according to the eschatological name of God. So now perhaps it is fair to repeat our refrain: *Who qualifies for such re-naming?* From this perspective it seems rather appropriate to baptize infants. Though they may one day reject this renaming process, our children are never too young to be a part of the church whose identity is no longer its own. In fact, it seems deeply appropriate to *christen* our children and then allow them to be nourished and nurtured in their understanding and appropriation of their "new" identity. As Paul writes in Romans, "we have been buried with him by baptism into death, so that, just as Christ was raised from the dead by the glory of the Father, so we too might walk in newness of life" (Rom 6:4). To be baptized, whatever one's developmental and cognitive capacity, is to walk with the church in the new life of this new name.

There is a distinct advantage to understanding infant baptism with primary reference to identity and naming. When we acknowledge that baptism is primarily about being a part of the un-named community of the Triune God, we can easily see that this covenant encompasses people who, because of trauma or medical problems, are never able to achieve the sort of independent "decision for Christ" that Anabaptists and their theological descendants use for a baptismal criteria. If baptism is about being renamed together, then we ought to eagerly allow people with mental handicaps to receive this new name. Like my daughter's last name, the identity of such baptized people is assumed because of their place within this community of the eschatological future. From such a theological perspective, children whose parents and church bear the name of the Triune God should be eager to enter their children into this christening ritual. No wonder Paul says that a child with at least one believing parent is "holy" (1 Cor 7:14).

This is not to deny that there is significant validity to the concerns raised by Karl Barth and company concerning the ease with which infant baptism can and has been abused and misunderstood. Those who are familiar with Christian history know that solid theology does not always translate into healthy Christian practices. Infant baptism has often led to people identifying themselves as "Christian" who have no connection whatsoever to Christianity or the "eschatological church" discussed here. The practice of baptizing infants can and has created great misunderstanding about the nature of sin, redemption, conversion, and grace. These problems appear to arise out of a failure to translate theology into practices that reinforce the richness of baptismal sacramental imagery. Infant baptism *must* be followed and completed by a childhood and adolescence that is rich in intimate nurture and instruction. The baptism of infants is completed by the ritual of confirmation, wherein the infant *confirms* the choice of her church and parents to give her this name. The failure of churches and families to nourish baptized children is a profound failure to cherish the Triune name, which is God's great gift to the church. The church who names its children in baptism is called to guide these children into the profound understanding of what it means to be identified with the unusual "name" that is Father, Son, and Holy Spirit.

AVOIDING MISREPRESENTATIONS

We must say a few words about the notion of "original sin," which has often been a dominant factor in discussions of infant baptism. I would agree with Augustine, Luther, Wesley, and others who have claimed that original sin is cleansed in baptism. I do not, however, believe that original sin is substantive or that it is transmitted through sexual intercourse. It seems that the notion of "original sin" must refer to a way of being that is profoundly opposite to the manner in which humans were created to live. Jesus sums up the Law and the Prophets with the two commandments: "You shall love the Lord your God with all your heart, and with all your soul, and with all your mind" and "You shall love your neighbor as yourself" (Matt 22:37–40). These commandments call for a doubly outward orientation of human life, of selfless love for God and neighbors. I call "original sin" the opposite of this: a universal, inward, self-centered orientation. Adam's curse is the curse of being curved in upon ourselves, as Luther classically defined sin. "Original sin" is reversed by God and others; we are called out of our self-fixation by the love of God and by the faces of others. In this sense, the church lives out the reversal of original sin. The stain of original sin is "removed" by the kind of love that, by grace, flows in Christian community. So I am not arguing that we should baptize children in order that they might have a substance called "original sin" removed from their lives. I am rather arguing that we baptize infants so that we can mark them as members of the community of grace, which denies the efficacy of original sin by abiding in Jesus's great commandments. Infants are born with original sin, which is addressed and removed by God within the baptized community.

This leads me to some fundamental and important clarifications about my disagreement with those who argue for "believer-only" baptism. When children are baptized, and this baptism is not remembered for them vibrantly, the baptism is incomplete and "original sin," as I am defining it, goes un-addressed. It is important to note that infant baptism, when not connected to a rearing in the context of Christian community, is a travesty unbefitting of this sacrament. On the question of rebaptism, it seems that what is needed is not another *mark* but a chance for people to seize and embrace a baptism that was given but not activated (as it should have been) in childhood.

A Baptist Response

Dereck F. Stone

IT IS NOT MY intention to answer the lengthy, philosophical, and some-what involved paper by Professor Severson, but rather to try and address the broad theme and thrust of it.

Professor Severson begins his essay by using the words "baptismal ritual," which immediately presents a problem. As believers we do not have "rituals" that we follow—we seek to be obedient to the teachings, commands, and practices of the Scriptures in all things. We have a living, dynamic relationship with the Lord Jesus Christ that excludes the concept of religion and ritual. The baptism of a believer is clearly an act of obedience, a step willingly and sincerely taken by one who knows Christ, understands his commands and obeys them (Matt 3:13–15; 28:18–20; John 14:23a). As I have pointed out in my essay, the Greek word for "baptize" means to totally immerse, and in the New Testament only believers were baptized by immersion. Infant baptism was neither taught nor practiced in the Old or New Testaments. "Infant baptism" requires the sprinkling or pouring of water on the head of an infant who has neither heard nor can understand the gospel and, therefore, has made no response by faith to Christ.

The great danger of such a practice lies in the words contained in many service books of various churches that have led multitudes into a false hope of salvation, myself included, until my conversion at the age of seventeen. Let me give two examples: The Presbyterian Church of Southern Africa states the following in their "Order Of Baptism For Children":

> "In bringing our children before Almighty God, we believe that
> the act of baptizing them signifies God's cleansing and acceptance
> of them. We look to God's grace that they will, one day, by faith

confirm for themselves, their salvation in Christ." The preamble
to those words acknowledges that although the children [infants]
may not understand these things, the promise [of eternal life] is to
them also.[26]

Likewise, in "The Baptism of Children" at St John's Parish, Wynberg,
points 2 and 5 state:

N, when you are baptized, you become a *member* of a new family.
God takes you for his own *child*, and all Christian people will be
your brothers and sister. Bless this water, that your *servants* who
are washed in it may be made one with Christ in his death and
resurrection, to be cleansed and delivered from all sin. Send your
Holy Spirit upon *them* to bring *them* to new birth in the family of
your church, and raise *them* with Christ to full and eternal life.

Professor Severson's reasoning is based on several factors, and not
on an exegesis of relevant Scriptures. For example he says, "Like most of
the religious rituals, baptism has its origins behind the mists of early human civilization" (p. 98). The point must be made that we don't begin
with man, nor with customs and cultures—we begin with God and his
revelation, which is his word. He continues by asking, "What aspects of
ancient water rituals are active in the Christian sacrament?" Professor
Severson gives the impression in his paper that he believes Scripture and
Christian practices were possibly influenced by extra-biblical customs,
traditions, and practices. However, he does acknowledge, "Scripture
provides an abundance of baptismal events and references that appear to
show a strong connection between baptism and adult decisions of faith"
(p. 105). He goes on to say, "One is almost certain to find in Scripture
some sound support for whatever position on infant baptism one brings
to the text . . . Ultimately, the Bible both muddies and clears the baptismal waters" (p. 106)—a statement I cannot agree with, except to say that
Scripture certainly "clears the waters" on the subject of believer's baptism
by immersion. Professor Severson's reasoning wanders in and out of the
detours of custom, culture, church history, debates, some other issues,
and on the meaning of original sin.

To sum up, my personal view is that although he has done a great deal
of research, he has ultimately missed the point by not going to Scripture
and doing a simple and clear exegesis of all the relevant passages and,
thereby, presents a case that is vague and extra-biblical in its conclusions.

26. *Service Book And Ordinal*, 17.

8

Believer's Baptism

Dereck F. Stone

WHO IS A CHRISTIAN?

I BELIEVE THE STARTING point when considering believer's baptism is the question: *Who is a Christian?* A Christian is not someone born into a particular race, culture, or religion. Christianity is not hereditary—you are not a Christian because your parents or grandparents were Christians. Even today in South Africa, as in many western countries, there are those who believe that a white person born into a white church-going culture would be a Christian as against, for example, being a Hindu or a Muslim.

We do not become Christians through christening ("infant baptism" as some call it), baptism by immersion, communion, church membership, or through any ritual or tradition of a particular church—Protestant or Roman Catholic. Good works and a good character do not make us Christians either.

Who is a Christian? A Christian is one who has had a personal, spiritual, life-changing encounter with the Lord Jesus Christ. A Christian is one who has been "born again, born anew" through the work of the Holy Spirit. We are born again, born into God's family, when we repent and turn from our sin and from all that we have trusted in, and when we personally place our faith and trust in Christ and his substitutionary work on the cross (John 3:1–18). We then become a new creation in Christ (2 Cor 5:17). By the grace of God we are then cleansed of our sin. We die to the old life, that old life is buried, and we rise to walk in a new life in Christ (Rom 6:1–14; Eph 1:3–7).

A Christian is a follower of Christ, and that requires us to bear testimony to him and his saving grace the remainder of our days, and we do that in a multitude of ways—one of them being baptism. In fact, the New Testament clearly teaches that baptism was the next step taken by those who trusted in Christ. Hence the need to begin with the question: *Who is a Christian?*

THE MEANING OF THE WORD "BAPTIZE"

The Holy Spirit is the author of Scripture and is responsible for the words we have in the Bible. The Greek word *baptize* in all Greek Lexicons means *to dip, immerse, or submerge.* Several years ago I spoke with a Greek Orthodox priest who said that in their "baptismal ceremony" they immerse the infant because to baptize means exactly that—*to immerse.* Sadly, he missed the essential gospel truth of personal trust and faith in Christ as the biblical prerequisite for baptism by immersion. Nevertheless, he insisted that the word means *to immerse,* and so, to be consistent with the Greek language and the meaning of the word, he immerses infants.

To pour or sprinkle water on an infant cannot be termed "baptism" for three principle reasons: (1) As stated above, the word *baptize* means to *immerse* while the words *sprinkle* or *pour* are entirely different both in English and in Greek. (2) We shall see that only *believers* may be baptized. (3) Baptism is meant to symbolize the spiritual death, burial, and resurrection of the believer with Christ, as well as their union with him. The sprinkling or pouring of water upon a person of any age cannot constitute New Testament baptism. More than that, such practice is not found in Scripture. I once came across a little booklet entitled, *What the Bible Teaches about Infant Baptism.* My curiosity aroused, I turned to the first page—it was blank, as were all the other pages, making the point that the Bible teaches nothing about "infant baptism."

THE MINISTRY OF JOHN

Baptism by immersion is first mentioned in Scripture when John exercised a brief ministry of baptizing people in the River Jordan in preparation for the coming of Christ. It was a unique and unusual ministry in that he did not baptize converts (those who had trusted in Christ), for Jesus had not yet died on the cross and risen from the dead—that still lay some three years ahead. John prepared people for Christ's ministry,[1] and when Christ commenced his public ministry, John ceased baptizing.

Several years later, the apostle Paul came across some disciples in Ephesus and asked them if they had received the Holy Spirit (Acts 19:1–5).[2] Those disciples replied that they had not even heard of the Holy Spirit, and upon Paul asking them about their baptism, they said John had baptized them. Paul then explained that John's baptism was a baptism of repentance—a preparation for the coming of Christ. Somehow this group of people had bypassed the ministry, death, and resurrection of Christ. It could be that they had traveled to Ephesus shortly after John had baptized them. Whatever the circumstances, the fact is clear that they had not heard the gospel, and so Paul had to evangelize them.

There can be no doubt that the apostle explained the truths of salvation to that group, for he then baptized them as they trusted in Christ. That would be consistent with the facts that we see in Scripture regarding baptism following conversion.

THE EXAMPLE OF CHRIST

As Christ approached John at the River Jordan where he was baptizing, Jesus made a startling request when he asked John to baptize him (Matt 3:13). John was totally taken aback that Jesus, the spotless Lamb of God whom he had just proclaimed and openly identified, should ask to be baptized—and by him! John had just said to the gathered crowd, "Look, the Lamb of God, who takes away the sin of the world!" He went on to say he was not worthy to untie the thongs of Christ's sandals (John 1:27, 29).[3] Now the Messiah asked John to baptize *him*!

Jesus had no need of an outward testimony of cleansing and new life. He had no need to prepare for the coming of the Savior, as was the purpose of John's ministry of baptism, for he *was* the Savior. Christ was pure and sinless; he had no need to be born again, and yet he requested to be baptized! Why? The answer is that he was identifying with us and was

1. See Matthew 3:1–17 and John 1:19–34.

2. In the early church that term was often used to enquire about a person's faith in Christ. One cannot be a Christian unless the Spirit indwells them; see Romans 8:9 and Acts 10:47—Peter testifying to the believers at Jerusalem about the Gentiles trusting in Christ.

3. Unless otherwise indicated, all Scripture quotations are taken from the *New International Version*.

setting us an example to follow. He said, "I must do all that is right" (John 3:13 LB). Likewise, Jesus set numerous other examples for us to follow: he prayed, he read the Scriptures, and he attended the house of God to worship and have fellowship. As the pure and perfect Son of God, Jesus did not have to do any of those things, but he set examples for us to follow in our daily living as he did in his baptism.

Note that after he was baptized, Christ "went up out of the water" (Matt 3:16). The sprinkling of a little water would not require him to go down *into* the water and *up out* of the water. The words used also confirm that Christ was immersed.

THE COMMAND OF CHRIST

In the passage we call "The Great Commission" (Matt 28:18–20), Christ gave a specific command to his disciples who would soon form the early church. He said:

> All authority in heaven and on earth has been given to me. Therefore go and make disciples of all nations, baptising them in the name of the Father and of the Son and of the Holy Sprit, and teaching them to obey everything I have commanded you. And surely I am with you always, to the very end of the age.

Christ gave his church a simple three-point plan:

1. *Make disciples.* Our first responsibility is to preach the gospel and to call men and women to faith in Christ. When people repent of their sins and trust in Christ, they are born by the Spirit into the family of God and become followers of Christ.

2. *Baptize them in the name of the Father and of the Son and of the Holy Spirit.* We are to baptize disciples, new converts—those who have faith in the Lord Jesus Christ.

3. *Teach them to observe all I have commanded you.* Newly baptized converts are to be taught and grown in the faith within the fellowship of the local church.

Jesus commanded us to make disciples, to baptize those disciples, and to continue to teach those disciples. Christ brackets this simple and dynamic three-point plan for the church with two great assurances: "[1] All authority in heaven and on earth is given to me . . . therefore go . . . [2] and I am with you always, to the very end of the age."

WHAT BAPTISM TEACHES

The person being baptized enters the water; they are lowered back into the water, totally immersed, and brought up out of the water. The picture is one of *death, burial, and resurrection*. Water in Scripture is also symbolic of cleansing. Believer's baptism graphically teaches the dynamic truths of our conversion experience and, in particular, Paul's teaching in Romans 6:1–7.

It is important to note that in the first five chapters of Romans, Paul teaches on justification (i.e., being declared right with God). We are justified through faith in Christ and through our spiritual union with him. Paul also teaches that same truth in 1 Corinthians 12:13 where he says, "We were all baptized by one Spirit into one body" (the body of Christ). This is a spiritual baptism, and Paul repeats that great truth in Galatians 3:27, Ephesians 4:4–5, and Colossians 2:12.

In the next three chapters of Romans (6–9), Paul teaches on sanctification (i.e., the progressive living out of our spiritual union with Christ in a new life). That new life is made possible at conversion by our spiritual union with Christ in his death, burial, and resurrection.

In chapter 6, the pivotal chapter of Romans, Paul simply and clearly teaches what happens when we repent and place our trust in Christ. He says:

> Don't you know that all of us who were baptized into Christ Jesus [spiritually] were baptized into his death? We were therefore buried with him through baptism into death in order that, just as Christ was raised from the dead through the glory of the Father, we too may live a new life. If we have been united with him like this in his death, we will certainly also be united with him in his resurrection. (Rom 6:3–5)

The apostle then goes on to argue that this spiritual union meant a death blow to our old self, resulting in us being set free to live out our new resurrection life in Christ. The baptism of the believer by full immersion does not *achieve* these things but clearly and graphically *portrays* and *teaches* these great spiritual truths and realities. Baptism tells the story of personal cleansing from sin, death, burial, and resurrection.

As a young person I heard a missionary from China tell of a unique baptismal service in that land. It was a time of severe drought. The rivers and wells had dried up and there was hardly enough water for drinking, never mind for baptism. The new converts wanted to obey the Scripture and testify of their new faith in Christ. So in a public place, they dug a deep grave with steps leading down into it. On the day advertised for their baptism, they all gave testimony of their faith in Christ to the assembled villagers. Dressed in their oldest and dirtiest clothes, one by one they entered the grave. New white robes had been laid in the grave, and out of sight they slipped these new robes over the dirty clothes and then came up out of the grave. *Death, burial, resurrection,* the death of the old life and the putting on of the Christ life—that is what believer's baptism teaches.

BAPTISM IS A PLEDGE

Believer's baptism is not only an outward identification with Christ and a graphic testimony of new life in him, it is also, as the apostle Peter adds, "the pledge of a good conscience toward God" (1 Pet 3:21). In his commentary, William Barclay points out that the word "pledge" is the Greek word *eperotema,* which was commonly used in the business world of that day: "In every business contract there was a definite question and answer which made the contract binding."[4] Before the contract was entered into, the question was asked, *"Do you accept the terms of this contract, and bind yourself to observe them?"* The answer was, *"Yes, I accept the terms and bind myself to them."* This reply was required to be given publicly before witnesses. Baptism is thus my reply to God, saying that I understand his terms and call upon my life (all of which are set out in Scripture) to follow him unreservedly during all of my days.

BAPTIZING IN THE NAME OF THE FATHER, SON, AND HOLY SPIRIT

Attention is seldom drawn to the words Christ used in Matthew 28:19: "baptizing them in the name of the Father and of the Son and of the Holy Spirit." "In" or "into" is the Greek word *eis,* which signifies the union of the believer not only with Christ but also with God the Father and the Holy Spirit. When John baptized Jesus in the River Jordan, the voice of the Father was heard from heaven, and the Spirit descended on Jesus like a dove (Matt 3:16–17). The Father, Son, and Holy Spirit are all involved in our conversion. Many verses could be quoted, but the following cover the essential truths: God loves us and gave us his Son (John 3:16), Christ died for us to

---

4. Barclay, *The Letters of James and Peter,* 243.

purchase our forgiveness (Eph 1:7–8), the Holy Spirit convicts us of our sin (John 16:8), and by the Spirit we are also born anew (John 3:3–8).

The words we use, when baptizing the new convert, emphasize the Trinity and also point to the fact of our salvation and spiritual union with God the Father, God the Son, and God the Holy Spirit—a full and all-inclusive salvation!

BAPTISM IN THE EARLY CHURCH

On the day of Pentecost, the birthday of the church, the apostles and disciples immediately obeyed the Great Commission Christ had given them: They began to preach the gospel, to call people to faith in Christ, and to make disciples. And as a sign of their faith in Christ, those disciples were baptized. These disciples formed churches and began to grow in faith and maturity.

Acts 2:41. On the day of Pentecost, Peter preached the gospel to a vast crowd of people gathered in Jerusalem for the feasts. "Those who accepted his message were baptized, and about three thousand were added to their number that day." I have visited Israel and Jerusalem many times and there is ample evidence of the pools that were in and around the city at that time that would have been used for public baptisms.

Acts 8:12–13. Philip was greatly used of God in Samaria, with many placing their trust in Christ. The new converts were then baptized.

Acts 8:26–39. The Ethiopian eunuch, treasurer of Candace the Queen of Ethiopia, or Chancellor of the Exchequer as one British commentator called him, had made the incredibly long and difficult journey from Ethiopia, down the River Nile to Egypt, and then across to Jerusalem. A black African, he was obviously a Jewish proselyte, and if not circumcised he would have been called a "God-fearer." He had come to Jerusalem for the great annual Feasts of Passover and Pentecost. On his return journey to Ethiopia, in the vicinity of present day Gaza, he was reading from the fifty-third chapter of the prophet Isaiah.

The Lord sent an angel to instruct Philip the evangelist to leave his very successful ministry in Samaria and go down to Gaza to meet this man. Approaching the chariot, Philip asked the eunuch if he understood what he was reading, to which he replied, "How can I, unless someone explains it to me?" The passage he was reading was Isaiah 53:7–8, which prophetically speaks of Christ being led as a sheep to the slaughter. The eunuch asked Philip who the prophet was speaking about—himself or someone else. "Then Philip began with that very passage of Scripture and told him the good news about Jesus" (v. 35). The evangelist preached the gospel to the Ethiopian eunuch who immediately requested to be baptized. (The *New International Version* footnote adds the words of Philip: "If you believe with all your heart, you may.") Philip then baptized him.[5] The baptism was a public testimony. A man as important as the treasurer of the Queen of Ethiopia would have traveled with a large entourage of soldiers and servants.

Some ask how the eunuch would have known about baptism. There are two possible answers; in fact, both may pertain: (1) Philip may have told him that baptism followed trusting in Christ. The early church linked baptism directly with conversion (Acts 2:38). (2) Another reason is that as the eunuch was in Jerusalem for the great feasts, he in all likelihood would have witnessed, or at least heard about, the baptisms of the three thousand converted on the day of Pentecost. Besides that, every day in Jerusalem people were coming to faith and being baptized publicly (Acts 2:47). However he knew about baptism, one thing is certain: in that day there was no question about public baptism by immersion following faith in Christ.

Acts 9:1–19. Traveling to Damascus and being intent on persecuting the church, Saul had an encounter with the risen Christ. A great light from heaven suddenly flashed around him, blinding Saul and causing him to fall to the ground. After Jesus spoke to him, Saul's companions led him into Damascus, as Christ had instructed them. A disciple named Ananias laid his hands on Saul, and as his sight was restored, "He got up and was baptized." His name was later changed to Paul, the great apostle whom Christ was to use so mightily.

Acts 10:47–48. This is the account of the first Gentile (non-Jewish) converts. Although a Gentile by birth, the Ethiopian was a Jewish proselyte. The apostle Peter had to be convinced that he could go and preach to the Gentiles through a vision of a large sheet being lowered from heaven

---

5. Note that verse 39 says, "When they came up out of the water"—underscoring the fact it was baptism by immersion. See Matthew 3:16 again—the same words used for Christ's baptism. Those who argue that there is not enough water in the desert for a person to be immersed, overlook the location of Gaza and the ancient highway to Egypt in relation to the Mediterranean Sea. If sprinkling was the mode, a few drops from the eunuch's water supply would have made it unnecessary for him to go *into* the water, and then to come *up out of the water.*

by its four corners. The sheet contained all kinds of four-footed animals, reptiles, and birds—all unclean under Jewish law. Peter was hungry and when told to eat he objected, saying he had "never eaten anything impure or unclean." Three times he was told by a voice from heaven not to call anything impure that the Lord had made clean. Following that came the request to go to the home of Cornelius. Verses 34–48 provide us with the account of Peter's evangelistic message and the subsequent baptism of the Gentile converts.

Acts 16:14–15. Paul preached to a group of women gathered at a riverside in Philippi. Lydia, a trader in purple cloth from Thyatira, "opened her heart to respond to Paul's message." Then she and the members of her household were baptized. The members of her household were obviously also present; they listened to Paul and responded to his message and were also baptized.

Acts 16:30–34. Paul and Silas were cast into prison in Philippi, and the Lord sent an earthquake to shake up the prison building and release them. The jailer was distraught and prepared to take his life because he thought they and all the other prisoners had escaped. He would have received severe punishment, even death at the hands of the authorities for not preventing the escape of his prisoners. Paul and Silas called out that he was not to harm himself, for they were all still in the building. The jailer asked what he should do to be saved, and the two preachers replied, "Believe in the Lord Jesus, and you will be saved—you and your household." They then explained the gospel to the jailer and all who were in his house. The whole family came to faith in Christ and was baptized.

Acts 18:8. In Corinth, Paul preached to the family and all who were in the home of Crispus, the synagogue ruler.[6] They trusted in Christ and were baptized.

Acts 19:1–5. The conversion and baptism of "John's disciples"—this was dealt with earlier when we considered John's ministry.

Note the order in each instance: (1) the gospel was preached and explained; (2) people responded and placed their trust in Christ, that is, they were converted and became disciples; (3) these new converts (disciples) were then baptized. The early church followed the command and simple three-point plan Christ had given them in Matthew 28:18–20.

---

6. The word "household" refers not only to immediate family but also to servants in the home.

HOUSEHOLD BAPTISMS

Some Christians reason that because the New Testament records several "household baptisms" (i.e., all in the house being baptized), and that logically little children and even infants would have been present, the mode of baptism could not then have been immersion. Therefore, water was sprinkled or poured on them.

In response to this argument, notice that in each instance of a household baptism it was clear that all in the house *heard* the gospel, *responded* to the good news, and placed *personal* faith in Christ.[7] That tells us something about the age of understanding and ability of those believing and being baptized; they were able to make an intelligent, responsible, and personal commitment to Christ.

In 1 Corinthians, Paul—in dealing with the issue of believers choosing their favorite preacher and teacher whom they would follow (Apollos, Cephas, or himself)—says he was grateful that he baptized only two people, Crispus and Gaius, in case some believers would say they had been baptized into his name. Paul then remembered he had also baptized the household of Stephanas—a household baptism that would have included little children and infants, or so some would argue. In 1 Corinthians 16:15 Paul settles the issue when he says, "the household of Stephanus were the first converts of Achaia, and they have devoted themselves to the service of the saints." Household baptisms referred to people in that house or family who could understand the gospel, its challenges, and its claims. As already stated, they were of an age where they could make a meaningful, responsible, and personal commitment to follow Christ.

AM I BEING BAPTIZED A SECOND TIME?

This question is often asked by those who were "baptized as infants" and who later in life are considering baptism by immersion. I can personally identify with people who face this dilemma. I grew up in a church that practiced infant baptism. And when I came to faith in Christ in my teens, I began to devour the Scriptures and the New Testament in particular. It wasn't long before I came across believer's baptism in the book of Acts, and two things became very clear as I read on: (1) only believers were baptized, and (2) the word baptism meant immersion, even in English.

7. See Acts 10:44; 16:14, 34; 18:8.

Obeying the clear teaching of Scripture, I made preparation to be baptized by full immersion. My parents and minister insisted that I was going to be baptized "a second time" and that I was disregarding the vows my parents had made on my behalf when I was baptized as an infant. In fact, my minister was adamant that I had "been accepted into the church" through my infant baptism. I was a Christian because of that baptism, he said, and should I now be baptized by immersion, I would be showing great disrespect toward the church and my parents.

Many face that same pressure today. Some are even asked to leave the church if they are baptized by immersion. Our approach must always be to go to God's word, and once again I must repeat that the Scriptures are simple and clear on this issue: (1) only believers were baptized—those who had taken a personal step of faith in Christ in response to hearing the gospel. No other person can make promises, vows, or place faith in Christ on our behalf; (2) baptism is by immersion—that is what the word means; (3) baptism by immersion graphically shows new life in Christ—the spiritual death, burial, and resurrection of that person when they trusted in Christ.

As the Scriptures do not teach "infant baptism," whatever ritual one passed through as an infant was not biblical or New Testament baptism. When baptized by immersion after trusting Christ, one is therefore not repeating any previous baptism—it is not "a second baptism." I was, in fact, extremely grateful for the sincere promises made to God by my parents on my behalf, and they did their very best to be faithful to those promises, which meant I grew up in the church. It was a heritage I was most grateful for, *but that did not make me a Christian.* I had to take a personal step of faith in Christ, and, following that, I was baptized "for the first time."

AN HISTORICAL NOTE

For at least the first two hundred years of the early church's life, only believer's baptism by immersion was taught and practiced. Having tracked early church history and the records of the early church fathers, T. E. Watson quotes the German historian, Dr. L. Lange, who stated, "It must now be granted by every unprejudiced reader of holy Scripture and Christian antiquity, that the baptism of new-born children was altogether unknown to primitive Christianity."[8]

8. Lange, *History of Protestantism*, 221, quoted in Watson, *Should Infants be Baptized?*, 64.

At some point after the close of the second century, the tradition of "infant baptism" was introduced and took hold, and baptismal regeneration soon began to take root. What was known as "clinic baptism" was practiced (from *kline—a couch*), which referred to people close to death, lying on a couch or bed because of illness and having water poured on them to "have their sins washed away." Henry C. Vedder says, "It was, however, a short and easy step to diminish the quantity of water, and then apply it to other than sick persons."[9] It was not long before infants were being "baptized" in this manner. Vedder then traces the development of this tradition until it became the doctrine of baptismal regeneration taught by the Roman Catholic Church. However, despite growing persecution, a remnant of faithful and true believers continued down the years to preach the biblical gospel of redemption by grace and faith alone, testified to in believer's baptism.

With the great Reformation of the 1400s and 1500s came the restoration of biblical truth and with it a return, by a growing number in the emerging evangelical congregations, to the practice of believer's baptism by immersion. This resulted in widespread persecution by the Roman Catholic Church, with those holding to New Testament truth and practice being put to death in the cruelest of ways: being burnt alive, tortured to death, or drowned.

Today almost every evangelical church, denomination, or group of churches baptizes believers by immersion because it is the clear teaching of God's word.[10] However, infant baptism, and even the teaching of baptismal regeneration, is still taught and practiced. The following is an extract from the "Order Of Service" for the baptism of a child in one of the major denominations:

> *Priest:* (Standing in front of the waters of baptism); Almighty God, whose Son Jesus Christ was baptised in the River Jordan: We thank you for the gift of water to cleanse and revive us . . . bless this water,

9. Vedder, *A Short History of the Baptists*, 48.

10. Some examples of denominations and groups: Pentecostal and Charismatic churches, Christian Brethren, New Covenant Fellowship, Faith Community of Churches, Evangelical non-denominational churches (sometimes called "free churches" in the UK), Independent Bible-based churches of the third world, and almost all non-denominational mission organization. There are also a good number of Methodist and Presbyterian churches across the world (depending on their affiliation to parent bodies in their constituencies) who will baptize believers if so requested in private ceremonies, and some will baptize converts on the mission field, although not in their western (white) churches.

that your servants who are washed in it may be made one with Christ in His death and resurrection, to be cleansed and delivered from all sin. Send your Holy Spirit upon them to bring them to new birth in the family of your Church, and raise them up with Christ to full and eternal life.

Upon pouring water on the child, or dipping him in the water, the Priest then says; "I baptise you in the name of the Father, and of the Son, and of the Holy Spirit."

The Priest and the congregation, representing the whole Church, welcome the newly baptised infant.

Priest: God has received you by baptism into His Church.

This brings us back to the question I posed at the beginning of my essay: *Who is a Christian?* Baptism, however it is seen, must never be confused with the simple gospel.

A BROAD SUMMARY

1. The Greek word *baptizo* means to *immerse,* to *submerge* and also carries the idea to *merge* and *identify* with.

2. Christ identified with us and set us an example when he was baptized by John in the River Jordan at the commencement of his public ministry.

3. Christ gave us a command and a simple, dynamic three-point plan for his church: (1) make disciples; (2) baptize those disciples; (3) continue to teach those disciples (Matt 28:18–20).

4. Baptism does not remove sin; it is a testimony to others and a pledge to God.

5. The early church, from its birth on the day of Pentecost, obeyed Christ's command, baptizing believers by immersion. This continued for at least 200 years until tradition entered the life of the church.

6. Believer's baptism is an important aspect of our ongoing discipleship. Jesus said, "If you love me, you will obey what I command" (John 14:15).

AVOIDING MISREPRESENTATIONS

The Scriptures are consistently clear that salvation is by grace through repentance and faith alone. However, there are some who teach that baptism is an essential element of our conversion experience.[11] They insist that passages like Acts 2:38 and 1 Peter 3:18–22 are saying that to believe without being baptized is insufficient for eternal life.

In answering that, I begin with the teaching of Scripture and the testimony of the gospel. The gospel of Christ teaches us that salvation and regeneration is by grace, repentance, and faith in the person and finished work of Christ *alone*, and that trust in Christ is preceded by the Holy Spirit's convicting and convincing work regarding sin, righteousness, and judgment (John 16:8–11). If baptism was an essential element of our salvation, then it follows that the Spirit would also convict and convince us of baptism, as well as the need of a saviour. Nowhere do we find that link of Christ's work and our baptism equalling salvation. Nothing can be added to his work. Christ and his redemptive work stand alone. We have no merit, action, good intention, or anything else we can add to what he has already accomplished. When Jesus cried out on the cross, "It is finished," he meant that his work for our redemption was complete (John 19:30). Salvation is not a partnership with Christ. To suggest that we cannot be saved until we are baptized is totally anti-gospel.

Then there is the logical question that must be asked: If I trust Christ today, but I am only baptized by immersion later—be it an hour later, or a week later, or even longer—am I saved during that time gap between believing and being baptized? Am I *partially* saved? What if I should die before being baptized—am I lost? Was Christ's work alone not sufficient? Space will not allow for the long list of verses that could be referred to in showing that baptism plays no active part in my salvation, but the following will suffice: John 1:11–13; 3:16, 36; Romans 5:1; Ephesians 2:8–10.

Acts 2:38 is sometimes used to support the teaching that baptism must accompany faith in order for a sinner to be saved. In context, Peter preached to the gathered crowd that Jesus was the promised Messiah, and that he was accredited by God to them by his miracles, wonders, and signs. He further preached that Jesus was put to death on a cross, raised from the dead, exalted to the highest place, and is both Lord and Christ (Acts 2:22ff cf. Joel 2; Pss 16; 110). The people were then cut to the heart and cried out, "Brothers, what shall we do?" (v. 37) Peter answered, "Repent and be

---

11. For example, the New Apostolic Church, Oneness Pentecostalism, and some branches of the Churches of Christ.

baptised, every one of you, in the name of Jesus Christ for the forgiveness of your sins. And you will receive the gift of the Holy Spirit" (v. 38).

Warren Wiersbe points out, "It is unfortunate that the *King James Version* suggests that people must be baptised in order to be saved."[12] He notes that the Greek word *eis* (translated *for*) can mean *on account of* or *on the basis of* "the remission of sins" (KJV). Peter was in fact preaching that baptism, while closely linked to trusting in Christ, is the outward indication of that trust in Christ. If Peter believed that faith *and baptism* were essential for conversion, he would have taught that, but he didn't.[13]

12. Wiersbe, *The Bible Exposition Commentary*, 410.

13. See Acts 3:12–26; 5:29–32; 10:34–43; 1 Pet 1:18–19. Notice that in Acts 10:47–48 the Gentiles received the Holy Spirit *at* their conversion, and were thus saved, before being baptized.

A Wesleyan Response

Eric Severson

Pastor Stone has indeed pointed us in the right direction when exploring the concept of Christian baptism. This sacrament is about identity, about Christian identity, and there should be no question concerning the intimate connection between the question, "Who is a Christian?" and the question, "Who should be baptized?" Furthermore, I have nothing but high praise for the articulate way that Pastor Stone outlines the way baptism is interpreted by Anabaptists and others who oppose the practice of baptizing infants. To disagree with this articulation one must start at the beginning. So it is here that I'll begin.

Stone answers the question, "Who is a Christian?" with a resounding answer, pointing a consistent finger toward the individual "who has had a personal, spiritual, life-changing encounter with the Lord Jesus Christ" (p. 117). Who could deny the responsibility of the Christian community to baptize such individuals? Still, is this the bedrock answer to the question, "Who is a Christian?" I'm not so sure.

THE INFLUENCE OF MODERN REDUCTIONISM IN CHRISTIANITY

The fundamental problem with Stone's argument is the pervasive modernist and individualistic assumptions loaded into the understanding of personhood, sin, salvation, and Christian identity. I am the first to agree that these categories are deeply informed by very personal connotations. However, we only see a distorted version of Christianity when we subtly shift from a *personal* understanding of Christianity into an *individualized* understanding. The difference is subtle, but perhaps this issue of infant baptism rides on this subtlety.

In his tormented journey into his own soul, Rene Descartes undertook to doubt all things doubtable and to reconstruct philosophy and theology on the foundation of that which is indubitable. Though he was able to doubt all sense data, the value of all stories, and even the existence of the desk at which he pondered, Descartes was unable to doubt the fact that he was a doubter. Whether or not it is justifiable to blame (or credit!) Descartes for the revolution that followed his meditations, it is fair to say that his "I think therefore I am" turned a key page in the history of Western thought. His meditations were dedicated to the faculty at the school of theology in Paris.[14] His purpose was to reconstruct theology on a firmer foundation to "prove" God, beginning with a new and more stable logic. Theology would never, indeed *will* never, be the same. Descartes gets a fair amount of unwarranted blame for the theological changes that follow his groundbreaking meditations. For our purposes here, I will not attempt to exonerate Descartes but to show how a little tract written in 1641 has come to influence the way we answer the question, "What is a Christian?"

As significant as the discovery of the indubitable *cogito ergo sum*[15] is, is the way that Descartes' doubting process assigned new levels of value to various religious categories. Of lesser value are the shifty, instable narratives and relationships that have been so important to Christians from the beginning. These foundations have proven to be unsteady during an era where rationalism demands more concrete and unchanging data. What matters more—perhaps *most*—is the individual and his or her "mind." The problem with *stories* is their openness to new interpretations and scathing critical questioning. Relationships are equally difficult to quantify, always changing and depending on multiple parties and interpretations. It is much easier to measure the health of an individual than to measure the health of a relationship or even a society. A physician can say with scientific confidence, "this patient is sick." But how much less stable is the statement, "this community is sick"? Descartes was right; there is stability to be found in reducing things to the least-common-denominator. And

---

14. Descartes, *Meditations on First Philosophy*, 1.

15. The famous Latin phrase which translates "I think therefore I am."

this reduction moves even beyond personal senses and personal stories and into the quiet and solitary stability of the individual human mind.

The modern era, with its foundations in this "reduction," has found a new way of answering Stone's question, "Who is a Christian?" The new answer, offered by Stone and many others, joins Descartes in cutting past the complex layers of narrative and community and reducing what it means to be a Christian to the least-common-denominator. For the modernist this reduction leaves us with the *believing* self. Only a *believing* self can be Christian; all others should be denied the waters of baptism. It would be foolish to deny that baptism is appropriate for selves who believe. As Stone has outlined, baptism and belief are intimately related in Scripture and Christian history. Interestingly, the sorts of arguments made by Stone to support believer-only baptism begin to appear only during the era of rationalism that Descartes helped craft.

I concur with Stone that in the earliest centuries there is a silent ambiguity with regard to the baptism of infants. It is simply difficult to tell how widespread this practice may have been, though it seems to have reached general acceptance by the middle of the third century. From the third century until about the time of the Reformation, infant baptism was practiced by Christian churches all over the world. One would suppose that the hoards of Christians who participated in this sacrament occasionally pondered the fundamental question, "Who is a Christian?" How could they ask this question and still baptize squealing, unbelieving infants?

The practice of infant baptism is rooted in an understanding of Christian identity that is not beholden to the modern reduction of religion to the individual. The practice of infant baptism flourished in pre-modern times, before the philosophy of modernity drove Christians to define "who is a Christian" without respect to community. It is the shift into the modern era that made the practice of infant baptism uncomfortable to a minority of Christians, specifically the minority that appears to have been most enamored with modern and rationalist thinking. Descartes' reduction remains valuable, just as the *personal* aspect of Christianity identity is undeniable and irrefutable. But like Descartes' meditations, believer-only baptism is lopsided, leaning too far into the realm of individualism and ignoring the richness of a theological heritage that can, hopefully, guide us out of some of the other individualistic excesses of the modern era.

SO WHO IS A CHRISTIAN?

To answer Stone's question directly, a Christian is *a member of the believing community*. This includes, and has always included, the senile, the disabled, the mentally handicapped, and children. Baptism is an act of inclusion, bringing the one who is *outside* of the saved community into the body of Christ. That *belief* is a part of the *believing* community is significant. This community is nothing if not based in the story of Jesus Christ. This understanding of Christian identity focuses attention on the fact that we are not "saved" as individuals, but as a people, as a community, and as a church. Some modernists, the Anabaptists in particular, have felt profoundly uncomfortable with the lack of structure to this way of constructing Christianity identity. Is it not much easier to have a litmus test, a way to gauge a person's "mind" to determine whether they qualify for these baptismal waters? It may indeed be easier and fit comfortably into the "reductionist" method of the modern mind. But this ease makes me uneasy.

The question, "Who is a Christian?" can never be appropriately answered without reference to the church, to relationship, to community, and to the body of Christ. The final reduction that allows for Christian identity to be definable without mention of relationship is the pulling of the fish out of the water. In order to analyze the fundamental question of who is a Christian, modernists perform a scientific dissection of the concept of Christian identity. But living creatures do not survive dissection, and the definition of a Christian that comes from the modern reductionism is as incomplete as a heart without a body. This final reduction leaves us with an abstract version of Christianity; a religion whose primary "locus" of activity is somewhere inside the isolated human mind. Belief remains the "heart" of Christian identity, but it is a heartbeat we share and nourish together. Seen verbally, belief is something we "do" together. A Christian is anyone who is a part of this community, the body, which crafts its identity in Christ and his future. One need not pass an IQ test to "believe" in this richly communal sense.

INFANT BAPTISM: A RICH FORM OF GRACE

The baptism of children, the senile, the mentally disabled, and others who cannot pass the "mind" test of modernity is a part of the rich Christian tradition of locating salvation primarily in the believing community, not first of all in the believing mind. This tradition embraces a kind of foolish optimism of grace, a confidence that the movement of grace precedes and intercedes for cognitive inadequacies. The "foolishness" of infant baptism is a foolish hope, grounding the life of a child within the community of the redeemed. The "baptized" child is a part of the reoriented community, the community that is nourished by the sacrament of communion to live toward the coming kingdom of God.

The modern understanding of the "self" is ultimately incapable of capturing the complexities of Christian theology. The tensions between personal belief and corporate faith are impossible to dissect or completely unravel. The question of "infant baptism" is ultimately about *who we refuse to baptize*. We are not, fortunately, pondering whether Christians should attempt to baptize people against their will—an unfortunate strategy employed occasionally during Christian history. When parents bring a child to be baptized by the church, trusting God and the community to safeguard the place of this child within the redeemed community, on what grounds do we send the parents away disappointed? What of the family who has just joined the community and wishes to baptize a grandfather wracked by Alzheimer's disease? What of the adult whose mental disabilities prevent her from pronouncing her own name?

The richness of Christian baptism is that it prizes personal confessions of faith but sees them forever in the context of a richer form of grace that can be distilled into the narrowness of individualistic categories or mental capacities. Believing is something we do together, with and for one another. Baptismal grace never abandons the central place of belief; it expands "belief" into a relational category. We believe together, and by the depth and wonder of grace our belief includes those whose brains are not yet able (or who may *never* be able) to believe anything in the modern sense. Infant baptism repeatedly reminds the community that Christian faith is not something we possess but something we do, something we do together, with and for one another.

9

Israel and the Church:
A Dispensational View

BENJAMIN R. WEBB JR.

INTRODUCTION

PREMILLENNIALISM IS THE BELIEF that the Lord Jesus Christ will return to establish his kingdom at the start of the millennium. All dispensationalists are premillennialists. The basic tenets of dispensationalism includes the belief that "the inhabitants of Jerusalem" (Israel) will one day believe on the Lord Jesus Christ and rule many nations in the millennial kingdom.[1] Israel's former enemies will worship in Jerusalem; there will be peace because Satan will be bound for a thousand years; and the nations will not learn war any more.[2]

Dispensationalists make a clear distinction between Israel and the church, and most believe a pre-tribulation "rapture" is found in 1 Thessalonians 4:14—5:3. Yet some non-dispensationalists also believe in a pre-trib "rapture."[3] The pre-trib "rapture" is the doctrine that the church will be caught up (or "raptured") into heaven *before* the seven-year Great Tribulation period and the revealing of the Antichrist while Israel will be left behind to face it. In Daniel 9:24–27, the angel Gabriel stated that seventy "weeks" (weeks of years, or 490 years; see Gen 29:27–30) were

---

1. See Numbers 24:8–18; Deuteronomy 15:6; Zechariah 8:13–23; 12:10; 14:16; Acts 1:6–8.

2. See Isaiah 2:2–4; Micah 4:1–3; Zechariah 14:16; Revelation 20:1–6.

3. Although the pre-trib "rapture" doctrine may not be the "official" position of the non-dispensational churches they attend, I have had many Christian friends who have disagreed with their particular church over this issue.

determined upon Israel and Jerusalem. In verse 26, he stated that Messiah (the Lord Jesus) would be "cut off, but not for himself: and the people of the prince that shall come shall destroy the city and the sanctuary."[4] Then he stated in verse 27, "he shall confirm the covenant with many for one week: and in the midst of the week he shall cause the sacrifice and the oblation to cease." Most dispensationalists believe "he" who confirms "the covenant with many for one week" refers back to "the prince that shall come" in verse 26 (this belief is not shared by non-dispensationalists). In turn, this evil "prince," the Antichrist, will stand up "against the Prince of princes" and destroy many "by peace" (Dan 8:25) and will be responsible for the false "peace and safety" that will usher in the destructive day of the Lord (1 Thess 5:2–3). The final "week" of Daniel 9:27 (the final seven-year period) will be a future time of tribulation caused by this "prince that shall come." It is believed that today this prophecy has temporarily been halted. Based on 1 Thessalonians 4:15—5:3, it is believed that Christians will be "raptured" to escape this future seven-year period of tribulation and "day of the Lord."

In addition, a small number of dispensationalists believe in a post-trib "rapture."[5] Other dispensationalists distinguish the "rapture" of 1 Thessalonians 4:16–17 from the resurrection of the dead in Philippians 3:11, known as the "out-resurrection."[6] So dispensationalists do not exclusively claim every tenet commonly associated with dispensationalism, and non-dispensational doctrines are often mixed with dispensational beliefs. But I shall try to be as fair as possible to all views here and inform the reader before I comment on more controversial views within dispensationalism. Most dispensationalists should therefore agree with many of my statements, even if they fail to agree with everything I write.

I shall also try to honestly represent opposing, non-dispensational viewpoints because misrepresentations would only undermine my own credibility. And I shall always be respectful to those who honestly disagree with me. I shall also quote as many passages as space permits, but quoting all passages would make my article far too lengthy. So every Scripture I reference should be looked up, in its context, for verification.[7]

---

4. Unless otherwise indicated, all Scripture quotations are taken from the *King James Version*.

5. Baker, *A Dispensational Theology*, 598.

6. Bullinger, *The Foundations of Dispensational Truth*, 106.

7. Many dispensationalists use various Bible versions, and do not limit their study

DISTINCT DISPENSATIONS

We dispensationalists are notorious for dividing Scripture into distinct dispensations: usually seven, often more, sometimes fewer.[8] Each dispensation is characterized by specific acts of obedience the Lord requires of humankind. God himself never changes, but his requirements do. Malachi 3:6 even states, "For I am the LORD, I change not" and Hebrews 13:8 also states, "Jesus Christ the same yesterday, and to day, and for ever." But just as an earthly father has different requirements for his eight-year-old son than he does for his eighteen-year-old son, so our heavenly Father also had different requirements for Old Testament Israel (Deut 6:24–25—"it shall be our righteousness, if we observe to do all these commandments") than he does for us today (Gal 2:21—"if righteousness come by the law, then Christ is dead in vain"). Faith is always required for obedience, but God's requirements must still be met on *his* terms. A man gathering sticks on the Sabbath learned this the hard way, when God ordered him to be put to death for doing so (Num 15:32–36). Paul therefore uses Romans 10:4–10 to contrast God's former requirement of Deuteronomy 6:24–25 with the fact that Christ is the end of the law for righteousness to every one who believes (cf. Gal 3:23–26). As Paul also explained when he was at Antioch in Pisidia, ". . . by [Jesus] all that believe are justified from all things, from which ye could not be justified by the law of Moses" (Acts 13:39). Therefore, a change in God's requirements generally indicates a dispensational change.

There are three major dispensational views regarding the "birth" of the church: *(1) Classic dispensationalists*[9] believe that the present church (the body of Christ) began sometime between the birth of Christ and

---

to a single version. Personally, I use the King James; but many other versions also verify the points I will be making. In fact, I have verified that my Scripture references are also supported by the Amplified, the A.S.V., and the New King James.

8. We are also criticized frequently for using charts or time lines, such as those drawn by Larkin, *Dispensational Truth*. But there are valid reasons for these practices. Charts and time lines are simply visual aids ("a picture is worth a thousand words"). Like notes in a reference Bible, they are *not* inspired. Scripture alone is the final authority. Nor are we the only ones who use visual aids; some non-dispensationalists have also drawn some detailed charts and time lines, for similar reasons. The ones drawn from a Covenant Theology perspective by the Puritan William Perkins are also quite notable—available from Dr. C. Matthew McMahon, *A Puritan's Mind*, 4101 Coral Tree Circle #214, Coconut Creek, FL 33073.

9. Also known as "Traditional" or "Acts 2" dispensationalists.

the day of Pentecost; *(2) Mid-Acts dispensationalists* believe it began with Paul in the Mid-Acts period; and *(3) Acts 28 dispensationalists* believe it began sometime around Acts chapter 28. Most classic dispensationalists also believe that the New Testament epistles of James through Jude were written directly to the body of Christ. By contrast, Mid-Acts and Acts 28 dispensationalists do not believe these epistles were written directly to the church today but to future Israel after she repents and returns to the Lord.[10] Acts 28 dispensationalists also distinguish themselves from the other two groups with their belief that the book of Acts, along with Paul's Acts-period epistles, does not record the beginning of church history but "the Biblical conclusion of Israel's past history."[11] So Mid-Acts and Acts 28 dispensationalists are also known as *ultra-* or *hyper-*dispensationalists because they make additional divisions in Scripture. The prefixes "ultra" and "hyper" simply mean "farther than," and are not derogatory terms although many critics use them as such.

THE MESSIANIC KINGDOM

Dispensationalists and non-dispensationalists agree that God has translated us into the kingdom of his dear Son (Col 1:13) and that flesh and blood cannot inherit the kingdom of God (1 Cor 15:50). But each draws a different conclusion here. Many non-dispensationalists believe that the kingdom has been taken from Israel and is now spiritual. So the church, as "spiritual" Israel, has replaced the nation of Israel and inherited her promises.[12] By contrast, dispensationalists believe Israel's kingdom (the messianic kingdom) has only been delayed. One day believers will be changed at the "rapture" (1 Cor 15:51–52). Afterward, there will also be a physical change for Israel in the millennium. Children will "die an hundred years old; but the sinner being an hundred years old shall be accursed" (Is. 65:20). The Lord will write his law in the hearts of Israel (Isa 51:7; Jer 31:33), and they shall *all* know him (Jer 31:34, Zech 12:10).

Therefore, dispensationalists do not believe that the church today is the messianic kingdom, although it is still part of the kingdom of God.

---

10. They also like to point out that all Scripture is *for* our learning and admonition (Rom 15:4; 1 Cor 10:11); but not all Scripture is *to* us. For example, both groups read James 1:1 literally, in view of Galatians 2:7–9.

11. Bullinger, *Foundations*, 195.

12. Baker, *A Dispensational Theology*, 476.

Charles Baker likens the kingdom of God to the United States, with individual states representing the body of Christ and the messianic kingdom: "One may be in New York or California and be in the United States, but one cannot be in New York while he is in California. And just as New York and California are separate and distinct parts of the United States, so the Body of Christ and the Messianic Kingdom are separate and distinct parts of the Kingdom of God."[13]

The prophet Hosea also saw a day when God would call Israel "Lo-ammi" (1:9—"not my people"). Today, Israel is fulfilling this prophecy by rejecting the Lord Jesus Christ, the only way to the Father (John 14:6). But we believe her rejection is only temporary. Because Paul states in Romans 11:25 that Israel is blinded "in part" *until* "the fullness of the Gentiles" comes in, she will no longer be blinded after that time. After the Lord's resurrection, the apostles also expected him to restore Israel's kingdom (Acts 1:6–8). He never denied that it would be restored, so we believe Israel's kingdom has only been delayed and not permanently taken away. One day we will see Romans 11:26 being literally fulfilled ("all Israel shall be saved") when Israel is provoked to jealousy and believes on the Lord Jesus Christ (Rom 11:11; Zech 12:10). So if we can show from Scripture that Israel will still receive her kingdom, we have a good case for dispensationalism.

Deuteronomy 15:6 and Zechariah 14:16–17 shows us that Israel was promised a literal kingdom. God also promised to place her above all people (Exod 19:5–6), and she would be a *kingdom* of priests—a priest mediates between God and man. Israel would be a "peculiar people . . . above all the nations" (Deut 14:2), "special . . . above all people" (Deut 7:6), and "above all nations of the earth" (Deut 28:1).

But Israel rebelled and was scattered among the nations (Deut 4:27–28, 28:64; Neh 1:8). So again, many non-dispensationalists believe the Lord is finished with Israel. Dispensationalists, though, believe that passages such as Leviticus 26:44–45 and Deuteronomy 4:30–31 prove that the Lord has only *temporarily* forsaken Israel. Also, Zechariah 12:10 states that one day the house of David and the inhabitants of Jerusalem "shall look upon me whom they have pierced, and they shall mourn . . . as one that is in bitterness for his firstborn" (i.e., they shall mourn for the Lord Jesus Christ, whom they pierced when they crucified him). Isaiah

13. Ibid., 318.

54:7 states, "For a small moment have I forsaken thee; but with great mercies will I gather thee." Jeremiah 29:14 also states, "I will gather you from all the nations, and from all the places whither I have driven you." And finally, Ezekiel 11:17 states, "I will even gather you from the people, and assemble you out of the countries where ye have been scattered, and I will give you the land of Israel."[14] Taken literally, these passages show that the Lord still has plans for Israel. Therefore, we believe Israel will repent and be gathered back into the land.[15]

In fact, at least one restoration of Jerusalem has already taken place. After the Lord had scattered Israel for being disobedient, and Nehemiah the son of Hachaliah was the king's cupbearer (Neh 1:11), he received word that the Jews of Jerusalem were "in great affliction and reproach"; the wall of Jerusalem had been broken down and the gates of Jerusalem had been burned (Neh 1:1–3). But Nehemiah believed the Lord literally meant what he had promised in Deuteronomy 30:1–5:

> And it shall come to pass, when all these things are come upon thee, the blessing and the curse, which I have set before thee, and thou shalt call them to mind among all the nations, whither the LORD thy God hath driven thee: And shalt return unto the LORD thy God, and shalt obey his voice according to all that I command thee this day, thou and thy children, with all thine heart, and with all thy soul: That then the LORD thy God will turn thy captivity, and have compassion upon thee, and will return and gather thee from all the nations, whither the LORD thy God hath scattered thee: If any of thine be driven out unto the outmost parts of heaven, from thence will the LORD thy God gather thee, and from thence will he fetch thee: And the LORD thy God will bring thee into the land which thy fathers possessed, and thou shalt possess it; and he will do thee good, and multiply thee above thy fathers.

So Nehemiah asked the Lord to remember his promise to gather Israel, even from "the uttermost part of the heaven" (Neh 1:9). Thus began an earlier restoration of Jerusalem. But men have short memories, and Israel again rebelled. So again, Israel was scattered among the nations.

14. Also see Deuteronomy 30:1–5; Jeremiah 30:10–24; 31:7–11; Ezekiel 28:25–26; 36:24–28.

15. Many dispensationalists believe the Lord Jesus was referring to this promise of gathering Israel out of the nations and back into the land, when he stated in Matthew 24:31 that *after* the tribulation, his angels will gather together his elect "from one end of heaven to the other." See Baker, *A Dispensational Theology*, 594.

Yet, as we've seen above, the Lord has not permanently forsaken Israel. We know the Lord is able to forgive Israel more than once because even Peter was to forgive his brother "seventy times seven" (Matt 18:22). The Lord's ways are so much higher than our ways (Isa 55:8–9), so he would be even more willing to forgive Israel "seventy times seven." One day Israel must repent because the Lord will "set his hand again the second time to recover the remnant of his people" (Isa 11:11); and Israel will actually *loathe* herself for all the evils that she has committed (Ezek 20:43).

Israel must also return to the land because Deuteronomy 30:1–5 was only partially fulfilled by Nehemiah's restoration of Jerusalem. Indeed, there are many other cases where a prophecy had been partially fulfilled, yet that same prophecy would still await a complete fulfillment. One example is the prophecy that the day of the Lord will come as *destruction* (Isa 13:6, 9; Joel 1:15ff). God promised to "stir up the Medes" in the day of the Lord (Isa 13:17), and Scripture proves that he did so (Dan 5:31; 9:1; 11:1). Yet the day of the Lord itself was not completely fulfilled by the Medes because, five centuries later, Paul and Peter both stated that the day of the Lord was still a *future* event (1 Thess 5:2; 2 Pet 3:10). Therefore, because Deuteronomy 30:1–5 was only partially fulfilled by Nehemiah's restoration of Jerusalem, the Lord repeated his promise to restore Israel.[16]

Just as Israel and Judah have been a curse among the heathen, so will they also be a blessing one day: "And it shall come to pass, that as ye were a curse among the heathen, O house of Judah, and house of Israel; so will I save you, and ye shall be a blessing . . . So again have I thought in these days to do well unto Jerusalem and to the house of Judah: fear ye

---

16. Another Scripture that has only been partially fulfilled is Zechariah 12:10. Most dispensationalists believe this prophecy will be ultimately fulfilled at the Lord's second coming (after the "rapture" and tribulation have taken place), when "every eye shall see him, and they also which pierced him: and all kindreds of the earth shall wail because of him" (Rev 1:7). It is believed that this Scripture was only partially fulfilled after the Lord's crucifixion. According to John 19:34–37, one of the soldiers who came to remove the body of Jesus from the cross pierced his side with a spear, "and forthwith came there out blood and water . . . that the scripture should be fulfilled, A bone of him shall not be broken. And again another scripture saith, They shall look on him whom they pierced." Most Bible versions that use the "formal equivalence" (word-for-word) method of translation (KJV; ASV; NASB) do not have John 19:37 stating that the prophecy in Zechariah 12:10 was fulfilled. Instead, according to these translations, only Psalm 34:20 was fulfilled (the prophecy that the Lord's bones would not be broken); and John is simply referencing Zechariah 12:10. In *The Companion Bible*, E. W. Bullinger's notes on John 19:37 state that Zechariah 12:10 ". . . was fulfilled in the case of those who looked upon Him, but waits for its complete fulfillment when the spirit of grace and supplication is poured out on repentant Israel."

not" (Zech 8:13, 15 cf. Jer 44:8). Later in this passage, the Lord promised that "many people and strong nations" will seek him in Jerusalem: "Yea, many people and strong nations shall come to seek the LORD of hosts in Jerusalem, and to pray before the LORD . . . it shall come to pass, that ten men shall take hold out of all languages of the nations, even shall take hold of the skirt of him that is a Jew, saying, We will go with you: for we have heard that God is with you" (vv. 22–23). This passage is *not* referring to the church because verse 13 states that Israel and Judah were a "curse" among the heathen, just as Jeremiah 44:8 states that the Jews have been a curse among the nations (the heathen). Yet the church was never a curse. Nor does "him that is a Jew," whom God is "with," refer to the Lord Jesus because he *is* God (John 1:1). One day Israel and Judah will truly be a "blessing" when "strong nations . . . seek the LORD of hosts in Jerusalem." Just as Nehemiah literally interpreted Deuteronomy 30:1–5, so dispensationalists also believe that the above passage is literal.

THE GOSPEL OF THE KINGDOM AND THE MILLENNIUM

Earlier, I promised to notify the reader before I depart from making more than general comments on dispensationalism, and some may consider my following statements to be such a departure:

Many (but not all) dispensationalists believe the gospel of the kingdom preached in the four Gospels was different from today's gospel of grace. This is because the gospel by which we are saved is that Christ died for our sins (1 Cor 15:1–4). But in the four Gospels, the apostles did not know that the Lord had to die (Luke 18:31–34), and yet they had been preaching "the gospel" for quite some time (Luke 9:6 cf. vv. 44–45). Therefore, they could not have been preaching the gospel by which *we* are saved. In Matthew 16:21–23, Peter even rebuked the Lord who had stated that he would be killed and raised again on the third day. Even on the morning of the Lord's resurrection, Peter and John still did not know that he would rise from the dead (John 20:9). How, then, could they have been preaching the gospel by which we are saved, that "Christ died for our sins"? Indeed, the fact that Christ was going to die *had* to remain hidden from "the princes of this world"; otherwise, "had they known it, they would not have crucified the Lord of glory" (1 Cor 2:8). Therefore, the gospel preached in the four Gospels is called the "gospel of the kingdom" (Matt 4:23, 9:35).

Basically, the content of the gospel of the kingdom concerns the "good news" that the kingdom prophesied in the Old Testament was "at hand" (Matt 3:2). Israel would receive her kingdom if she repented and believed on the Lord Jesus Christ. By taking the gospel of the kingdom to the rest of the world, they would establish the messianic kingdom (Matt 28:18–20). That is why, in the four Gospels, as well as in the first part of the book of Acts, Peter and the other apostles did not expect the nation of Israel to reject the Lord Jesus Christ. Nor did they know that salvation would eventually "come unto the Gentiles" through the "fall" of Israel, "to provoke them [Israel] to jealousy" (Rom 11:11).

When the Lord stated that "the meek" shall inherit *the earth* in Matthew 5:5 (a quote from Psalm 37:11), many dispensationalists believe he was speaking only to the Jews, and not to the church today.[17] If so, this further proves that Israel stands to receive a literal kingdom in the millennium. For one reason, if the kingdom were spiritual, why would the meek inherit the earth?

Even after the Lord's resurrection, his apostles asked if he would at *that* time "restore again the kingdom to Israel" (Acts 1:3–7). Because they expected the kingdom to be restored *to Israel,* they were still looking for a real kingdom (the millennial kingdom) and had not been preaching a "spiritual" kingdom for the church. When this kingdom is established, "the dragon, that old serpent, which is the Devil, and Satan" will be bound for a thousand years, and those who were beheaded for Christ will reign with him (Rev 20:1–4). This resurrection is also mentioned in the Old Testament (Isa 26:19–21; Ezek 37:12–14; Dan 12:1–3). Many dispensationalists believe the Lord was referring to this resurrection into the millennial kingdom when he stated, ". . . in the regeneration when the Son of man shall sit in the throne of his glory [and the 12 apostles] shall sit upon twelve thrones, judging the twelve tribes of Israel" (Matt 19:28).[18] Some also believe that the Lord was referring to this in Isaiah 1:26, when he told Jerusalem that he would "restore thy judges as at the first."[19]

---

17. Baker, *A Dispensational Theology,* 323.

18. With Matthias replacing Judas: see Acts 1:20–26, where Peter gives a "composite" quotation of Psalms 69:25 and 109:8 (a practice followed by many New Testament writers).

19. In turn, this is a reference to passages such as Deuteronomy 16:18–20, where the Lord originally set up judges over Israel.

THE PRE-TRIBULATION "RAPTURE" VIEW

As stated earlier, most dispensationalists also believe in a pre-trib "rapture." One criticism of the "rapture" doctrine (even from non-dispensational *Trinitarians*) is that the word "rapture" is not in the Greek text or in the English Bible. But this is not a valid argument because neither is the word "Trinity" in the Greek text or the English Bible. Instead, the word "rapture" is a transliteration of the Latin word for "caught up" (*raeptius*) in the Latin Vulgate translation of 1 Thessalonians 4:17. Paul originally wrote these words in Greek. Later, Jerome translated these words from Greek into Latin for his Vulgate, which in turn has been translated from Latin into English. When *raeptius* is carried over into English, the word becomes "rapture." So I shall always put the word "rapture" in quotation marks to show that I realize the word is only a transliteration.

The events of 1 Thessalonians 4:15—5:3 are chronological, so the pre-trib "rapture" is indeed a scriptural doctrine—contrary to the claims of its critics. Translators inserted chapter divisions to make verses easier to find. But chapter divisions can also be a hindrance because they encourage us to start reading at the beginning of a chapter and to stop reading at the end of it. However, when the passage is read in its entirety, we find that we who are alive will one day be *caught up* ("raptured") together with the dead in Christ to meet the Lord "in the air." Paul does *not* say that the Lord will come to earth at this time. So he is not referring to the prophesied second coming of the Lord, when his feet "shall stand . . . upon the mount of Olives, which is before Jerusalem on the east, and the mount of Olives shall cleave in the midst" (Zech 14:4). The prophesied second coming of the Lord, often confused with the "rapture" of the church, is truly a separate event.

Paul then describes the day of the Lord, which will take place after we are caught up, as sudden "destruction" that will come "as a thief in the night" upon "them" (those left behind after the "rapture"). As we saw earlier, Old Testament prophets such as Joel and Isaiah also describe the day of the LORD as "destruction" from the Almighty (Isa 13:6, 9; Joel 1:15). It will only be *after* we are "caught up" to meet the Lord in the air, and "they" (those left behind) say, "Peace and safety," that the destruction shall suddenly come upon *them* (not us), "and they shall not escape." This sequence of events should be read without chapter divisions in 1 Thessalonians 4:14 through 5:3.[20]

Paul states in verse 15 above that he was writing by the word of the Lord. Therefore, many dispensationalists believe he wrote this by special revelation. Only Paul states that living believers will be caught up together with the dead in Christ "in the clouds, to meet the Lord in the air," *prior* to the day of the Lord. Indeed, Paul actually stated in 1 Corinthians 15:51–53 that he was showing the Corinthians a "mystery" (something not previously revealed). As further proof that Paul wrote about things not previously revealed, he was to continue receiving visions and revelations; so he was given a "thorn in the flesh" to keep him from being "exalted above measure" (2 Cor 12:1–7). This explains why many dispensationalists do not believe any other Bible writer mentions the pre-trib "rapture." Nobody else received the revelations that Paul received.

One day, when the people of Israel return to God, he will gather them from the nations wherein they are scattered, even if they have been driven to "the outmost parts of heaven" (Deut 30:1–5). Some dispensationalists believe the Lord Jesus was referring to this gathering of Israel *from* "the outmost parts of heaven" when he stated that his angels shall gather together his elect "from one end of heaven to the other":

> Immediately after the tribulation of those days shall the sun be darkened, and the moon shall not give her light . . . And then shall appear the sign of the Son of man in heaven: and then shall all the tribes of the earth mourn, and they shall see the Son of man coming in the clouds of heaven with power and great glory. And he shall send his angels with a great sound of a trumpet, and they shall gather together his elect from the four winds, from one end of heaven to the other. (Matt 24:29–31)

Because this gathering together of the elect occurs after the tribulation, many non-dispensationalists believe the Lord was referring here to a *post*-trib "rapture." But as we have seen, when Nehemiah petitioned the Lord about his promise to gather Israel from "the uttermost part of the heaven" (Neh 1:8–9), he was clearly referring to Deuteronomy 30:4 5 where the Lord promised to gather Israel from "the outmost parts of heaven." So the Lord's promise to gather his elect "from one end of heaven

---

20. Before continuing with the rest of this essay, I would urge the reader to read 1 Thessalonians 4:14 through 5:3.

to the other" could also be a reference to Deuteronomy 30:4–5 instead of a reference to a post-trib "rapture."

But even if the Lord was not referring to Deuteronomy 30:1–5, he still explained a parable in Matthew 13, indicating that he will actually allow the "children of the wicked one" and the "children of the kingdom" (Matt 13:38) to coexist, until the wicked are gathered *out* of his kingdom (Matt 13:41). In the parable, a man sows good wheat seed in his field, but an enemy secretly sows tares among the wheat. When his servants find the tares and wheat growing together, he tells them not to gather the tares in case they pull up the wheat with the tares. Instead, they are to let both grow together until the harvest. Then, they are to *first* gather the tares for *burning* and gather the wheat into his barn (v. 30). Later, the Lord explains the parable to his disciples:

> He answered and said unto them, He that soweth the good seed is the Son of man; The field is the world; the good seed are the children of the kingdom; but the tares are the children of the wicked one; The enemy that sowed them is the devil; the harvest is the end of the world; and the reapers are the angels. As therefore the tares are gathered and burned in the fire; so shall it be in the end of this world. The Son of man shall send forth his angels, and they shall gather out of his kingdom all things that offend, and them which do iniquity; And shall cast them into a furnace of fire: there shall be wailing and gnashing of teeth. (Matt 13:37–42)

Just as the servants in the parable first gather the tares for burning, so the Lord's angels will gather *out* of his kingdom "them which do iniquity." In both the parable and the explanation, the undesirable are destroyed from *among* the desirable. This is the post-"rapture" destruction that most dispensationalists believe Paul was writing about in 1 Thessalonians 5:2–3.

The Lord also stated that just as the flood destroyed the wicked in Noah's day, so would the wicked be destroyed in the days of the Son of man:

> And as it was in the days of Noe, so shall it be also in the days of the Son of man. They did eat, they drank, they married wives, they were given in marriage, until the day that Noe entered into the ark, and the flood came, and destroyed them all. Likewise also as it was in the days of Lot; they did eat, they drank, they bought, they sold, they planted, they builded; But the same day that Lot went out of

Sodom it rained fire and brimstone from heaven, and destroyed them all. Even thus shall it be in the day when the Son of man is revealed. In that day, he which shall be upon the housetop, and his stuff in the house, let him not come down to take it away: and he that is in the field, let him likewise not return back. Remember Lot's wife. Whosoever shall seek to save his life shall lose it; and whosoever shall lose his life shall preserve it. I tell you, in that night there shall be two men in one bed; the one shall be taken, and the other shall be left. Two women shall be grinding together; the one shall be taken, and the other left. Two men shall be in the field; the one shall be taken, and the other left. (Luke 17:26–36 cf. Matt 24:37–42)

Those who are "taken" at the Lord's second coming will not be "raptured" but destroyed (2 Thess 1:7–9). Again, many dispensationalists disagree with those who teach that this passage refers to a post-trib "rapture." Instead, we believe it refers to the post-"rapture" *destruction.*

FUTURE FULFILLMENT OF PROPHECY

Going back to a point made earlier, dispensationalists do not believe prophecies concerning Israel are being ultimately fulfilled by the church today. Many also believe that the "last days" of Acts 2:16–20 were temporarily interrupted by this present dispensation for several reasons. On the day of Pentecost, for example, Peter told the Jews in Jerusalem that the "last days" prophesied in Joel 2:28–31 were already beginning:

But this is that which was spoken by the prophet Joel; And it shall come to pass in the last days, saith God, I will pour out of my Spirit upon all flesh: and your sons and your daughters shall prophesy, and your young men shall see visions, and your old men shall dream dreams: And on my servants and on my handmaidens I will pour out in those days of my Spirit; and they shall prophesy: And I will shew wonders in heaven above, and signs in the earth beneath; blood, and fire, and vapour of smoke: The sun shall be turned into darkness, and the moon into blood, before that great and notable day of the Lord come. (Acts 2:16–20)

According to verses 16–17 above, Peter realized Joel's prophesied "last days" were starting to be fulfilled and expected those "last days" to continue through the prophesied "day of the Lord." But many years later, when he wrote his second epistle, this same apostle Peter stated that there *shall come* scoffers in the "last days" (2 Pet 3:3–4). In other words, the "last days" had somehow become a *future* event.

Therefore, at some point between the day of Pentecost and the writing of Peter's second epistle, the "last days" of prophecy were interrupted. Many dispensationalists believe that shortly after Joel's prophesied "last days" began in Acts 2, the Lord temporarily halted them and began this non-prophesied dispensation. When he did so, the "last days," along with the tribulation and the day of the Lord, all became future events (1 Thess 5:2–3; 2 Pet 3:10). After the "rapture," prophecy will resume with the sun and moon being darkened. Then the LORD will "roar out of Zion":

> Multitudes, multitudes in the valley of decision: for the day of the LORD is near in the valley of decision. The sun and the moon shall be darkened, and the stars shall withdraw their shining. The LORD also shall roar out of Zion, and utter his voice from Jerusalem; and the heavens and the earth shall shake: but the LORD will be the hope of his people, and the strength of the children of Israel." (Joel 3:14–16)

Paul, by inspiration of God, makes a "composite" quotation of this passage by combining Joel 3:16 above with Isaiah 59:20–21 and 27:9. By doing so, he shows that this entire event is still future. The result is his statement that "the Deliverer" will come out of Zion *when* "the fulness of the Gentiles" has come in and "all Israel" shall be saved: ". . . blindness in part is happened to Israel, until the fulness of the Gentiles be come in. And so all Israel shall be saved: as it is written, There shall come out of Sion the Deliverer, and shall turn away ungodliness from Jacob: For this is my covenant unto them, when I shall take away their sins." (Rom 11:25–27)

The second passage in Paul's composite quotation states, "And the Redeemer shall come to Zion, and unto them that turn from transgression in Jacob, saith the LORD. As for me, this is my covenant with them" (Isa 59:20–21). And the third passage in Paul's composite quotation states, "By this therefore shall the iniquity of Jacob be purged; and this is all the fruit to take away his sin" (Isa 27:9). Paul therefore connects the Deliverer (the Lord) coming out of "Sion"[21] with "all Israel" being saved, and Joel connects this event (the LORD roaring out of Zion) with the darkening of the sun and moon.[22] So the fact that Israel is blinded "until the fulness

---

21. New Testament spelling for "Zion."

22. This occurs *after* the tribulation; see Matthew 24:29.

of the Gentiles be come in" shows that Israel's temporal blindness will end when the Deliverer comes out of Zion. Dispensationalists and non-dispensationalists alike believe we could soon see the stage being set, but dispensationalists do not believe we will see the day of the Lord while we are on this earth.

The prophet Ezekiel also states that the Lord will one day gather the people of Israel out of the countries wherein they are scattered (20:34–43).[23] Verse 43 states that Israel will one day loathe herself for her past evils.[24] Verses 37–38 also state that the rebels and transgressors will be purged *out* when the Lord brings Israel into "the bond of the covenant."[25] Those who are purged will not enter the land of Israel. Ezekiel does not say what will happen to them, but they will probably be destroyed.[26] Verse 37, which states that the Lord will bring Israel "into the bond of the covenant," is a reference to the "new covenant" the Lord will one day make with the house of Israel and the house of Judah (Jer 31:31–37). In that passage, Jeremiah states that the status of the "seed of Israel" as a *nation* before the Lord is as permanent as the sun and the moon, and the Lord will not "cast off all the seed of Israel." Although many opponents of dispensationalism believe the Lord is finished with Israel, Jeremiah states otherwise. The "new covenant" with Israel and Judah still awaits a future fulfillment.[27]

AVOIDING MISREPRESENTATIONS

As Michael Meiring states elsewhere, a misrepresentation is not a disagreement over doctrine, but rather, "an inaccurate or distorted presentation of someone else's belief" (p. 12 ft. 7). In this section, I will address certain misrepresentations of dispensationalism, which cause it to be looked upon negatively by some Christians.

Our belief that the gospel of the kingdom and the gospel of grace are different is misrepresented in an article entitled *Moses or Christ? Paul's Reply To Dispensational Error*, which equates us with the "false brethren"

23. Again, I would urge the reader to first read Ezekiel 20:34–43 before proceeding with the rest of my essay.

24. Dispensationalists believe this will take place at the fulfillment of Zechariah 12:10, when the house of David and the inhabitants of Jerusalem "look upon me [the Lord Jesus] whom they have pierced, and mourn . . ."

25. See Matthew 13:37–42 and Luke 17:26–36.

26. See Isaiah 13:6–9; Joel 1:15; 1 Thessalonians 5:3; 2 Peter 3:10.

27. Along with the promises in Deuteronomy 4:29–31; 30:1–5; Ezekiel 20:34–43.

in Galatians 2:4 (whom Paul soundly rebuked). The author claims that our "error" comes from "the same Judaistic root whose fundamental ground is that Jewish privilege and priority are perpetual and that the New Testament Church at best is only a makeshift arrangement of providence to tide over the time until the resources of a baffled and well-nigh impotent Godhead are assembled in sufficient force to compel at last a Jewish solution of the problem of redemption." This is nothing more than inflammatory rhetoric because we do *not* believe that the church "at best is only a makeshift arrangement of providence." And to state that "a baffled and well-nigh impotent Godhead" is the head of our church is absolutely dishonest. We proclaim the same all-powerful Trinity as believed in by the Lutherans, Presbyterians, and other non-dispensational brethren.

The article then goes on to say:

> The theory has become sinister and subversive through its elaboration into a succession of "ages" to which belong certain well-defined segments of Holy Scripture, all combining to exclude "the church" from all but a fragment of the Divine Word. The Jewish theory predominates. A variety of second comings and last judgments has been invented. The abolition of the gospel has been proclaimed with great enthusiasm for it is fundamental to pre-millennialism that another gospel known as "the gospel of the kingdom" will take the place of the gospel of grace when "the church" is safety removed out of the way.[28]

At least the author accurately describes our belief that the gospel of the kingdom will replace the gospel of grace after the "rapture." Yet he destroys his credibility by portraying our belief as a "theory . . . sinister and subversive." Our belief is valid because the apostles never knew the Lord would die at all. So they could not have been preaching the gospel "by which [we] are saved," that Christ died for our sins (1 Cor 15:1–4).

But then, the author even misrepresents Paul's own words in Galatians 1:8 ("But though we, or an angel from heaven, preach any other gospel unto you than that which we have preached unto you, let him be accursed"). Because dispensationalists believe the gospel of the kingdom was different from today's gospel of grace, the author concludes from Galatians 1:8 that the gospel preached by dispensationalists is also different from the gospel that Paul preached. But this is obviously not what Paul meant. The gospel by which we are saved, and the gospel that Paul preached, is that Christ

28. Alexander, "Moses or Christ?" 32–36.

died for our sins. If anyone preaches a gospel *today* that fails to proclaim this fact, he is accursed. The gospel of the kingdom was certainly relevant during the four Gospels; it's just not relevant for *this* dispensation. Today, the gospel of grace has replaced the gospel of the kingdom. The gospel of the kingdom will again replace the gospel of grace (Matt 24:14) after the "rapture" and prior to the "end of the world" (Matt 24:3).

Michael also asked me to review a booklet written several years ago by another prominent non-dispensationalist, which also contains flagrant misrepresentations of dispensationalism. Upon reading the booklet, I found that this brother uses very little Scripture in his attempted refutation. Instead, he relies heavily on philosophical arguments to arrive at his conclusions. Personally, I believe this is because he *cannot* refute dispensationalism from Scripture alone, and so he must resort to philosophy. But Paul warns us in Colossians 2:8 to beware, lest any man spoil us "through philosophy and vain deceit, after the tradition of men, after the rudiments of the world, and not after Christ." I believe this brother has fallen into this trap. For example, he claims that our dispensational distinction between Israel and the church, along with our concept of predestination, imply a different "way" of salvation.[29] In fact, after accurately stating that Jesus Christ "is the same yesterday, today, and forever" (quoted from Hebrews 13:8), he even misrepresents what the passage itself says by stating that the Lord's *salvation* "is the same yesterday, today, and forever."[30] Yet the passage does not say this, nor does any other passage in the Bible. Instead, 1 Peter 1:9–12 indicates just the opposite: Peter states that the prophets "enquired and searched diligently" regarding the salvation of the souls to whom he was writing. This indicates that the salvation of the prophets actually was different from the salvation of these saints.[31] So if the Old Testament saints had the same salvation as Peter's audience, why would the prophets inquire about this salvation?

29. Gerstner, *A Primer on Dispensationalism*, 17.

30. Ibid.

31. Nor is this belief only supported by the King James Bible. Concerning the salvation Peter wrote about, the Amplified also states, "10 The prophets, who prophesied of the grace (divine blessing) which was intended for you, searched and inquired earnestly about this salvation. 11 They sought [to find out] to whom or when this was to come which the Spirit of Christ working within them was indicating when He predicted the sufferings of Christ and the glories that should follow [them]."

Let me be absolutely clear here. The Lord Jesus Christ is "the way, the truth, and the life." No man comes to the Father except through him (John 14:6). Peter also stated, "Neither is there salvation in any other: for there is none other name under heaven given among men, whereby we must be saved" (Acts 4:12). Non-dispensationalists and dispensationalists agree on this point, known as "Solo Christo" (Christ Alone). So our dispensational distinction between Israel and the church cannot imply a different "way" of salvation. Rather, we believe salvation itself in this present dispensation is different from salvation under the law, and salvation in the next dispensation (the millennial kingdom) will be different from salvation today.[32]

Unfortunately, I don't have enough space to address other misrepresentations in these booklets. In fact, it could take an entire booklet to properly refute them. But I can summarize other misrepresentations, where it is alleged that we believe a gospel of works will be preached in the millennium. Although there may be a few dispensationalists who believe this, most would disagree. We do, however, view Jeremiah 31:31–34 literally: "saith the LORD, I will put my law in [Israel's] inward parts, and write it in their hearts." Therefore, we believe the Lord will *supernaturally* enable Israel to keep his law in the millennium. But this does not mean a "gospel of works" will be preached at that time. We fully realize that faith in the Lord Jesus Christ alone will be required. Besides, if God supernaturally empowers his people to keep his law, they would not be the ones performing a "work" because he will be the one doing the empowering!

The same applies to our literal interpretation of Ezekiel 44:9: "No stranger, uncircumcised in heart, nor uncircumcised in flesh, shall enter into my sanctuary." Many dispensationalists take this to mean that in the millennium circumcision will again be required as an act of obedience, but *not* for salvation. Because we believe this passage literally means what it says, we are accused of teaching that a gospel of works will be preached at that time. Yet we actually believe circumcision may serve the same purpose that water baptism serves for most Christians today. With the exception of hyper-dispensationalists, most Christians view water baptism as an "act of obedience." In fact, some churches even *require* water baptism for those who would join the church. A few churches do not even consider someone to be a "true" Christian unless he is baptized with water. Although they realize water baptism is not a work of salvation, they still

---

32. Baker, *A Dispensational Theology*, 280.

require it as an act of obedience. In like manner, many dispensationalists believe Ezekiel 44:7–9 literally means what it says, and circumcision will also be an act of obedience in the millennial temple.[33]

It should be noted that today's regeneration of *uncircumcised* Gentiles was also unthinkable in Old Testament times. Even though Gentile sanctification was prophesied throughout the Old Testament, it was never implied that the sanctified would include uncircumcised Gentiles. The book of Isaiah alone is full of prophecies that the Lord will one day bless Gentiles,[34] but neither Isaiah, nor any other Old Testament writer, stated that circumcision would no longer be required, as is the case today. Instead, the Lord told Abraham, "the uncircumcised man child . . . shall be cut off from his people" (Gen 17:14). He also told Moses, "when a stranger shall sojourn with thee, and will keep the Passover to the LORD, let all his males be circumcised . . . for no uncircumcised person shall eat thereof" (Exod 12:48). There is no implication anywhere that circumcision was to be done away with, yet it is no longer necessary today.

Therefore, critics should not be so quick to accuse us of teaching that a "gospel of works" will be preached in the millennium just because we believe Old Testament passages, such as Ezekiel 44:7–9, literally mean what they say. God is sovereign; he is all-powerful, but he cannot violate his word. He may not fulfill it in the expected way, but he will always keep his promises. Just as the Old Testament saint could not imagine that the Lord would ever sanctify the uncircumcised—even Peter had difficulty accepting this in Acts chapter 10—we also may not fully understand how the Lord will fulfill his promises.

And finally, some critics also misrepresent our beliefs by claiming that we throw away much of the Old Testament. But this chapter will hopefully prove their accusations to be false because I have probably quoted as many Old Testament passages as I have New Testament passages. In fact, the majority of this chapter is based on the Old Testament, just as the New Testament is based on the Old Testament. Therefore, dispensationalists are not throwing away any part of the Bible. Rather, those who misrepresent our beliefs are the ones who effectively throw away much of the Old Testament by denying the literalness of the passages in which the Lord promised a kingdom to Israel after she believes on the Lord Jesus Christ.

---

33. Granted, this is an obscure passage, but we are not building an entire doctrine upon this one passage.

34. See Isaiah 2:2–4; 11:10; 42:1–6; 49:6–22; 54:3; 60:3–16.

A Continuity Response

Adrio König

I WANT TO COMMEND Mr. Benjamin Webb for his gracious attitude toward other theological viewpoints, which is what one can expect of a professing Christian but often is missing in many theological debates.

However, I have serious problems with his theology, as I have with dispensationalism in general. If my understanding is correct, there are at least three main pillars on which dispensationalism rests: the literal fulfillment of prophecy, the discontinuity of Israel and the church, and the rapture. To my mind none of these are substantiated in Scripture.

THE LITERAL FULFILLMENT OF PROPHECY

Many Old Testament prophecies are fulfilled in the New Testament. So we have ample examples of how prophecies are indeed fulfilled. In my essay I have shown that these prophecies are not fulfilled literally but rather in a remarkably free way. The point I then made is that we cannot predict the future in terms of the prophecies (as dispensationalists try to do). No one beforehand would have predicted the time and/or the way the Spirit was poured out in light of the prophecy in Joel 2:28–32. One would have expected a much more dramatic, warlike event of blood and fire and smoke, a solar eclipse and a blood red moon. None of these, however, occurred literally, only the coming of the Spirit (which in the end made a much bigger impact on world history than yet another bloody war)!

In response to this clear biblical testimony of non-literal fulfillment, dispensationalists, like Webb himself, claim that prophecies may be fulfilled in part, with some detail in suspense for a future fulfillment. In this way they try to handle the fulfillment of Joel 2 in Acts 2, claiming that merely the coming of the Spirit has been fulfilled, not the more warlike parts. However, dividing the prophecy of Joel in this way is not supported by Peter, who is reported to have said (without any qualification): "This is what was spoken by the prophet Joel." But even more important is that in this way dispensationalists concede that one cannot predict the future in light of the prophecy, as one never knows what part will be fulfilled when. So the point has been made: according to the New Testament, prophecies are not fulfilled literally but in a remarkably free way.

In terms of prophecy, there is yet another very strange view in dispensationalism. It is part of a larger phenomenon—what I call a "dramatic rift" cut right through the New Testament. According to Webb, soon after Pentecost prophecy was temporarily halted and the messianic kingdom was delayed, the last days were temporarily halted—as was the final "week" of Daniel 9:27—and a new gospel was introduced: the gospel of grace in place of the gospel of the kingdom. All this seems to imply that after Pentecost nothing that happened in the New Testament or since has been "covered" by Old Testament prophecy! Webb himself calls our time "a non-prophesied dispensation," as only "after the rapture [the fulfillment of] prophecy will resume" (p. 150).

But what of the New Testament prophets? Didn't they prophesy? Haven't these been fulfilled? What of clear references after Pentecost to the fulfillment of specific Old Testament prophecies in the mission of Paul (Acts 15:15–17)? Are these really not prophesied in the Old Testament? What of the central place the flocking of Gentiles to Jerusalem holds in the psalms and the prophets?[35] What of the central place the blessing to the Gentiles (from the start) occupies in God's covenant with Abraham (Gen 12:3), the covenant into which even we, Gentiles by origin, are still included by baptism (Gal 3:26–29)? What of the clear words of James that Amos 9:11–12 is fulfilled in Paul's mission (Acts 15:16–17)?[36]

In short, neither the literal fulfillment of prophecy nor the suspense of prophetic fulfillment is supported by Scripture.

---

35. E.g., Isaiah 2:2f; 55:5; 60:3; Jeremiah 3:17; 4:1–2; Psalm 22:28; Micah 4:1–2.

36. Also, would the majority of dispensationalists agree that what happened in 1948 and afterward to Israel is not a fulfillment of prophecy?

THE CHURCH AS NEW, UNEXPECTED, NOT FORESEEN IN OLD TESTAMENT PROPHECY, IN NO MEANINGFUL RELATIONSHIP WITH ISRAEL

Neither do I see any support for this view in the New Testament. In my essay I have heaped up the New Testament references in which a clear, strong relationship between Israel (as the true Old Testament people of God) and the church is put forward. The Gentile believers are "heirs *together with* Israel, members *together* (with Israel) of one body, and sharers *together* (with Israel) in the promise" (Eph 3:6); the New Testament believers are grafted into the olive trunk which is the true Old Testament Israel, and this trunk is continually supporting the church (Rom 11); the Gentiles are, through baptism, included in the promises and covenant God made with Abraham (Gal 3:26–29). Promise after promise, prophecy after prophecy, given to Israel in the Old Testament is fulfilled in the church (e.g. 2 Cor 6:16—7:1; Rom 9:24–29). Title after title, exclusively used for Israel in the Old Testament, are now applied to the church: a chosen people, a royal priesthood, a holy nation, a people belonging to God (1 Pet 2:9), God's chosen people, the holy ones (Col 3:12). Again Peter applies to the church the remarkable words that God spoke to Israel: "Once you were not a people, but now you are the people of God; once you had not received mercy, but now you have received mercy" (1 Pet 2:10 cf. Hos 1:10–12; 2:23).

Although it is clearly stated that the prophecy of the new covenant, given to Israel in Jeremiah 31:31, is fulfilled in the church (Heb 8:7–13), it is claimed by Mr. Webb that this promise is only fulfilled to Israel during the millennium.

Again, it seems to me that there is a total lack of evidence to support the idea of the church being totally new, unrelated to Israel and Old Testament prophecy. One of the reasons why this view is held by dispensationalists is their interpretation of Ephesians 3:5, an interpretation I have dealt with in my essay.

THE RAPTURE

Fundamental to dispensationalism is the twofold return of Christ; first, the rapture in which the believers (or according to some, only the special ones who have attained a specific level of sanctification) will be taken away to celebrate the wedding feast of the Lamb; and second, the visible coming of Christ only after the Great Tribulation. Now even dispensationalists concede that there is little evidence of such a twofold return in the New Testament. In fact, Webb states that this all-important teaching of the rapture was revealed only to Paul. According to Webb, it is referred to only once (1 Thess 4:15–18).

Now what seems utterly strange is the fact that this revelation is included in what is in all probability the earliest written New Testament book (1 Thessalonians), which was written well before all of the other Pauline epistles, including the letters of Peter and John, and the Gospels and Acts. Why is it that no other New Testament writer has picked up this teaching of Paul and included it in his own view of the future? In fact, not even Paul seems to refer to the rapture again, notwithstanding the fact that after 1 Thessalonians he wrote some twelve more epistles in which he again and again dealt with his future expectation.

Furthermore, we always warn against building a doctrine on merely one or two references. But, according to Webb, on this one and only reference, and an unclear one at that, this cornerstone of dispensationalism is built. It is not clear why 1 Thessalonians 4:15–18 cannot be interpreted as referring to the visible second coming of Christ. The main reason given is that the passage says that the believers will meet the Lord *in the air* (v. 17), whereas at his second coming Christ will come down and stand on the earth.

But what a small detail for a cornerstone doctrine! What if Paul meant that we will meet Christ in the air, and from there he and we will come down and live on the (renewed) earth? This view cannot be excluded, especially if one seriously considers the subsequent words in verse 17: "And remain with him *forever*."[37] Do not these words speak against the idea of a *temporal* wedding feast of the Lamb after the rapture and during the Great Tribulation? Aren't they rather applicable to the final return and eternal stay with the Lord on the new earth? "Remain with him *forever*."

And to add to all these questions: Why assume that at 1 Thessalonians 5:1 there is introduced a new event, the visible second coming, when there is no grammatical or theological hint to support this changing over from what is called the "rapture" to the second coming? Instead, it seems clear that Paul is simply adding some remarks to the one and only event he was dealing with.

---

37. Emphasis mine in *italics*.

In conclusion, I am not sure that Webb's article is representative of the majority of dispensationalists. It is true, as he has pointed out again and again, that there are a variety of different views among them, but there are "main lines" and "side lines," and it is possible that at least some of his views are rather representative of a sideline.

Counter Response

Benjamin R. Webb Jr.

I DO NOT UNDERSTAND why Dr. König claims that according to me the rapture "is referred to only once (1 Thess 4:15–18)." I never stated any such thing. On the contrary, in my essay I cited 1 Corinthians 15:51–52 as referring to the rapture. I also believe that Paul refers to the rapture elsewhere. Maybe Dr. König just misunderstood my intent.

When Dr. König concludes that prophecies are not fulfilled literally, he seems to ignore those that have obviously seen a literal fulfillment. Large parts of Psalm 22 were literally fulfilled at the crucifixion and resurrection of Christ, along with Isaiah 50:6, Psalm 69:21, Zechariah 11:12–13, and so on.[38] On the road to Emmaus, the resurrected Lord criticized Cleopas and his companion for not believing *all* that the prophets had spoken (Luke 24:25–27). Because this is not for us to decide, it is my belief that all prophecy must be fulfilled literally unless Scripture states otherwise.

Suppose a person living a hundred years before the crucifixion claimed that Psalm 22 and Isaiah 53 would not be "fulfilled literally but in a remarkably free way" (p. 156), as Dr. König views prophecy, no one at that time could have proved him wrong because the crucifixion was still future. I believe this is the problem with Dr. König's example of Acts 15:15–17, where James stated that the words of the prophets agreed with what was taking place. Although he mentioned Amos 9:11–12, he never stated that this prophecy was fulfilled. Likewise, Peter referred to Joel 2:28–32 in Acts 2:16–21, stating that God would pour out *of* his Spirit

---

38. Today, I also believe Hosea 3:4 is being fulfilled literally: "For the children of Israel shall abide many days without a king, and without a prince, and without a sacrifice . . ." But this prophecy is only for "many days," not forever. One day I see an end to this prophecy when the millennial kingdom is established, and Israel believes on the Lord Jesus Christ.

161

upon all flesh. But Joel 2:28 only states, "I will pour out my spirit upon all flesh." Quoting from a prophecy does not mean that *that* prophecy has been totally fulfilled.

I disagree with Dr. König's claim that the present salvation of Gentiles was prophesied in the Old Testament.[39] According to prophecy, Gentiles will only be converted when *Israel* is converted (Isa 11:6–16; 61:3–11; Zech 2:10–13; 8:22–23; and 14:16). This has not yet taken place.

By contrast, today's Gentile salvation is through the temporary *fall* of Israel (Rom 11:11–15). No prophecy ever states that uncircumcised Gentiles will be saved through the fall of Israel. Even though Dr. König refers to passages such as Jeremiah 3:17 for support, all nations have *not* ceased from walking "after the imagination of their evil heart." He also refers to Psalm 22:28, but again, the LORD is not "the governor among the nations"; nor do "all the kindreds of the nations worship before [him]" (v. 27). Likewise, Dr. König refers to Isaiah 2:2f and Micah 4:1–2 for support, yet the Law does *not* currently go forth "out of Zion," nor does the word of the LORD "from Jerusalem," and neither have the nations "beat their swords into plowshares, and their spears into pruninghooks." Isaiah 2:4 and Micah 4:3 also state that nation shall not lift up sword against nation; "neither shall they learn war any more." But as I write this, in July 2006, one look at the present conflict between Israel and Lebanon, as well as the war in Iraq, will prove that this prophecy has not yet been fulfilled.[40]

Nevertheless, I do see an agreement with Dr. König's continuity view—to an extent. I think it's really just a matter of definition. Whereas dispensational authors see a clear distinction between Israel and the church, many of these same *dispensational* authors still take certain passages that apply to other dispensations and make spiritual applications to the present church.[41] Others admit that the church partakes of the same spiritual blessings contained in the covenants that God made with Israel.[42] And like Israel, the church today also tends to wander away, turning to idolatry (i.e.,

---

39. Salvation of the *uncircumcised* was never prophesied in the Old Testament; see Genesis 17:14 and Ezekiel 44:9.

40. Nor do I believe that "what happened in 1948 and afterwards to Israel" is a fulfillment of prophecy since Israel does not yet believe on the Lord Jesus Christ; see John 14:6. We may see the stage being set, but I do not believe the Lord will actually fight for Israel until she believes on him.

41. See R. B. Shiflet, "Ultradispensationalism."

42. Baker, *A Dispensational Theology*, 89, 103.

serving mammon). In reality, the church today is no different than Israel was. Although I still draw a clear *literal* distinction between Israel and the church, these other dispensational authors' spiritualization of certain Old Testament promises still constitutes an agreement of sorts.

10

Israel and the Church: A Continuity View

ADRIO KÖNIG

INTRODUCTION

MY ESSAY QUESTIONS THE two main pillars on which dispensational-ism builds its doctrine of a future millennium: (1) the discontinu-ity between Israel and the church, and (2) the unfulfilled prophecies of the Old Testament.

The word "Israel" has different meanings in the Bible. In this essay "Israel" mainly has two meanings: In section one (*"The Israel–Church Relationship"*) "Israel" refers to the true Old Testament people of God; in sections two (*"The future of Israel"*) and three (*"The millennium"*) it refers either to the true Old Testament people or to the present nation of Israel.

THE ISRAEL–CHURCH RELATIONSHIP

Summary

There are two extreme views regarding the relationship between Israel and the church. One is that there is a radical break or discontinuity: in that the church is an altogether new phenomenon, is in no way foreseen in the Old Testament, and has no positive relationship with Israel. The other view is that there is an absolute identity between the two, and there is a seamless transition from the Old Testament to the New, from Israel to the church. The position taken in this essay is that there is a very strong continuity, but that there is also a specific structure in this relationship in that Israel enjoys a certain priority.

In terms of the image used by Paul, Israel is the root of the olive tree onto which the church is grafted. This means that Gentiles have to unite with Israel—the true people of God in the Old Testament—in order to become part of the church, the people of God in the New Testament, which is itself called "the Israel of God" (Gal 6:16).[1]

The Gospels

In the Gospels we read of twelve disciples and eventually twelve apostles—a clear reference to the twelve tribes. John refers to two groups of sheep (probably Jews and Gentiles) that should become one flock with one shepherd (John 10:16).

Ephesians 2:11—3:6

Content wise, this is an extraordinarily rich section. Formerly the Gentiles were separated from Christ, "excluded from citizenship in Israel." But now in Christ they have been brought near as Christ has destroyed the barrier and on the cross has created "one new man out of the two"—Jews and Gentiles. The implication is that, indeed, they now have become part of "the citizenship of Israel." Thus, both Jews and Gentiles now have "access to the Father by one Spirit" (2:11–18). It can scarcely be said stronger and clearer that now Jews and Gentiles are one in Christ.

However, it is not simply two separate groups united into one people of God. Already God had a people, the true Israel of the Old Testament. They already were the citizens of the kingdom. The Gentiles were excluded from this citizenship. But now, through Christ, the Gentiles have become *fellow* citizens with Israel who are the original citizens. Thus, the Gentiles are included into an existing people. This refers to continuity between Israel and the church and a certain priority of Israel.

In Ephesians 3:6 this is stated even more emphatically. The great mystery that has now been revealed is that the Gentiles are "heirs *together with* Israel, members *together of* one body, and sharers *together in* the promise" God gave to Abraham.[2] Israel has the priority, while we, the Gentiles, are the latecomers. They are the true people of God. God does not create a new people in the New Testament; he adds us to an existing people.

---

1. Unless otherwise indicated, all Scripture quotations are taken from the *New International Version*.

2. Emphasis mine in *italics*. See Gnilka, *Der Epheserbrief*, and Grosheide, *De Brief van Paulus aan de Efesiërs*.

Romans 11

All this is even clearer and more emphatic in Romans 11. Paul is facing the strange situation that, while Jesus is the Messiah of *Israel*, the *Gentiles* are flooding the church (Rom 9:1–5). He concludes that Israel, by rejecting their Messiah, is rejected themselves (Rom 11:12, 15).[3] They are the broken-off branches while the Gentiles who came to faith in Jesus are the branches from the wild olive tree that are grafted onto the natural root, which is the true Israel of the Old Testament (Rom 11:17).

This again implies both the unity between Israel and the church and the priority of Israel in this unity. Paul tells the Gentiles, "You have been grafted in among the others and now share in the nourishing sap from the olive root" (11:17). And again he emphasizes, "Do not boast . . . You do not support the root, but the root supports you" (11:18). This means that we as Gentile Christians should be humble and grateful toward Israel, the true Old Testament people of God. The generation that rejected Jesus as Messiah are the natural branches that were broken off, and the believing Gentiles were grafted on. But we should take heed. If we, Gentiles, do not persevere in the faith, we will also be broken off. And they, if they accept Jesus as their Messiah, will again be grafted on, in fact much easier than we were because they are the *natural* branches.[4]

This means that the rejection of the now living Jews is not total. They are rejected from the special place Israel had occupied in terms of salvation history but not in terms of personal salvation.

It seems fairly straightforward to draw the following conclusions:

- There is a very strong unity between Israel and the church, that is, between Israel as the true Old Testament people of God and the New Testament church consisting of all believing Jews and Gentiles.

- This unity is a fruit of the cross (Eph 2:16).

- However, there is a very specific structure in this unity. Israel has an obvious priority above the Gentiles. We are united to them, not they to us. We are grafted onto an existing tree and are nourished by its root. What should fill us with amazement is the mystery of Ephesians 2 that we are accepted on an equal footing! Christ opened up this way on the cross.

---

3. Also see Matthew 21:43; 23:37f.

4. See Ridderbos, *Aan de Romeinen*.

Galatians 3

The continuity view is strongly supported from another angle: the meaning of Abraham and the covenant with Abraham in the New Testament.

Abraham plays an important role throughout the Bible. Though his name does not occur that frequently in the Old Testament (some twenty times), the formula of the Abrahamic covenant ("I shall be your God, and you shall be my people") is the one sentence that occurs the most by far in the Old Testament. In the New Testament Abraham is mentioned more than fifty times. Additionally, there are negative references to virtually every important Old Testament figure mentioned in the New, except to Abraham—just think of Moses and Joshua (Gal 3:1–6; Heb 3:1–6; 4:8).

There are two main reasons why Abraham comes to the fore so emphatically: (1) his personal faith, and (2) the covenant with him. In fact, the two are so interwoven that they cannot be separated. Galatians 3 and Romans 4 are the classic chapters on Abraham's personal faith and on the Abrahamic covenant.

In Galatians 3 Paul contrasts two groups: Moses, law, and human effort on one side, and Abraham, Holy Spirit, and the gospel on the other (vv. 1–6). This introduces Abraham into a very important context: the gospel itself! Paul then continues that all those who believe are children of . . . *God*? Of course, yes. But that is not what Paul writes. Rather, he refers to them as children of *Abraham*! He also writes that the gospel had already been proclaimed to Abraham and that we who have faith are blessed *along with Abraham*, the man of faith (vv. 7–9)!

All of this is part of Paul's letter to oppose the Judaists who claimed that the Gentiles had to keep the law of circumcision in order to be saved. Over against this claim, he puts faith in Christ as the one and only requirement. And it is in this context that he places Abraham in the center, for no other reason than that "Abram believed the LORD" (Gen 15:6). He did not even have the Law of Moses. This means that Paul places the gospel of the Old Testament (which to him is Abraham!) against those who want to be saved by the works of the law.

But this is not all. Now the covenant of Abraham is put on the table. On the cross Christ opened up this covenant for the non-Jews (3:14).[5] Paul then ends the chapter with the remarkable statement that baptism includes us into this Abrahamic covenant. Through baptism we are united

---

5. See Van Stempvoort, *De Brief van Paulus aan de Galaten*.

to Christ, and "if [we] belong to Christ, then [we] are Abraham's seed, and heirs according to the promise" (3:26–29).[6] The same perspective is found in Romans 4. Again Abraham is used as the example of how we are saved (vv. 1–5). Circumcision is then mentioned as a sign and seal of righteousness through faith (vv. 9–12), and Abraham is called "the father of us all"—all believers, Jews and Gentiles (v. 16).

Both Galatians 3 and Romans 4 lend strong support for the unity between Israel—as the true Old Testament people of God—and the New Testament church. Abraham is the father of us all, we are blessed together with him, we are included by baptism into the Abrahamic covenant, and as baptism is a sign and seal of righteousness through faith, so circumcision has been. All these constitute overwhelming witness to the continuity between Israel and the church.

Old Testament Titles for Israel and Promises to Israel Applied to the Church

In light of the above, it comes as no surprise that many of the titles used for Israel in the Old Testament are applied to the church. Remarkable in this regard is the first letter of Peter.[7] He calls the church "a holy priesthood, offering spiritual sacrifices" (1 Pet 2:5)—phrases immediately reminding one of old Israel. But then he heaps up the titles used for Israel in the Old Testament. The church is a chosen people, a royal priesthood, a holy nation, and a people belonging to God (1 Pet 2:9). As if these are still not enough, he immediately applies the remarkable words that God had spoken to Israel to the church: "Once you were not a people, but now you are the people of God; once you had not received mercy, but now you have received mercy" (2:10 cf. Hos 1:10–12; 2:23).

The rest of the New Testament reveals the same tendency. The church is called "God's chosen people" (Col 3:12). In many of the epistles the believers are called "saints" or "holy ones," and elsewhere the faithful are called the "children of Abraham."

Also, regularly, promises given to Israel are repeated or fulfilled for the church. Paul includes a whole list and then, writing to a Gentile church, he emphasizes: "Since *we* [the church] have these promises . . ." (2 Cor 6:16—7:1). He does the same in Romans 9:24–29. Here he quotes four

6. See Schlier, *Der Brief an die Galater.*

7. See Beare, *The First Epistle of Peter.*

promises to Israel and applies them to the Gentiles. Again he emphasizes that these promises are for those that are called from the Gentiles (v. 24). There is, therefore, a definite continuity between Israel and the church.[8]

This Continuity Comes as No Surprise

This continuity can be no surprise to anyone who knows the Old Testament. God does not choose Abraham because he turns his back on the nations. Prophet after prophet foresees the day when the nations will flock to Jerusalem to serve the God of Israel (Isa 2:2f; Mic 4:1f; Zech 8:23). This vision is as clear in the Psalms: "The nobles of the nations assemble as [with] the people of the God of Abraham . . . So the name of the LORD will be declared in Zion and his praise in Jerusalem when the peoples and the kingdoms assemble to worship the LORD" (Pss 47:9; 102:21–22).

This continuity between Israel and the church is no peripheral phenomenon. It is part of the central message of the Bible and reflects the faithfulness of God.

A Misunderstanding

A few times Paul refers to "the mystery of Christ" (Eph 3:1–6; Col 1:24–27). This mystery is often misunderstood.

Ephesians 3:1–6. Here we have the clearest and most elaborate exposition on the mystery of Christ. Some see this mystery as the fact of the church's existence. They are convinced that Paul is writing here that the church's existence, consisting of both Jewish and Gentile Christians, is a mystery that was never foreseen in the Old Testament, and that in fact there is no indication anywhere in the Old Testament of anything like the church. But exactly what is this mystery?

First, Paul wrote in verse 5 that the mystery was not made known *as it has now been revealed*. This doesn't seem to imply that it has never been revealed, but rather that it has now been revealed in a special way. That is also the implication of what follows. The mystery is not that there will be a church consisting of Jewish and Gentile members, but rather that the Gentile members will be included on exactly the same level as the believing Jews. The triple "together" shows this. Everything that is true of the Jewish members is as true of the Gentile ones: heirs together, members together, sharers together (v. 6). The Gentiles will not simply be allowed

8. See Ridderbos, *Paulus*.

into the citizenship of the Jewish members but will be on an absolute equal footing.

Colossians 1:24–27. The content/meaning of the mystery is not as clear here as in Ephesians 3. Literally the content is given as: "Christ in you, the hope of glory" (v. 27). Immediately thereafter, it is emphasized that it concerns all and everyone. And again, immediately before, we read about the glorious riches of this mystery that should be made known among the Gentiles.

So as in Ephesians it concerns a mystery for the Gentiles. But the mystery is not merely that the gospel is also intended for them or that they too will become part of the people of God. All these are clear both in the Old Testament and in the mission command of Jesus (Matt 28:19).

It seems that the mystery is, like we found in Ephesians, that the Gentiles will enter the people of God on the same level and the same status as the Old Testament Israel of God. Remember that "Christ" means Messiah. The mystery therefore is that "the Messiah is in you Gentiles." This is so much more than what could have been gathered from the Old Testament. They would fully enjoy the riches and glory of the Messiah and his kingdom, while according to the Messianic prophecies the Messiah would only restore the glory of Israel.

THE FUTURE OF ISRAEL

The Problem

Even if Dispensationalists would concede that the Gentiles are grafted onto the root of the true Old Testament people of God, they may still be convinced that God has a special program ahead for the nation of Israel, that the unfulfilled promises of the Old Testament are still to be fulfilled to them, and that the millennium is the only time this could happen.

So what is the future of the nation of Israel? It is not so easy to formulate the meaning of "Israel" in this connection. In the Old Testament many promises were given to Israel as the true people of God. Do they still hold true for the present state and nation "Israel"?

Romans 9–11: Paul's View on the Future of Israel

Let us begin with these classic chapters on Israel. Paul wrestles with the problem that the Gentiles flood the church, while Israel on the whole has rejected their Messiah (Rom 9:1–6). Does that mean that God's promises to Israel have failed (9:7)? He answers emphatically, No! He starts out with some distinctions. Not all who are "descendants" from Israel are true Israel. There is a distinction between Isaac and Ishmael, and again between Jacob and Esau. These distinctions are solely in the hands of God as he has mercy on whomever he pleases and hardens whomever he pleases (9:6–18). Now, do we know who will receive his mercy and who will be hardened? Yes. He has mercy on the Gentiles who accept Jesus in faith, and he hardens the Jews who pursued righteousness by works (9:22–33). So the unbelieving Jews are the branches that are broken off, while the believing Gentiles are grafted onto the natural root.

What now is the status of these Gentiles in this new unity? Paul clarifies this question by applying a whole range of promises that were initially given to Israel to the Gentile believers. And he even emphasizes the fact that these are for them (9:24).[9] So they are now part and parcel of the Israel of God.

In Romans 11 he deals with the future of Israel as a nation. Because Israel rejected her Messiah, she stumbled and was rejected (vv. 11–12, 15). In explaining this, Paul uses the image of the two olive trees mentioned earlier. Here we receive the wonderful assurance that Israel's rejection is not total and is only a rejection from their special place in salvation history, not from salvation itself. Whoever of them comes to accept Jesus as Messiah are again grafted onto the Old Testament root. However, in the meantime, their hardening continues, "until the full number of the Gentiles has come in. And so all Israel will be saved" (vv. 25–26).

It is important to make sure exactly what is written here: Not *when* all Israel will be saved but *how*: "And so . . . " What does this mean? It seems to mean that the hardening of Israel will continue until the Gentiles have come in, which means until the return of Christ, and that in this way "all Israel" will be saved. Will "all Israel" be saved while the hardening continues? Yes, because "all Israel" does not mean every individual, just as "the full number of Gentiles" does not mean every Gentile. In fact, the view that "all Israel" will be saved *after* the Gentiles have come in is truly a strange one, as this would involve only that generation who happens to live at that moment. How can merely one last generation be "all Israel"?[10] Nothing is said here on what is to happen *after* the full number of Gentiles

---

9. Compare my exposition of Galatians 3 above.

10. Berkouwer, *De Wederkomst van Christus II*, 138ff.

has gone in. And Paul's argument is concluded by the remarkable double "now": Israel have *now* become disobedient in order that they too may *now* receive mercy, not *after* the Gentiles have gone in (v. 31).

So for the conversion of Israel, Paul does not have the distant future in mind but the time in which he lives and the work he is doing among the Gentiles. This is emphasized by other details in the chapter. Earlier on Paul sees the aim of his mission as bringing the Gentiles to faith so that they may arouse the Jews to envy. In this way he hopes to bring back the mass of Jews, easily, and in his own time. This is his view for Israel. He has the *mass* of Jews in mind. The "some" he hopes to save are in fact the *mass* as we see from the same Greek word elsewhere (Rom 11:17 cf. 3:3). Moreover, he is confident that it will be *easy*. If wild branches were grafted onto the natural root, "how much more readily" would natural branches (11:24)! Israel's whole history is drenched in the presence and works of God. Jesus is *their* Messiah, while the Gentiles are absolutely ignorant and have to accept a new, unknown God (Acts 17:23). Also, Paul is working towards this conversion of Israel *in his own time*. This is his life task (Rom 11:13–14). All this supports the "so" instead of a "then" in 11:26.

It seems Paul's vision for Israel is that, while their hardening continues, the majority will be aroused to envy by the conversion of the Gentiles, so that in this way "all Israel will be saved" while the time/conversion of the Gentiles continues.

To summarize: Paul does not have an apocalyptic vision of a miraculous conversion of merely the last generation of Israel but a continuing conversion of the masses while the Gentiles go in.[11] In the meantime, this did not happen. Why? This, the Lord will ask the Gentile church on the day of Judgment.

What Happens after the Hardening?

Dispensationalists hold that the hardening is temporal, that it will eventually be followed by the millennium when all the unfulfilled prophecies for Israel will be literally fulfilled to the nation of Israel. Let us look at the New Testament references they believe support this notion.

Acts 3:19–21. Though Israel itself is rejected from the unique position they have occupied in salvation history because of their rejection of Jesus as Messiah, there is indeed a door of grace open for their salvation.

---

11. Ibid., 141–42. Also see Beker, *Paul the Apostle,* 328ff.

Acts 3 testifies to this. It correlates with Paul's view on their future: they are called to conversion, then God will forgive their sins, and then they wait together with all God's people on Christ's return, which is here called "times of refreshing." These words can scarcely refer to something else than the time that God "will restore everything" at Christ's return (cf. Rev 21:5). It surely cannot refer to the millennium that we are told will be on the old, unrenewed earth where everything surely will not as yet be restored or refreshed.

Luke 21:24. "Jerusalem will be trampled on by the Gentiles until the times of the Gentiles are fulfilled." Some believe that after "the times of the Gentiles" there will again be a time of the Jews (Israel) as it has been in the Old Testament (i.e., the millennium). But there seems no clear reference to support this interpretation and no reason not to accept that "the times of the Gentiles" will be followed by Christ's return. As in Romans 11:25, nothing is said of the time after these times.

Matthew 10:23. "I tell you the truth, you will not finish going through the cities of Israel before the Son of Man comes." This is one of the rather difficult sayings of Jesus. It seems to suggest that the evangelization of Israel will continue till Christ's return. But on a special future of Israel nothing is said.

Matthew 23:39. "For I tell you, you will not see me again until you say, 'Blessed is he who comes in the name of the Lord.'" Does this refer to a special future time when Israel would en masse have accepted the Messiah? There seems no reason not to see it as a reference to Christ's return. Elsewhere we read that on that day everyone, wherever in the universe, will confess Jesus as Lord (Phil 2:10–11).

Matthew 24:32–33. This reference to the fig tree has been given a very special meaning. The budding of the fig tree is seen as a symbol of the return of Israel to Palestine, the present land of Israel. And so it was said to have been fulfilled in 1948 with the inauguration of the modern state of Israel. One problem with this interpretation is that in Luke 21:29 reference is made to "the fig tree *and all the trees.*" Does this mean that all peoples will have to return to their native lands?

The real point, however, is that the trees are not symbolizing anything. It is merely a point of comparison: From the budding of the trees we can draw the conclusion that the summer is at hand. So we have to conclude from certain signs that Christ's return is at hand.

It thus seems clear that in the New Testament we do not have an indication of an apocalyptic mass conversion of the last generation of Jews nor of a special future place of Israel in salvation history. This place and role has been terminated by their rejection of Jesus as Messiah. What is certain is that the responsibility of the believing Gentiles is to call Israel back to their Messiah.

THE MILLENNIUM

The New Testament

Dispensationalism holds to the view that there will be a special thousand years of peace on this unrenewed earth. Jesus will return from heaven and will reign over the entire world from the throne of David in Jerusalem where the temple will be rebuilt and, according to some, even the entire sacrificial system will be restored. In this period Israel will en masse have accepted Jesus as their Messiah and will be the missionaries to the Gentiles.[12]

Without going in detail into this topic, we should distinguish between the Old Testament and the New. Concerning the New Testament, it should be said in general that neither Jesus nor Paul, nor any other New Testament writer, specifically refers to a future time of peace under the rule of Messiah from the throne of David in Jerusalem. In fact, none of their references to the future even allows or merely leaves room for such a period of time. The one reference used in this regard, Revelation 20, is so incidental and contentious that it is not advisable to build an entire doctrine on it.[13]

The Fulfillment of Old Testament Prophecies

The foregoing conclusion implies that the entire doctrine of the millennium, as a future time of a thousand years on the unrenewed earth, is to be built on the unfulfilled prophecies of the Old Testament. This makes it all important to determine how prophecies are fulfilled.

Dispensationalism makes a strong case for the literal interpretation of the Bible in general, and more specifically the literal fulfillment of

12. See Price, *Jerusalem in Prophecy*, 179ff; Walvoort, *Israel in Prophecy*, chap. 7; Ice and Demy, *Prophecy Watch*, 221ff; Pache, *Die Wiederkunft Jesu Christi*, 319ff.

13. See Hoekema, *The Bible and the Future*, 223ff.

prophecy. Now we know that there are quite a number of Old Testament prophecies that were fulfilled in New Testament times. The best way to learn how prophecies are fulfilled is to look at the fulfillment of these. In these cases we can compare the prophecy and its fulfillment and learn how prophecies are fulfilled.

Joel 2:28–32 is fulfilled in the outpouring of the Spirit. In his sermon, Peter specifically refers to the Joel prophecy as being fulfilled in the Spirit's coming, and he fully quotes the prophecy (Acts 2:16–21). But a comparison of the details of the prophecy and what really happened in the fulfillment shows that the details of the prophecy are not literally fulfilled. In fact, one is struck by the huge differences. There is no blood, fire, and billows of smoke (all war images). The sun did not turn to darkness or the moon to blood. Many of the other details also did not happen. Only the essence of the prophecy was fulfilled: the Spirit was poured out. There is no way in which someone could have drawn a picture of the fulfillment of this prophecy before it happened. Prophecies are not history written beforehand.

Jeremiah 31:15 is fulfilled in the murder of the baby boys by Herod (Matt 2:17–18). A careful look at Jeremiah 31 tells us that the prophecy is, in fact, much longer than the section quoted by Matthew. It continues through verses 16 to 17. The prophecy concerns the Exile (31:15) *and* the Return (31:16–17). This prophecy was indeed fulfilled when the Babylonians took Judah captive and when the Jews returned in 539 BC.

Now part of the prophecy is repeated as being fulfilled in the murder of the baby boys. Only this part is quoted because the second part, on the return, could in no way fit the new situation. In fact, even the first part has only a faint analogy to the murder. In the Exile "weeping Rachel" refers to the tears of the mothers of the young men and women who were taken as slaves to Babylon (31:15). These young people could of course return after the Exile (31:16–17). However, the situation in Matthew is totally different. "Weeping Rachel" is still applicable to the mothers. But here ends the analogy. These "children" are not young people but infants, and they are literally murdered, so there can be no return in any case. Once again there is no way in which we can defend the view that this prophecy is literally fulfilled, not even the half quoted by Matthew.

Amos 9:11–12, as fulfilled in Acts 15:16–18, is all the more complicated. James quotes this prophecy of Amos to explain and support Paul's Gentile mission. But virtually no detail is included in the fulfillment. The fallen tent of David has not been rebuilt (9:11), and Israel did not conquer what was left of Edom and all the other nations (9:12). In fact, James even quotes Amos "wrongly," or rather, quotes a "wrong" version of Amos from the Septuagint, which turned a nationalistic prophecy into a mission one. It is well known that there were at least two tendencies in the Septuagint: to "Messiah-nize" and "mission-ize" some nationalistic prophecies. The only detail in the original prophecy of Amos that is more or less applicable to Paul's mission work is the phrase about the nations that bear the Name of the Lord.

Therefore, prophecies are not fulfilled in detail. A picture of the fulfillment cannot be drawn beforehand by using the detail of the prophecy. One can consider prophecy after prophecy, and the result will be the same. Prophecies are not fulfilled literally but rather in a very free, surprising way. In most cases there are only one or two points of agreement or analogy.

A counter argument may be that prophecies are fulfilled in phases or parts, and that in the case of Joel's prophecy only the part of the Spirit's coming is fulfilled while the warlike parts will be fulfilled only in the future. But this is not what we hear Peter saying. He quoted the entire prophecy as being fulfilled. But let us go the second mile. The argument of prophecies being fulfilled in part relates to the position that prophecies are fulfilled more than once, which is a sound theological principle. But this immediately reinforces the question: How would it be possible beforehand to know how the fulfillment will look, whether a part or the entire prophecy would be fulfilled? And after the first (partial) fulfillment, how to know how the following second (full) fulfillment(s) would look like, especially in light of the fact that we know prophecies are not fulfilled literally?

Again it may be said that Jeremiah 31:15–17 has already been fulfilled in the Exile and Return, and that it has always been God's intention that only the first part is again to be fulfilled in the baby murder. But again: how would it have been possible to know this before the second fulfillment, and how is it even now possible to know if and how the second part will ever again be fulfilled? *This means that the counter argument in fact further underscores the point that we cannot beforehand know how specific prophecies will be fulfilled.*

Conclusion: God is free in fulfilling his promises. We are in no position beforehand to determine exactly what will happen when unfulfilled prophecies are fulfilled. Prophecies are not history written before it happens. They are faint, dotted lines indicating the way God is moving into the future.[14] In fact, the fulfillment is often much richer than the promise. Instead of yet another bloodbath, Joel 2 is fulfilled by the Spirit's coming—not to win wars but the people's hearts. And instead of yet another bloody victory of Israel over her enemies, Amos 9 is fulfilled in Paul's missionary journeys.

The implication seems clear: There is no way in which prophecies can sustain:

- the notion of a future millennium on the unrenewed earth;

- the details offered by dispensationalists as to this millennium;

- the notion that all the prophecies they refer to are to be fulfilled in a coming millennium.

ABOUT WHAT CAN WE BE CERTAIN?

Does this view leave us in total uncertainty? Yes and no. It leaves us uncertain about the details of the future. But we can rest assured that we know where God is heading: the new earth, full of righteousness. Instead of a detailed scheme, the future expectation of but four basic events is sober and well founded in Scripture:

- The return of Christ

- The resurrection of the dead

- Judgment

- The new heavens/earth[15]

Even of these, no clear blueprint can be made beforehand. Some wonderful surprises are awaiting us. What we have is the dotted lines of the prophecies yet to be fulfilled. And to this fulfillment we look forward with "outstretched necks."[16]

---

14. König, *The Eclipse of Christ in Eschatology*, 182ff.

15. Hell should not be dealt with under eschatology which (if derived from "the eschatos," a reference to Jesus; see Rev 22:13) relates to the *goal* of God with creation. Surely hell has no part of this goal! It should rather be dealt with in Anthropology as part of our not-reaching-the-goal-of-God. See König, *Gelowig Nagedink Deel 4*, 228ff.

16. A literal translation of the Greek for "eager expectation" in Romans 8:19 (NIV).

A Dispensational Response

Benjamin R. Webb Jr.

F IRST, I WOULD LIKE to thank Dr. König for allowing me to respond
to his essay, and I pray that I do not offend him in my response.
Although I will be writing from a mid-Acts perspective, I do not claim
to speak for all mid-Acts dispensationalists. Due to space limitations, I
can only address certain parts of his essay. So I will try to combine those
portions that deal with similar subjects.

"THE ISRAEL OF GOD" AND THE "NATURAL BRANCHES"

To begin with, I question the claim being made that the church is called
"the Israel of God" in Galatians 6:16 because the church is not even mentioned in this chapter. Instead, I see "the Israel of God" as a literal reference to those of *national* Israel who believed.[17] This "Israel of God" would
also be the *saved remnant* in Romans 9:27, which literally refers to the
"remnant" of "thy people Israel" in Isaiah 10:22. Likewise, this "Israel of
God" would be the "all Israel" of Romans 11:26, the "little flock" (Luke
12:32), and possibly the remnant of Romans 11:5.

Dr. König's claim that Old Testament Israel is the "root" of the olive
tree in Romans 11 seems to be more of an assumption that leaves no future
hope for *national* Israel. But as I understand Romans 11, national Israel

---

17. Dispensationalists make a literal distinction between the church and Israel. As
a *mid-Acts* dispensationalist, I believe those who were saved under the ministry of the
Twelve stood to inherit God's Old Testament promises to Israel; so *they* were "the Israel
of God" in Galatians 6:16. As believers, they were "in Christ" (1 Pet 5:14), where there is
neither Jew nor Greek, as Paul states in Galatians 3:28 (also see Rom 10:12; Col 3:11). But
as "the Israel of God," they were not members of the present church.

still has a future hope,[18] even though it is currently in a fallen state.[19] As a result, I fail to see why Christ himself could not be the root in Romans 11. Indeed, Paul also calls Christ a "root" of Jesse in Romans 15:12 (quoted from Isaiah 11:10), and Revelation 22:16 calls him the "root and the off-spring of David." Therefore, if the root is Christ, *national* Israel could be the natural branches instead of the root, and the grafted-in branches could be the present church. Even though national Israel is now broken off, they will be grafted in again once they believe (Zech 12:10 cf. Rom 11:23–26) because "the root and fatness" of the tree is Christ (Rom 11:17).[20]

JOINT-HEIRS WITH CHRIST

Romans 8:17 states that we are "joint-heirs" *with Christ.* Ephesians 3:6 also states that Gentiles are "fellowheirs, and of the same body, and partakers of his [God's] promise in Christ by the gospel."[21] However, Dr. König quotes Ephesians 3:6 from the *New International Version*, which states that the Gentiles are heirs together "*with Israel.*" But the NIV could very well be misleading here because the words "with Israel" are not found in Greek manuscripts containing this passage. The translators of the NIV added them because they used more of a "dynamic equivalence" (thought-for-thought) method, which is based on the translators' own understanding. By contrast, the "word-for-word" method used by the KJV and many other versions, such as the *New American Standard Bible*, is less dependent on the translators' understanding, and therefore, gives a more literal reading.

---

18. Verse 12 states that if their fall is "the riches of the world," and their diminishing is "the riches of the Gentiles; how much more their fulness?" Verse 15 states that if their "casting away" is "the reconciling of the world, what shall the receiving of them be, but life from the dead?" And verses 23–24 state that if they abide not in unbelief, they "shall be grafted in: for God is able to graft them in again . . . how much more shall these . . . natural branches, be grafted into their own olive tree?"

19. For example, verse 25 states that Israel is partially blinded "until the fulness of the Gentiles be come in;" verses 11–13 indicate that Gentiles are now saved through Israel's temporary fall; and John 14:6 shows that Israel is in a fallen state today because national Israel rejects the Lord Jesus Christ, and thus she can no longer come to the Father.

20. Some mid-Acts dispensationalists may not agree that the root is Christ because they believe in eternal security. However, since verse 23 states that God can graft these branches back on again, I do not believe the passage concerns salvation.

21. Unless otherwise indicated, all Scripture quotations are taken from the *King James Version.*

Accordingly, Ephesians 3:6 in the NIV highlights a serious flaw with this "thought-for-thought" method. If the translators misinterpret a passage as they translate it, they could unwittingly change the meaning of the entire passage. Such, I believe, is the case with Ephesians 3:6 in the NIV. So Romans 8:17 and Ephesians 3:6 both tell me that we are joint-heirs with *Christ*, not Israel.

OLD TESTAMENT TITLES FOR ISRAEL
APPLIED TO THE CHURCH

Dr. König points out a flaw with traditional (Acts 2) dispensationalism that is also recognized by mid-Acts dispensationalists; yet our solution is different. Dr. König states, "many of the titles used for Israel in the Old Testament are applied to the church . . . [Peter] calls the church 'a holy priesthood, offering spiritual sacrifices' (1 Pet 2:5)—phrases immediately reminding one of old Israel" (p. 168). Although most mid-Acts dispensationalists would agree with Dr. König, we agree for a different reason. We believe there is more than one church in the Bible, and Peter was not writing to the present church.

One reason we believe this is because today's church operates in a different manner. Today, parents should "lay up . . . for the children" (2 Cor 12:14), and 1 Timothy 5:8 states, "if any provide not for his own, and specially for those of his own house, he hath denied the faith, and is worse than an infidel." By contrast, Peter's church sold their possessions and made distribution according to men's need (Acts 2:44–45; 4:32), in obedience to the Lord's commandments to sell everything (Luke 12:32–33; 14:33). This was because the *kingdom of God* was taken from the chief priests and elders (Matt 21:43) and given to this "little flock" nation (Luke 12:31–32; 1 Pet 2:9).[22]

One reason for this separation of churches is found in the Lord's statement: "He that receiveth whomsoever I send receiveth me; and he that receiveth me receiveth him that sent me" (John 13:20). So Galatians 2:9 shows that James, Peter, and John confined their ministry to "the circumcision" (the Jews) and that Paul went to "the heathen." James therefore addressed his own epistle, "to the twelve tribes which are scattered abroad" (1:1), thereby honoring the Galatians 2:9 agreement.

---

22. Another reason we recognize multiple churches is because *Old Testament* Israel was also a distinct church (see Acts 7:38).

CONTINUITY OR FUTURE FULFILLMENT?

Dr. König makes another point here with which I agree, but for a different reason. He states, "Prophet after prophet foresees the day when the nations will flock to Jerusalem to serve the God of Israel," and he references Isaiah 2:2f; Micah 4:1f; Zechariah 8:23; Psalms 47:9 and 102:21–22 (p. 169). While Dr. König views these passages as evidence of a continuity between Israel and the church, I see them as awaiting a literal fulfillment in the millennium of Revelation 20:1–6. They prophesy of a time when Jehovah God will be king over all the earth and reign over the heathen, which I believe is still future. At that time, I believe Zechariah 14:16–21 and Deuteronomy 15:6 will also be literally fulfilled along with many other prophetic passages. Because I touched upon this in my essay, and I don't see Dr. Konig disproving any of it in his own essay, I won't cover the same material here.

THE FULFILLMENT OF OT PROPHECIES
AND PAUL'S VIEW ON THE FUTURE OF ISRAEL

I disagree with Dr. König's statement that Gentiles are now "part and parcel of the Israel of God" (p. 171). Yes, Paul does take some of Israel's Old Testament promises and, by inspiration of God, makes a spiritual application to Gentiles today. But that doesn't mean these promises were totally fulfilled or that they no longer apply to national Israel. Like prophecy, God can also fulfill his promises more than once. And Dr. König admits this is true with prophecy because he states, "The argument of prophecies being fulfilled in part relates to the position that prophecies are fulfilled more than once, which is a sound theological principle" (p. 176). The same is true with God's promises. If he inspired Paul to take certain promises he gave to Israel, and make a spiritual application to the church today, who are we to say they no longer apply to Israel? Because God can fulfill them more than once, and in more than one way (spiritually and literally), he will do so in his own time, not ours. We simply haven't seen enough history to know for sure that these promises no longer apply to national Israel.

Also, Dr. König rejects the idea that Joel 2:28–32 was partially fulfilled in Acts 2 and claims that Peter "quoted the entire prophecy as being fulfilled" (p. 176). But Peter never claimed Joel 2:28–32 was fulfilled. He simply stated, "this is that which was spoken by the prophet Joel" (v. 16), and quoted *from* it. This means that Joel's prophecy was underway, not fulfilled. God certainly could have fulfilled only this first part of the prophecy, with the remainder to be fulfilled at a future time.[23]

I also disagree with Dr. König's assessment of Romans 11:25–26. I think this passage literally means that, one day, Israel will no longer be blinded. But Dr. König states, "the view that 'all Israel' will be saved *after* the Gentiles have come in . . . would involve only that generation who happens to live at that moment. How can merely one last generation be 'all Israel'?" (p. 171) However, I don't believe that "all Israel" can refer to "merely one last generation." The fact that Israel was only blinded "in part" means that, when Paul wrote those words, there were some in "Israel" (i.e., *national* Israel) who were *not* blinded.[24] As the "natural branches" of Romans 11:16–24, they would be members of "the Israel of God" in Galatians 6:16, as well as the "remnant" of Romans 9:27 and possibly 11:5.[25] Dr. König also makes the claim, "Nothing is said here on what is to happen *after* the full number of Gentiles has gone in" (p. 171–72). But again, the passage states that Israel is only partially blinded "until" the fullness of the Gentiles comes in. This clearly means that, one day, Israel will no longer be blinded and the remainder of "all Israel" will believe.

CHRIST'S MILLENNIAL REIGN ON AN UNRENEWED EARTH

Dr. König questions the dispensational belief in a special thousand years of peace on this "unrenewed" earth. But Revelation 20 shows an obvious time of peace during the thousand-year reign of Christ while Satan is bound in "the bottomless pit." This peaceful millennium clearly takes place on this "unrenewed" earth because it precedes the new heaven and new earth of chapter 21.

---

23. One example of a partially fulfilled prophecy is in Luke 4:16–21 where the Lord proclaimed only part of Isaiah 61:1–2 as being fulfilled (the acceptable year of the LORD) but stopped before proclaiming "the day of vengeance of our God," which will be fulfilled at some future date.

24. Also see verse 7, which states, "Israel hath not obtained that which he seeketh for; but the election hath obtained it, and the rest were blinded." Likewise, Romans 9:6 shows why there is a clear distinction between Israel after the flesh (*national* Israel) and "all Israel" ("they are not all Israel, which are of Israel").

25. For example, as a mid-Acts dispensationalist, I believe James was a member of "all Israel." By addressing his epistle to "the twelve tribes which are scattered abroad" (1:1), he was writing to *national* Israel, not the church; and those who believed were also members of "all Israel"—and I have already shown why I do not believe the church can be "Israel."

However, Dr. König makes what I consider to be a non sequitur argument here.[26] First, he limits any discussion of this topic to the New Testament alone, without explaining why he excludes the Old Testament as a reference. Then he claims, "neither Jesus nor Paul, nor any other New Testament writer, specifically refers to a future time of peace under the rule of Messiah from the throne of David in Jerusalem" (p. 174). But it should not matter if these three premises are not all mentioned together if each one can be verified elsewhere in Scripture. And all three premises can certainly be verified. Nor should they be limited to the New Testament for no apparent reason.

Next, Dr. König simply dismisses *all* of Revelation 20:1–6 by claiming that it is too "incidental and contentious" (p. 174). But Revelation 20:1–6 is still inspired Scripture. So I will cite it anyway but back it up with other Scriptures as proof for the following three premises that are verified elsewhere in the Bible: [1] "a future time of peace under the rule of Messiah [2] from the throne of David [3] in Jerusalem."

Nevertheless, I do want to be fair here. Even though I believe Revelation 20:1–6 is referring to a literal thousand-year reign of Christ, I realize this is the only place where the Bible specifically mentions this period. So I will focus instead on the other three premises that he questions:

1. *A future time of peace under the rule of Messiah.* Revelation 20:1–6 foresees a time when Satan will be bound and "cast into the bottomless pit," and those who were beheaded "lived and reigned with Christ." Verse 6 also states that they will be "priests of God and of Christ."

Isaiah 2:1–4 refers to this same event, adding that the word of the LORD will go out "from Jerusalem" when he rebukes "many people: and they shall beat their swords into plowshares, and their spears into pruninghooks: nation shall not lift up sword against nation, neither shall they learn war any more" (cf. Mic 4:1–3). And Psalm 46:9 states, "He maketh wars to cease unto the end of the earth; he breaketh the bow, and cutteth the spear in sunder; he burneth the chariot in the fire." This "time of peace under the rule of Messiah" is obviously still "future."

---

26. A non sequitur argument is one in which the conclusion does not follow from the evidence or the premise.

2. *The rule of Messiah from the throne of David.* The angel Gabriel states in Luke 1:26–33 that God will give to Jesus "the throne of his father David: And he shall reign over the house of Jacob for ever; and of his kingdom there shall be no end." Compare this with Isaiah 9:7, which states, "Of the increase of his government and peace there shall be no end, upon the throne of David, and upon his kingdom." And in 2 Samuel 7:12–13, God promised to set up David's "seed" (i.e., Christ) and "establish his kingdom. He shall build an house for my name, and I will stablish the throne of his kingdom for ever."

3. *Messiah's rule in Jerusalem.* There is every indication that *Zion* (or *Sion*, as it is spelled in the New Testament) and *Jerusalem* will be the same place.[27] And Romans 9:33, a composite quotation of Isaiah 8:14 and 28:16, refers to Christ's future reign in Sion (Jerusalem), "Behold, I lay in Sion a stumblingstone and rock of offence." Romans 11:26 also states, "There shall come out of Sion the Deliverer, and shall turn away ungodliness from Jacob" (cf. Joel 3:16; Amos 1:2).

These few passages show that all three premises questioned by Dr. König are indeed scriptural. There are many more passages to quote, but I don't have the space here.

I do not wish to be offensive, but I believe the only way Dr. König can deny "a future time of peace under the rule of Messiah from the throne of David in Jerusalem" is to confine any mention of all three premises to a single person in the New Testament and dismiss Revelation 20:1–6 as being too "incidental and contentious."

---

27. For example, in Isaiah 30:18–19, the LORD tells Israel that in the day when he is "gracious" and has mercy upon them, "the people shall dwell in Zion at Jerusalem." Likewise, Isaiah 10:32 states, "he shall shake his hand against the mount of the daughter of Zion, the hill of Jerusalem." And finally, when the Lord Jesus Christ rode into Jerusalem upon the colt of an ass, both Matthew 21:5 and John 12:15 tells the daughter of "Sion" that "*thy* King cometh." Emphasis mine in *italics*.

Counter Response

Adrio König

JOINT-HEIRS WITH CHRIST IN EPHESIANS 3:6?

Mr. Webb's view is that Christ is the heir so that we are joint-heirs with him, not with Israel. First, I have seventeen Bible translations on my shelf—English, German, Dutch, Afrikaans—and seven commentaries on Ephesians, and none give any support for this view. By far the majority identifies Israel as the heir, while the others do not identify or mention the heir. Second, if Mr. Webb is right, Paul would be writing something like: Christ is the original heir, he is also the original member of his own body, and he is the original partaker in his own promise, and all of these because he, Christ, is in Christ!

CHRIST THE ROOT IN ROMANS 11:17?

Mr. Webb rejects the interpretation of Israel being the root on which the Gentile Christians are grafted. He sees the root as Christ.

Now again not one of the translations or commentaries on my shelf mentions this interpretation—to say nothing of accepting it. Neither do I find this meaning in the dispensationalist literature I have available. Further, it seems to me that the context does not support the idea of Christ being the root. It is true, as Mr. Webb argues, that elsewhere Christ is called a root. But the context is totally different. Here the entire section (chapters 9–11) is about two groups: Israel and the Gentiles. It is about Israel being rejected, although a remnant has kept true, and the Gentiles coming in exactly because Israel is partly hardened. The verses directly preceding verse 17 are about Paul being made an apostle to the Gentiles with the aim of saving Israel. If in this context two things are interrelated, one can be fairly certain that it is Israel and the Gentiles. Jesus is nowhere referred to in the chapter.

THE ISRAEL OF GOD—GALATIANS 6:16

According to Mr. Webb "the Israel of God" (Gal 6:16) is not the church "because the church is not even mentioned in this chapter" (p. 178). First, what could that mean? The church in Galatia is addressed in this chapter and in the rest of the epistle. Never is it formally addressed as "the church." Second, he states that "the Israel of God" refers to "those of national Israel who believed." But they are in no way addressed in this letter. In fact, Paul emphasizes the unity of all believers (3:28), but Mr. Webb sees in "the Israel of God" a separate church, as it seems he sees a number of distinct churches in the Bible.

His interpretation highlights the interesting feature of duplication in dispensationalism. Even the smallest of distinctions in wording in the Bible leads to differentiating between events, groups, and objects. They accept two second comings, two resurrections (or even three), two judgment seats (or even three), and two or more judgments. And now even two or three different churches!

MR. WEBB'S VIEW OF MULTIPLE CHURCHES

I am fully aware of the radical difference dispensationalists make between Israel and the church—it is one of the pillars of dispensationalism. But part of this view is that the Jews who came to faith in the early church became part of the one church, the body of Christ, wherever they lived. However, Mr. Webb accepts a number of churches quite independent from each other and even functioning in terms of different principles. He is convinced that the church, which Peter addresses in his epistles, is such a "different" church. But we know Paul was the missionary planting the churches in these areas (Acts 13–16), and we know very well that to him the entire gospel was at stake with the unity of Jewish and Gentile Christians in one church. So it seems difficult to accept that the Old Testament titles for Israel, which Peter so abundantly uses for the church, is used for a different type of church, "the Peter church," than the ordinary one. But even if that were true, these titles are still used for a New Testament church, meaning that there is indeed a relationship between

Israel and the church—the point I have made in my essay—unless Mr. Webb accepts that this "different" church is no Christian church at all.

In conclusion, I find Mr. Webb's theology very strange and would have liked to sit with him for some hours. Maybe I simply do not understand his views but his faith I do and share with him in the confession of Jesus as the Savior of the world.

11

The Sign Gifts of the Spirit: Cessationism

WILLEM BERENDS

INTRODUCTION

A T THE TIME OF the Reformation, Protestant leaders urged people to return to the Bible as the only word of God. They voiced their rejection of all claims to further revelations, by way of papal pronouncements or church councils, with the slogan: *Sola Scriptura*. They also opposed the veneration of saints and relics, and the claims of wonders and miracles associated with them were denounced as mere superstitions. But the Reformers did not deny miracles as such.[1] Thus, John Calvin observed that God daily continues to perform miracles to preserve his church.[2] But he warned, "Miracles must never be separated from the word."[3] With other Reformers, Calvin realized that only by keeping God's word central to the Christian faith could the kind of deviations found in the pre-Reformation church be prevented from reoccurring.

---

1. Martin Luther believed that the gift of miracles would continue till the end of time: "They [Christians] prayed for their enemies, and, in addition, performed many and great miracles. That has lasted uninterruptedly from that time on down to the present day, and it will endure to the end of the world." (*On the Jews and their Lies*, chap. 19). But Calvin was less certain and wrote: "Though Christ does not expressly state whether he intends this gift to be temporary, or to remain perpetually in the Church, yet it is more probable that miracles were promised only for a time." (Commenting on Mark 16:17; see Calvin, *Synoptic Gospels III*, 389.)

2. Calvin, *Commentary on Acts I*, 203.

3. Calvin, *Commentary on Jonah-Nahum*, 275. Calvin was commenting on Micah 4:6–7.

188

Calvin's concern that revelations, miracles, or other spiritual gifts should in any way detract from the centrality of God's word is one that is shared by many Christians today. Often they identify themselves as "cessationists" because they believe certain gifts have ceased. These Christians see practices such as tongues with translation, and especially some forms of prophecy, as challenging the full revelation in God's word. Many would also oppose practices like faith healing and events surrounding the so-called "Toronto blessing." Claims to these extraordinary gifts are perceived as undermining the centrality of the word of God in Christian worship.

Unlike liberal Christians, cessationists would not deny that the gifts of tongues, prophecies, and miracles occurred in the early church but would see them as limited to this earlier era. Some would also add that the biblically recorded events were inherently different from the events we witness today—that biblical tongue speaking, for example, involved real languages.

The term "cessationism" should not be used to include all positions that recognize some limit to the occurrence of miraculous gifts. There are different opinions on *when* the miraculous gifts came to an end, *which* gifts are included, and *why* they have ceased. I will begin by briefly examining the range of opinions on these questions so that we may clearly distinguish my cessationist position. Following this, we will study the biblical materials on the gifts of the Spirit.

DIFFERENT CESSATIONIST OPINIONS

When the Gifts Ceased

The position that some gifts have ceased does not date from the time of the Reformation but has a history going back to early Christianity. Among the Church Fathers some, like Irenaeus, upheld the continuation of the charismatic gifts, while others, like Arnobius, limited them to apostolic times.[4] Augustine asserted that miracles like those found in the Bible ended with the close of the apostolic era. He wrote that such miracles "were no longer

---

4. Irenaeus recognized various charismatic gifts as present in his days, including exorcism, healing, predictive prophecy, and even raising of the dead; *Against Heresies* 32:4. But Arnobius argued that Christ gave the gift of miracles only to the simple fishermen who followed him; *Against the Heathen*, 1:50, quoted in Roberts and Donaldson, *The Ante-Nicene Fathers*.

permitted to continue in our time, lest the mind should always seek visible things, and the human race should be chilled by the customariness of the very things whose novelty had inflamed them."[5]

More recently, Benjamin Warfield has vigorously defended the view that miraculous gifts ended with the passing of the apostles. For him the miraculous gifts "were distinctively the authentication of the apostles."[6] However, Warfield also chronicles different positions on this question. Here he mentions some scholars who see the gifts as disappearing by way of a gradual waning over the first three centuries and others who posit a more abrupt cessation at the establishment of the Christian church under Constantine. Explanations for this timing vary from the position that miraculous gifts were no longer needed when the church came into power to the view that the church had become so corrupt that it forfeited such gifts.[7]

Which Gifts Have Ceased

Those who believe that some spiritual gifts are no longer in evidence today do not always agree about the identity of the gifts that have ceased. Many would identify specifically the revelatory gifts, like prophecy and tongue speaking with translation, on the basis that the closing of the canon precludes all further revelation. Some of them would also include gifts like miracles, arguing that all such gifts are signs, and therefore, revelatory.[8]

Others hold that the gifts that ceased were all the extraordinary gifts, in that these belonged uniquely to the apostolic office. Which gifts are included here depends on how these gifts are understood. Thus, "prophecy" as *preaching* will be seen as a continuing gift but "prophecy" as *revelation*

---

5. Augustine of Hippo, *On True Religion*, 25:47. This book was written c. AD 390. However, it would appear that he had a much more positive attitude to the continuation of miracles after he moved to Northern Africa, where claims to miracles were commonplace. Augustine describes a number of miracles from around Hippo in *The City of God*. For a full discussion on Augustine's view of miracles see Van der Meer, *Augustine, the Bishop*, 527–57.

6. Warfield, *Miracles*, 6.

7. Ibid., 7ff.

8. This is the position of the Association of Reformed Baptist Churches of America, see "A Position Paper Concerning the Continuance of Revelatory Gifts in the Present Day" (Reported by the ARBCA Ad Hoc Committee on Revelatory Gifts & Unanimously Adopted at the General Assembly on March 8, 2000).

will not. On the matter of prophecy as *prediction* there is no consensus, and we will deal with this phenomenon below.

Why the Gifts Have Ceased

In the positions described above, we have already come across some of the different reasons given for the cessation of certain gifts. For some, God limits miraculous gifts to those times and places where the church is challenged with opposition of heathenism. For others, God only provides these gifts to those who are faithful to their Christian calling. But the term "cessationism" does not really fit either of these positions. Cessationism recognizes that all, or at least some, of the miraculous gifts have forever ceased to be available to the church because they were given only for the foundational phase of the church. This is variously explained as the time of the apostles or the time before the completion of God's revelation in Scripture, or both.

DIFFERENCE BETWEEN LIBERALISM AND "STRONG" AND "WEAK" CESSATIONISM

Before we go on to look at the biblical material on the gifts of the Spirit we should make it clear that there is another position that has denied the possibility of miraculous gifts today, and that is liberalism. Liberalism is well described in the Bible as "having a form of godliness but denying its power" (2 Tim 3:5).[9] Liberals rule out the miraculous, including miraculous gifts, on their presupposition that such things cannot occur. Because liberals do not hold the Bible as normative, we are not interested in interacting with their position on the gifts of the Spirit.

In contrast to liberals, cessationists fully recognize God's omnipotent power to do any kind of miracles. However, some cessationists would hold that God himself ceased to do miracles with the completion of the canon on the grounds that miracles served specifically to authenticate the word as communicated by his messengers, the apostles and prophets. Elsewhere I have termed this position "strong cessationism."[10] A more common position recognizes that God continues to do miracles but no longer bestows the *gift* of miracles on specific people. All of God's people

9. Unless otherwise indicated, all Scripture quotations are taken from the *New International Version*.

10. See Berends, "Cessationism," 44–54.

may pray for and expect miracles, but today none can perform them on demand, the way the apostles could. This position I have termed "weak cessationism."

I am defending here "weak cessationism" and will seek to demonstrate that Christ had given the apostles certain gifts that uniquely belonged to their office, and that these disappeared from the church along with the apostolic office. A key verse in understanding this position follows:

> The things that mark an apostle—signs, wonders and miracles— were done among you with great perseverance. (2 Cor 12:12)

Along with that, I will defend the position that revelatory gifts ended with the completion of the biblical canon, in the sense that there is no "prophecy" today that in any way can add to the revelation we have in God's word.

THE APOSTOLIC OFFICE

Jesus Christ selected twelve ordinary men for an extraordinary office, that of apostleship (Mark 3:14). For some three years he discipled these men to prepare them for their task, and at the end of his ministry he commissioned them by anointing them with the Holy Spirit:

> Again Jesus said, "Peace be with you! As the Father has sent me, I am sending you." And with that he breathed on them and said, "Receive the Holy Spirit. If you forgive anyone his sins, they are forgiven; if you do not forgive them, they are not forgiven." (John 20:21–23)

It would be wrong to interpret this passage as an alternative to the Pentecost account in Acts.[11] What is portrayed here reflects the Old Testament practice of a call to office through an anointing with the Spirit. Appointments to the offices of prophet, priest, and king took the form of an outward anointing with oil, which symbolized the bestowal of God's Spirit (Exod 29:7, 9; Zech 4). In the above passage, Christ uses his own *breath*, rather than oil, to signify a divine anointing. The symbolism would have been clear to the apostles and the early Gospel readers because the Hebrew and Greek have only one word to denote *breath, wind,* and *spirit* (cf. John 3:7–8).

---

11. For an example see Bernard, *International Critical Commentary on St. John*, 516.

The passage in John also speaks of the apostolic power to forgive sins. This reminds us of Christ's words to Peter upon his profession that Jesus was the Messiah:

> Blessed are you, Simon son of Jonah, for this was not revealed to you by man, but by my Father in heaven. And I tell you that you are Peter, and on this rock I will build my church, and the gates of Hades will not overcome it. I will give you the keys of the kingdom of heaven; whatever you bind on earth will be bound in heaven, and whatever you loose on earth will be loosed in heaven. (Matt 16:17–19)

The words spoken to Peter here are repeated to all the apostles in Matthew 18:18. To each of them was given the keys of the kingdom. And so each of them could have been named Peter, or *Rock*, because what was true for Peter was true for all of them: the apostles who professed Christ to the world were the *rocks* on which Christ built his church. Thus, the church is "built on the foundation of the apostles and prophets, with Christ Jesus himself as the chief cornerstone" (Eph 2:20).

There are two additional facts that the Ephesians 2:20 passage teaches us: first, only Christ, as the "cornerstone," holds a special position in the foundation of the church, not Peter as a Pope; second, the apostles were not alone in laying the foundation of Christ's church but were aided by prophets. In the context, Paul speaks of New Testament prophets who, together with the apostles, made known the mystery of Christ (see Eph 3:4–6). This description of their task shows that we must here think of men like the inspired authors of the New Testaments who were not apostles, such as Mark and Luke. They, together with the apostles, laid the foundation of Christ's church. The foundation on which Christ builds his church can therefore be identified with the word of God revealed to the apostles and prophets.

Because the apostles and New Testament prophets (of the kind who were inspired to write Scripture) had a foundational function in Christ's church, this explains why we no longer have such apostles and (Scripture producing) prophets today. When their task was done, they vanished like the Old Testament offices of former years. Therefore, when we see their offices listed among the gifts of the Spirit (1 Cor 12:28), we should not take this to mean that we can expect people to continue in identical offices today. The foundational offices ceased when the foundation was complete.

That is not to say that the *terms* "apostle" or "prophet" were not used in other ways or cannot be used of people today—but never with the meaning these words have in Ephesians 2:20. The term "apostle" can simply mean *missionary*.[12] In the New Testament it is sometimes used in this sense for Paul and Barnabas, sent out as missionaries by the church at Antioch (Acts 13:1–4; 14:4). Similarly, the word "prophet" (with the root meaning "one who speaks forth") can simply be used for those who speak forth or *preach* the already revealed word of God to encourage and strengthen the church (Acts 15:32). But today we do not have the apostolic or prophetic office in the foundational sense of the word used in Ephesians 2:20.

THE GIFTS OF THE APOSTOLIC OFFICE

A reading of Acts will soon reveal that "the things that mark an apostle—signs, wonders and miracles" (2 Cor 12:12) were criteria that marked the *foundational apostles* (Acts 2:43; 3:1ff; 5:12, etc.). In the Old Testament, wherever men performed miracles, these served to affirm their credentials as messengers of God (Exod 4:1ff; 7:17; 1 Kgs 18:36). Christ's miracles also witnessed to his identity as God's Messiah (Matt 9:6; Acts 2:22).[13] Similarly, the miracles done by the apostles confirmed their status as official envoys of Christ (Acts 2:43; Heb 2:3–4).[14] Therefore, when Paul wants to prove his apostolic status, he appeals to the fact that his ministry demonstrated "the things that mark an apostle—signs, wonders and miracles."

Here it might be objected that there were others who did "signs, wonders and miracles" who were not apostles. For example, Stephen, a man "full of God's grace and power, did great wonders and miraculous signs among the people" (Acts 6:8 cf. 8:6–7). But we should note that Stephen's power is first mentioned immediately after it is said that the apostles had laid their hands on him. This is important because there are several passages that indicate the apostles could share some of their power through the laying on of hands. We see this in Paul's desire to impart spiritual gifts to the church in Rome (Rom 1:11) and with the gifts bestowed to Timothy (2 Tim 1:6).

---

12. The Greek word *apostolos* has the same meaning as the Latin word *missionarius*, namely "one who is sent."

13. Also see John 2:11; 10:25, 38; 14:11; 20:30–31.

14. Also see Acts 14:3 and 19:11.

Some deny this connection because there is no mention of Ananias receiving the gift to heal through an apostolic laying on of hands (Acts 9:17f.).[15] But we cannot argue from silence, and it is entirely possible, and even likely in those early years, that Ananias became a disciple through the ministry of one or more apostles who would have laid their hands on him. It is also argued that Cornelius received the signs of the Holy Spirit's presence without a laying on of apostolic hands.[16] But this argument misses the point of the story, which is that the Holy Spirit himself had to show Peter and the Jews that Gentiles were included in the promise of salvation (Acts 10:44–46).

There are several hints that the apostolic manifestation of spiritual power was qualitatively different from that enjoyed by other Christians at the time. Thus, Philip, despite his display of spiritual power in miracles performed, could not bestow the Holy Spirit on the Samaritans. This only happened after Peter and John laid their hands on them (Acts 8:14–17). In the same way, some Christian disciples baptized by John the Baptist did not receive the Holy Spirit until Paul laid his hands on them (Acts 19:6). A further confirmation of the superior spiritual power associated with the apostolic office is seen in the way even the shadows and handkerchiefs of apostles could bring healing (Acts 5:15; 19:11).

But should we take these stories in the book of Acts as guidelines for Christian living today? Should we use the handkerchiefs of holy men to bring healing? There are many who still look for miracles in association with religious relics. Included are the blood and bones of saints, vials of milk from Mary's breasts, weeping images of Jesus and Mary, nails that were used to crucify Christ, and the shroud allegedly used to wrap his body. By and large Protestants have rejected looking to relics for miracles for a number of reasons. First, many of the claims are simply absurd. For example, there are far too many crucifixion nails.[17] Second, these claims to miracles are little different from what we would find in pagan religions and the occult, and the Bible warns us against involvement in such practices (Deut 18:10–12). Third, it is recognized that such activities detract from the message of salvation in Christ (cf. Luke 10:20). But more

---

15. Turner, *The Holy Spirit and Spiritual Gifts*, 292.

16. Ibid.

17. One Catholic website acknowledges "thirty or more nails," see http://www.living miracles.net/Relics.html.

important, some events described in Acts are exclusive to the time and people involved.

The book of Acts is not *prescriptive* but *descriptive*, depicting what led to the founding of the church, and what took place in the church in its foundational phase. Some of these events are never to be repeated, like the ascension of Jesus (Acts 1:9), the replacement of Judas as the twelfth apostle (Acts 1:15–26), and the outpouring of the Holy Spirit on Jews, Samaritans, Gentiles, and the disciples of John the Baptist (Acts 2:1ff; 8:14–17; 10:44–46; 19:1–7). True, many other events have their counterparts in the life of the church and of the works of the Spirit today, including the occurrence of miracles. But some of the events were unique, precisely because as *Acts of the Apostles* they ended with the cessation of the apostolic office.

For guidance on the gifts and manifestations of the Spirit we would do better to turn to the epistles, which are largely *prescriptive*. But even here we have to keep it in mind that these letters were written to the church in its foundational phase and that not every instruction can be carried over into our situation today. We see development within the New Testament books, for example, in the frequency of Christians getting together (Acts 2:46; 20:7), the way Christians shared their possessions (Acts 2:44–45; 1 Cor 16:2), and in instructions about meat offered to idols (Acts 15:29; 1 Cor 8). Some instructions presuppose unique situations, like Paul's advice that the Corinthians abstain from marriage in the time of their persecutions (1 Cor 7:1, 8, 25–26). Others involve specific people and circumstances (1 Cor 5:1–5; 16:5–18). So we cannot simply presume that every instruction to the churches addressed in the epistles is equally applicable to Christ's church today.

THE SPIRIT'S GIFTS TO THE CHURCHES

Those who hold to the continuation of all the gifts of the Spirit frequently argue that the gifts exhibited in the church of Corinth were typical of the churches in apostolic times and also serve as a pattern for churches today. This is questionable for a number of reasons. First, none of the other lists of spiritual gifts mention the extraordinary gifts that caused division in Corinth (Rom 12:6–8; Eph 4:11; 1 Pet 4:10–11).[18] Second, the

18. Here we must keep in mind that the words "prophet" and "prophecy" are open to more than one translation.

lesser but more spectacular gifts were promoted in Corinth out of rivalry; they were sought after as outward signs of an inner spirituality. Third, if every church typically had the gifts listed for Corinth, why does James not tell the sick to seek out those who have the gift of healing? Instead, he tells them to call the elders to pray over them and rub them with medicinal oil (Jas 5:14–15).[19]

Paul's specific concerns in writing to the Corinthians about spiritual gifts is that the gifts caused divisions by casting doubt on some members' spirituality and that people favored gifts that did little or nothing to build up the church. In responding, Paul begins by reminding them that people cannot come to Christ unless they have the Holy Spirit (1 Cor 12:1–3). In other words, there is no such thing as a non-spiritual (non-Spirit-anointed) Christian. Next, he points out that there is both unity as well as variety among Christians as there is unity and variety within the Godhead. Even as the (Holy) Spirit, the Lord (Jesus) and God (the Father) work together in their own unique ways in providing for Christians, so Christians are to work together using their own unique gifts for the common good of the church (vv. 4–6).

After listing the variety of gifts (vv. 7–11), Paul again reminds Christians of the need for unity, using the metaphor of a body where every part is dependent on the other parts (vv.12–27). Having stressed the point that all members are important, he then goes on to identify the various members as they appear in the body of the church. Some members are indicated by their position or office, and others by their gift. However, they are listed in a specific order:

> And in the church God has appointed first of all apostles, second prophets, third teachers, then workers of miracles, also those having gifts of healing, those able to help others, those with gifts of administration, and those speaking in different kinds of tongues. (1 Cor 12:28)

Why the order? Because after noting, by way of a rhetorical question, that no Christian has all these gifts, Paul instructs his readers, "But eagerly desire the greater gifts" (v. 31).

---

19. The word for ritual anointing, *chriō* is not used here, but a word indicating a medical anointing. This was the common remedy for illness, but James points out that the means God provides must be used with prayer.

Then follows Paul's well-known digression, the ode to love, which is the "most excellent way" of Christian service (ch. 13). Without love even the greatest gifts are useless. And while love will last forever, gifts like prophecy and tongues will cease. Some cessationists have tried to argue that the words, "but when perfection comes, the imperfect disappears," indicate that such gifts were to cease with the perfection of the completed canon of Scripture. But this interpretation is doubtful. A possible interpretation is that the perfection refers to the spiritual maturity of believers as they grow in love.[20] But most commentators take the reference to perfection to indicate the coming of the kingdom in its fullness.[21]

What is noticeable is that when Paul returns to the subject of the greater gifts in the chapter that follows, he does not encourage people to seek the one that was at the top of his list: apostleship. Here again we have confirmation that this office was not to be perpetuated because it was foundational. Instead, Paul goes to the second on the list: prophecy. But here it is not defined in the same manner as we saw it defined in Ephesians 3 and 4 (i.e., Scripture producing prophecy). Rather, in 1 Corinthians 14:3 prophesying is said to strengthen, encourage, and comfort people. This is in line with how we saw prophecy described in Acts 15:32—the preaching of the word.

SPECIFIC GIFTS

Prophecy

In the Corinthian 14 passage there is an additional connotation to the word "prophecy," that of revealing situations and foretelling the future. Cessationists are divided on whether they recognize this function as a continuing one. Some reject it on the basis that any claim to revelation of any kind would detract from Scripture. Others have recognized prediction as a gift manifested throughout the church's history, including the time of the Reformation.[22] They would distinguish between revelation manifesting God's will, as something only to be found in Scripture, and the disclosure of future events or hidden truths. The advocates of both

---

20. This is acknowledged as a possible interpretation by several interpreters, and defended by Gustafson in *Authors of Confusion*, 32.

21. See Morris, *The First Epistle of Paul to the Corinthians*.

22. See Berends, "Prophecy in the Reformation Tradition," 30–43.

interpretations would agree, however, that any prophecy claiming to state the Lord's will for his people should be rejected as spurious because God's will for his people is revealed in Scripture alone.

The distinction between prophecy as *prediction* and prophecy as *revealing God's will* is one that is borne out in other passages of Scripture. Thus, we see that Agabus' prophecies regarding a future famine did not include a revelation of God's will on how to deal with this. That was decided by the church (Acts 11:28–29). The same was true when Agabus prophesied Paul's imprisonment in Jerusalem, at which time the church was divided on how to respond to this information (Acts 21:10–14). Such prophets were not on par with those who could be described as the mouthpiece of God, and they did not prefix their utterances with the claim, "thus says the Lord."[23]

In summary, we can say that Scripture identifies at least three types of prophecy: (1) Prophecy revealing God's will for his people, much of which was written down as Scripture. Prophecy of this type ceased after God's revelation was complete in the Scriptures. (2) Prophecy in the sense of predicting the future or revealing something hidden. On the continuation of this kind of prophecy, cessationists are divided. (3) Prophecy in the sense of proclaiming God's word from the Scriptures, commonly called preaching or exhortation. This is a form of prophecy all parties can agree to.

Tongue Speaking

The continuation of another gift that is disputed is that of tongues. *Glossolalia* is a topic all on its own and falls beyond the scope of this essay. Here I will confine myself to stating the cessationist position. Cessationists would agree that Paul allowed tongues by way of a concession (1 Cor 14:6ff, 19), and then, only where they could be translated so as to edify the church (v. 27). But most cessationists would add that the tongues spoken in Corinth were real languages that could be translated and not ecstatic utterances brought on by the repetition of certain words. The latter characterizes most, if not all, tongue speaking today. It represents a phenomenon sometimes identified as "automatic speech," which can be found in many religions and elsewhere.[24] It therefore cannot simply be taken as a sign of the presence of the Holy Spirit.

23. See Ezekiel 11–14, cf. 1 Thessalonians 2:13.
24. See Kildal, *The Psychology of Speaking in Tongues*.

As real languages, speaking in tongues were a sign that the gospel was to go out to all nations (Acts 2:4–12). It was a reversal of the curse at Babel (Gen 11:1–9). But for the Jews it was more than that, for they had a tradition that God spoke out of the fire at Mount Sinai in the seventy languages of the nations of the world (as listed in Genesis 10). They celebrated this occasion in the feast of Pentecost, the feast of God's covenant.[25] For the Jews, therefore, the tongues of fire and languages at Pentecost reminded them that God was making a new covenant with his people, a covenant that would include all the nations of the world (cf. Jer 31:31–34; Ezek 36:24–27).

Miracles

I will deal with the remaining extraordinary spiritual gifts under the heading of miracles. This allows room for the recognition that a gift such as healing can still occur as an ordinary or natural gift. Miracles still occur today, especially where the gospel is challenged by occult powers and heathenism. But the question that concerns us is whether these miracles occur through the exercise of a specific spiritual gift. Are there those today who, like the apostles of old, through a special unction of the Spirit, can do miracles and heal at will?

The miracles I have witnessed in many years of missions and in the home church have been sovereign works of God, often in answer to special prayer. Although this includes prayers by specific people, I would not see such people as blessed with a special gift of miracles and neither would most of them. Rather, this is a blessing that is available to all God's people. Christ said, "You may ask me for anything in my name, and I will do it" (John 14:14).[26] And, as noted above, the only special people we are instructed to approach in times of need are the elders of the church. The reason is not that they have special gifts but because "the prayer of a righteous man is powerful and effective" (Jas 5:16, see vv. 13–16).[27]

---

25. For a full explanation of the link between Pentecost and Sinai see Berends, "What Do We Celebrate at Pentecost?" 42–66.

26. Also see John 15:16 and 16:23–26.

27. There is no reason why such prayers should not be offered at worship services, or even special healing services. Churches holding to the cessationist position too often dismiss this as a "charismatic" practice, but it is more likely that an unscriptural modernistic division between the physical and spiritual sides of man prompts their dismissal. Christ clearly shows a more holistic approach when he forgives the sins of those who come for healing (Mark 2:5).

CONCLUSION

Cessationism is the view that some of the gifts of the Spirit listed in the New Testament ceased at the end of the first century. Cessationists hold that these were specifically associated with the apostolic office and the foundational phase of the church, being of a revelatory nature. Claims to the gift of prophecy are rejected where prophets claim to reveal God's will apart from the Bible. For knowing God's will for our life and faith we must rely wholly on the Scriptures and the illumination of the Spirit, as well as God's providential leading. Although most cessationists believe Christians today can pray for and expect miracles, they do not recognize a gift to miracles, such as was present with the apostles. *Signs, wonders, and miracles* produced on demand are identified as *things that mark an apostle*. These have disappeared from the church as gifts of the Spirit.

A Continuationist / Pentecostal Response

James D. Hernando

L
ET ME BEGIN BY commending Dr. Willem Berends on a clear and well-written essay on cessationism and the respectful manner in which he presents his position and its antithesis. He does not mock the counterpoint position, as has often been done on both sides of the debate. His obvious desire is to measure all things by the truth of Scripture, a posture I applaud. I respond to his essay with pleasure and hope that I can advance and bring clarity to the debate in the same irenic spirit.

Despite the laudable traits mentioned above, it is my assessment that Dr. Berends's zeal has led him to some misconceptions about the nature and purpose of charismata. Moreover, he has failed to make some key distinctions relative to redemptive history. Finally, he has engaged in some questionable exegesis of important biblical texts. Although it is impossible to deal with all the problems raised by his essay, I will deal with three broad issues that encompass many of them.

THE CESSATION OF THE GIFTS

Dr. Berends recognizes different kinds of cessationism that are united in the affirmation "that all, or at least some, of the miraculous gifts have forever ceased to be available to the church because they were only given for the foundational phase of the church" (p. 191). He favors *partial cessationism*, which holds that *some* but not *all* spiritual gifts have ceased,[28] in particular, the "revelatory gifts ended with the completion of the bibli-

28. This is implied in his introduction (p. 188) and explicitly stated in the conclusion (p. 201). Moreover, it is clear throughout the paper where he admits the continuance of the gifts of prophecy and miracles, but qualifies them as of a different status and purpose as those experienced in the early apostolic period.

cal canon" (p. 192). It is obvious that the author is zealous to admit no
gift that might in its exercise compete with the function and authority of
Scripture in the church's life—a concern that is also shared by the vast majority of Pentecostals. It was also shared by the apostles, Paul and John, in
their calls for judging prophecy (1 Cor 14:29; 1 John 4:1–2). Nevertheless,
neither called for the cessation of prophecy. The cessationist response
that they did so because the New Testament canon was not available only
raises the most formidable objection to their position. Where in all of the
New Testament (hereafter NT) does it teach that prophecy or any other
charismatic endowment given by the Spirit to the church was only for the
purpose of establishing the church? What evidence is there that the gifts
of the Spirit ceased?

With respect to the testimony of the early church, Berends pairs the
testimonies of Irenaeus (pro-continuationism) and Arnobius (pro-cessa-
tionism), as if the church was equally divided between these two positions.
In fact, the position expressed by Arnobius was at odds with numerous
apostolic and Ante-Nicene Church Fathers whose writings clearly give
evidence to the existence and regular practice of the charismata.[29] A half-
century after the apostle Paul wrote 1 Corinthians, Clement of Rome ad-
monishes the same church to be subject to one another with respect to the
gift (*charisma*) granted to each (1 Clement 38:1). Ignatius of Antioch (ca.
AD 117) echoes 1 Corinthians 1:7 in describing the Smyrneans as having
"received every gift" (*panti charismati*) and describing them as "lacking
in no gift."[30] The *Didache*, written in the first half of the second century,
also gives testimony to the existence of charismatic prophecy. The author
devotes chapters 10–13 to guidelines governing the prophetic ministry.[31]
Similarly, the *Shepherd of Hermas* (ca. AD 130–150) gives instruction on
how to detect a false prophet in distinction from the true prophet.[32] The
pseudepigraphal *Epistle of Barnabas* contains a very Pauline greeting in
which he rejoices that the "grace of the spiritual gift has been received"
and links it to "the Spirit poured out among you" (1:2–3). Later, at the end

---

29. See footnote 14 in my essay and the work of Ronald Kydd, *Charismatic Gifts in the Early Church.*

30. Ignatius, *Epistle to Smyrneans*, 6:1.

31. This disproportionate attention clearly indicates that there were problems with this charisma and ministry, but like the apostle Paul (1 Cor 14) the remedy was to instruct as to what constitutes authentic prophecy, not to forbid its exercise or posit its cessation.

32. See Hermas, *Mandate II*, vv. 2–12.

of his epistle, Barnabus describes the work of charismatic prophecy in building up the church as the temple of God, "He [God] himself prophesying [*propheteuōn*]in us" (16:9).

Here we have five Apostolic Fathers bearing witness to the existence of spiritual gifts. I can also mention Justin Martryr (ca. AD 100–165) who spoke broadly of spiritual gifts, prophecy in particular, that remained in the church in his day,[33] Tatian (ca. AD 110–172) who referred to exorcisms and healings that came from the "celestial Spirit,"[34] and the Church Fathers who represented the views of the orthodox churches at large: Tertullian,[35] Irenaeus,[36] and Hippolytus.[37] Is it any wonder that NT scholar, D. A. Carson, while not a charismatic, is forced to admit:

> There is enough evidence that some form of "charismatic" gifts continued sporadically across the centuries of church history that it is futile to insist on doctrinaire grounds that every report is spurious or the fruit of demonic activity or psychological aberration.[38]

33. See the *Dialogue With Trypho*, cc 82, 87; cf. *Apology* 2:6.

34. See *Address to the Greeks* in Roberts and Donaldson, *The Ante-Nicene Fathers* (hereafter ANF), 2:72.

35. See Tertullian, *De Baptismo*, ANF, 3:679; *On Patience*, ANF, 3:715. It is instructive that Tertullian, in opposing Montanus and his abuse of prophecy, does not deny the existence of charismatic prophecy. In fact, Eusebius recalls the words of anti-Montanist, Miltiades, who objected to the legitimacy of Montanist prophecy on the grounds that it had ceased after the prophetess Maximilla, 14 years before. If it was true prophecy, it would have continued, "For the Apostle lays it down that the prophetic gift ought to continue in the whole Church until the final coming" (Eusebius, *Ecclesiastical History*, 288). Similarly, Ephipanius of Salmis wrote against an obscure late 2nd century sect. One of his objections was that "they did not recognize the things of the Spirit . . . and did not acknowledge the charismata in the holy church" (*Refutation of All Heresies*, II, 1. *Heresy*, 51, 35, quoted in Piepkorn, "Charisma in the New Testament and Apostolic Fathers," 374).

36. See Irenaeus, *Against Heresies* (hereafter AH), 3.11.9, ANF, 1:429; AH, 2.32.4, ANF, 1:409. Cecil Robeck points out the faults of Marcion for rejecting the charismata, which in this instance was regarded as a badge of orthodoxy! See Robeck, "Ecclesiastical Authority and the Power of the Spirit," 21.

37. Hippolytus wrote, "We have duly completed what needed to be said about 'gifts,' describing those gifts which God by His own counsel has bestowed on men in offering to Himself." (Hippolytus, *The Apostolic Tradition*, 33).

38. Carson, *Showing of the Spirit*, 166.

APOSTLES, PROPHETS, AND NEW TESTAMENT SCRIPTURE

The evidence from church history is clear. The gifts of the Spirit did not cease after the foundational period of the first century. Why then do cessationists say they are not valid for today? The answer lies in their view that certain gifts (revelatory ones) were needed only for the church's formation and until the NT canon was complete. Regarding the latter purpose, the cessationists are without any explicit statement from the NT itself. Berends concedes that the "perfect" of 1 Corinthians 13:10 does not refer to the completion of the biblical canon (p. 193). Consequently, cessationists are left to build their case on inferential teaching from other NT texts. Their inductive arguments are, however, exegetically suspect. For example, the inference from Ephesians 2:20 is that the charismatic ministries of apostles and prophets are tied to the "foundation of the church." This foundation resulted from the proclamation of revealed truth, identified as the word of God (p. 193). Because the canon is complete and the church established, there is no longer any need for these gifts.

This line of argumentation fails to convince for a number of reasons. First, it is highly improbable that Paul's audience would have drawn a cessationist conclusion from this text. From verse 11 Paul has been talking about redemptive history, not spiritual gifts. To be sure, the NT apostles and prophets, to whom Paul refers, had a role in founding the church. However, were those apostles and prophets inclusive of all apostles and prophets in every context? As C. S. Storms has poignantly asked, "Why should we conclude that the only kind of prophetic activity is 'foundational' in nature, especially in light of what the New Testament says about the extent and effect of prophetic ministry?" He then adds, "It is simply not possible to believe that all prophetic utterances were a part of the once-for-all foundation of the church."[39] This Berends himself concedes when he acknowledges three types of prophecy, one of which he believes can be equated with preaching although denying any contemporary revelation of God's will (p. 199).[40] Berends is rightfully concerned to safeguard the unique revelation of Scripture, but he need not pursue this at

39. Storms, "A Third Wave Response to Richard B. Gaffin, Jr.," 79.

40. It is hard to imagine how the proclamation of God's word or predictive NT prophecy (e.g., Agabus) does not reveal God's will. Do not these forms of prophecy reveal the will of God to his people, even if only by inference? Agabus' prophecy of the famine was not only predictive, it led to the Church's action of making preparation for the poor (Acts 11:28–30). Are we to conclude that this inferred course of action was not God's will?

the cost of denying the revelational dimension of prophecy, something that Paul clearly acknowledges as a function of the charismatic prophecy in the church.[41]

The same criticism applies to the foundational role of the apostles. Most students of the Bible readily acknowledge that the NT describes more than one category of apostle.[42] In particular, there is the distinction between the so-called "dominical apostles," who received their apostolic call directly from the Lord Jesus, and a broader group of "ecclesiastical apostles," who are sent out by the church. Actually, it is possible to detect four categories of apostles in the NT: (1) the Jerusalem apostles: James and the Twelve; (2) the Antioch apostles: Paul, Barnabus, and Silvanus; (3) local (church) apostles: Andronicus and Junias, (cf. Phil 2:25—Ephaphroditus); and (4) Timothy and Titus, who functioned as apostolic delegates of Paul.[43] I have elsewhere argued that this distinction must grant that the category of elite apostles (the Twelve and Paul) is unique, in that they served an unrepeatable function within redemptive history. I had acknowledged that, "These first apostles were foundational to the church (Eph 2:20; 3:5), and acted as the authoritative bearers of and transmitters of Jesus' teaching, (Matt 10:1–7; Acts 1:2–8). Their teachings and writings became the standard and criteria by which the Early Church determined the content of the NT canon."[44]

Because the Early Church recognized other ecclesiastical apostles not of the status of Paul and the Twelve, and because not all who were called apostles were used to write Scripture, why should we assume the gift of apostleship was exclusively foundational? Such a conclusion is not sustainable when weighed against the evidence of the NT itself.

MIRACLES AND THE APOSTOLIC MINISTRY

In discussing the apostolic office, Dr. Berends is reluctant to equate the miracles done through the first century apostles with the miracles that God might do today. He says that the foundational apostles were given special

---

41. See 1 Corinthians 14:6, 24–25, 30.

42. Berends himself points this out (p. 194) in alluding to the apostles at Antioch (Acts 13:1–4; 14:4) and in stating that the Greek term *apostolos* can "simply mean *missionary*."

43. See Taylor, *The Gospel According to Mark*, 656. Also see Bittlinger, *Gifts and Ministries*, 51.

44. Hernando, "Paul and the Scope of Apostolic Authority," 98.

authority by God to establish his church, and that signs, wonders, and miracles were the authenticating marks of these apostles (p. 194). Because the church is now established, there is no longer any need for apostles or the miracles done by them. But neither history nor the Scriptures support this conclusion. Thus, Berends takes the position that "God continues to do miracles but no longer bestows the *gift* of miracles on specific people" (p. 191). What then is the difference between miracles today and miracles in the foundational period? We are told that all of God's people "may pray for and expect miracles, but today none can perform them on demand, the way the apostles could." This position, termed "weak cessationism," holds that Christ gave "certain gifts [to the apostles] that uniquely belonged to their office, and that these disappeared from the church with the apostolic office" (p. 192). Berends then quotes 2 Corinthians 12:12 to support his view that signs, wonders, and miracles mark these apostles.

The position above suggests an incorrect distinction of miracles done by the apostles and today's miracles done by God! Paul teaches that all the gifts listed in 1 Corinthians 12, which include miracles, are given sovereignly by the Spirit (1 Cor 12:11). They are often mediated through believers, but the gift is the Spirit's to give "individually as he wills." Pentecostal scholar, Gordon Fee, points out that *all* the gifts have their origin in the one God who works "all things in all of his people" (cf. 1 Cor 12:6).[45] Nowhere in the chapter is there even a hint that any of the gifts were restricted to a certain class of apostles. In his position, Berends assumes more than what the Scriptures state or teach. Where do we find evidence that the apostles were able to produce miracles on demand? Certainly miracles attended apostolic ministry as recorded in Acts, but nowhere do we find evidence that the apostles were able to do miracles *at will*.[46]

More important, the concentration of miracles surrounding apostolic ministry (cf. Acts 5:12–16) does not prove that signs, wonders, and miracles were done exclusively through the hands of the apostles. A survey of the NT evidence refutes this. Miracles were done through Stephen, Philip, and Ananias who were *not* apostles.[47] Berends counters this by suggesting that they must have received their gift through the "lay-

---

45. Fee, *God's Empowering Presence*, 160.

46. If that were the case, Paul would not have left Trophimus sick in Miletus (2 Tim 4:20).

47. See Acts 6:8; 8:5–7, 13; 9:11–12; cf. 22:12–13.

ing on of hands," as was mentioned with Stephen (Acts 6:6). However, the "laying on of hands" is not mentioned in the cases of Ananias or Philip, and arguing its probability from silence is hardly convincing. But even if we were to concede that these three were somehow apostolic associates, it would not prove that signs, wonders, and miracles were experienced exclusively in the ministries of the apostles. As Gary Grieg has poignantly asked:

> Who among the Corinthians (1 Cor. 12–14) with gifts of healing, miraculous powers, tongues, prophecy—all "signs" according to Mark 16:17–18 and 1 Cor. 14:22—was an apostle? Who among the Galatians, among whom God worked miracles (Gal. 3:5), was an apostle? . . . How many among the churches of Asia Minor, which 1 Peter 4:10 suggests were fully conversant with all the gifts of the Spirit, were apostles?[48]

Finally, I must take issue with the exegetical conclusion that 2 Corinthians 12:12 presents signs, wonders, and miracles as the authenticating mark of apostles. The NIV translation quoted by Berends is inaccurate: "The things that mark an apostle—signs, wonders and miracles—were done among you with great perseverance." A literal translation reads: "The *signs of a true apostle* were performed among you with all perseverance, *by signs and wonders and miracles*."[49] One might assume that the "signs of a true apostle" are the miraculous signs, wonders, and miracles of the second half. Although the word for "signs" (*semeia*) is the same in both places, there are good reasons to conclude Paul meant something different: (1) the word has a wider range of meanings than just "miracles";[50] (2) the grammar indicates that the terms at the end of the sentence describe the manner in which the signs of a true apostle were performed.

To what then do these "signs" refer? In chapters 10–13 Paul has been pointing out the marks of a true apostolic ministry. In addition to spiritual power to confront evil (10:3–4, 8–11; 13:2–4, 10), and divine revelations,

---

48. Grieg and Springer, *The Kingdom and the Power*, 143.

49. Rather than take "signs" (Gk *semeia*), "wonders" (Gk. *terata*) and "miracles" (Gk *dunameis*) as referring to distinct types of miracles, they are more likely different designations for the same thing. The terms point to the different effects produced. They are the divine acts that validate the message, bring a sense of wonder at the divine presence and display the mighty power of God at work. See Hodge, *An Exposition of the Second Epistle to the Corinthians*, 291–2.

50. See Romans 4:11—of circumcision; 2 Thessalonians 3:17—of Paul's signature; and Matthew 26:48—of Judas' kiss.

they include such traits as: (1) jealous care for the churches (11:2); (2) true knowledge of Jesus and his gospel (11:6); (3) sacrificial self-support so as not to burden the churches; (4) the absence of self-serving or heavy-handed discipline (11:20–21); (5) willingness to suffer for the cause of Christ (11:23–29); and (6) patient endurance of the "thorn in the flesh" (12:7–9).[51] In another work I have argued that the "imitation of Christ" is the distinguishing character of true apostolic ministry:

> Supernatural manifestations are integral to, but are not the definitive mark of New Testament apostolic ministry. Signs and wonders must be judged as to their true source or origin. One key way of judging is to discern the character of the minister . . . through whom these signs and wonders appear. They must be ministered in the moral and spiritual character of the *Crucified One*.[52]

---

51. For a thorough exegetical treatment of this issue, see Grudem, "Should Christians Expect Miracles Today," 63–66.

52. Hernando, "Imitatio Christi and the Character of Apostolic Ministry," 85.

Counter Response

Willem Berends

D R. HERNANDO CITES A number of Church Fathers and other early writings to show that "charismata" were present in the early church (p. 203). However, we cannot simply presume that these authors are speaking of the gifts claimed by charismatics today. When Clement and Barnabas speak of "the gift" (*charisma*) they use the singular, and the context suggests that they may be speaking of the Spirit himself. When Barnabas speaks of God "prophesying in us" he appears to be speaking of the illumination of the Spirit, because he applies this to *all* Christians as they are built up into the temple of God. Similarly, when Tatian speaks of "the breastplate of the celestial Spirit" (to give the full quote) that guards against the demonic, he is probably alluding to Ephesians 6:10–18, which again pertains to all Christians.

A major difficulty with an appeal to early Christian writings is that it raises the question whether we are ready to accept *all* the claims made by these authors. Most Protestants would be hesitant about claims to healings through the sign of the cross or the use of relics. Jerome recounts how the sign of the cross was used by St. Hilarion to heal three sick children, while Tertullian (c. AD 200) suggests "the sign" can serve as an antidote to scorpion stings.[53] Can we really appeal to such accounts to show that the charismatic gifts were acknowledged in the early church?

As to Dr. Hernando's second point, that the words "apostle" and "prophet" often had a wider connotation than those men God used to write the New Testament, this is something I have granted from the start. What concerns us is whether there is a class of apostles with special status,

---

53. Jerome, *Life of St. Hilarion,* 14 [AD 390]; Tertullian, *Antidote Against the Scorpion* 1 [AD 211].

namely the Twelve and Paul, and Dr. Hernando readily concedes this (p. 206). The question is whether 2 Corinthians 12:12 is speaking of apostles in this restricted sense, and if so, whether the signs, wonders, and miracles mentioned are the authenticating marks of these kinds of apostles.

Here we first note the context of the verse in question: Paul is concerned that some Corinthians have departed from the faith by following "super apostles," who claim they have more status than Paul (11:5). They have fooled the Corinthians with their airs of superiority, so different from the humility of Paul. Where Paul was willing to work for his own keep, these "super apostles" were claiming that their status gives them the right to exploit the Corinthians (11:20). Paul identifies these men as "false apostles, deceitful workmen, masquerading as apostles of Christ" (11:13). Paul is the true apostle because he displays the "marks" of true apostleship: "signs, wonders, and miracles."

I have no difficulty with Dr. Hernando's suggestion that the "signs" or "things that mark" an apostle may cover more than "signs, wonders, and miracles." The point remains. As J. Scott observes:

> in contrast to his opponents, he [Paul] performed the things that mark an apostle (lit. "the signs of the apostles") in their midst. These "signs" are accompanied by three manifestations that need not be sharply distinguished from one another: signs, wonders, and miracles. The combination "signs and wonders" occurs frequently in the OT in reference to the divine displays that attest to the sending of a human messenger.[54]

Cessationists fail to see how these three marks could attest to Paul's authenticity as an apostle if they were widely practiced by people apart from the apostles—hence, our claim that these special charismatic gifts were associated with the apostles who laid the foundation of Christ's church.

---

54. Scott, *New International Bible Commentary, in loc.* A more restrictive interpretation is followed by Victor Paul Furness who writes, "Here all three words stand in the dative case expressing the means by which the apostolic signs had been exhibited in Corinth" (Furness, *The Anchor Bible, in loc*).

12

The Sign Gifts of the Spirit: Continuationism

JAMES D. HERNANDO

INTRODUCTION: SOME QUALIFICATIONS AND DELIMITATIONS

THE ISSUE BEFORE US can be framed with a simple question: "Are the charismatic endowments or 'gifts' of the Holy Spirit (Gk. *charismata*)—mentioned by Paul in 1 Corinthians 12, Romans 12, Ephesians 4, and elsewhere—expected to be operative in the church today?" Those within the Pentecostal and charismatic traditions answer that question in the affirmative. Many outside those traditions believe that certain gifts were foundational for the establishment of the New Testament (hereafter NT) church and thereafter ceased, hence the view often called "cessationism."[1]

The present author writes as a classical Pentecostal and an ordained member of The Assemblies of God. Such a tradition was birthed by the modern Pentecostal revival that had its beginning on American soil at the dawn of the twentieth century. Quite commonly, early Pentecostals saw this revival as a divine "restoration" of "apostolic" NT Christianity,[2] holding that in their generation God was restoring and equipping the church to evangelize the world in the power of the Spirit. This global evangelization would inevitably hasten and usher in Christ's second coming.

---

1. This author recognizes that cessationism has many faces and variously argues this position. However, the above view seems to be shared by most cessationists. See Gaffin Jr., "A Cessationist View."

2. This explains the name the Apostolic Faith movement, given by Charles F. Parham, and William J. Seymour's Los Angeles newsletter, *The Apostolic Faith*. See Robeck, Jr., "Azusa Street Revival," 31–36; Goff Jr., "Parham, Charles Fox," 660–61.

Subsequent theological and historical reflection by Pentecostals gave rise to the conviction that the charismata, while neglected in segments of the church throughout church history, were nevertheless given by the risen and exalted Lord to his church as a permanent and abiding provision (Acts 2:33 cf. Eph 4:7–11). They were, in fact, the necessary equipping or empowerment for the Spirit-filled life. Most representatives of this perspective would be Gordon Fee's substantial work, *God's Empowering Presence*. On the day of Pentecost, recorded in Acts 2, the "promise of the Father" was delivered (1:4). This universal provision of the Holy Spirit was nothing less than God's eschatological gift to the NT church, marking them as his end-time people (Acts 2:16). This eschatological community was endowed by his Spirit and distinctively constituted as a "prophetic" people.[3]

From the above perspective proceeds the conviction that the end-time anointing of the Spirit upon the NT church continues until the *parousia* or second coming of Christ. Of this provision, Peter stated, "For the promise [i.e., the gift of the Holy Spirit—v. 38] is for you and your children and for all who are far off, as many as the Lord our God will call to Himself" (Acts 2:39).[4]

A major problem presents itself to anyone wishing to defend the above position, contra the position of "cessationism," in the limited format of this work. The issue is multifaceted and complex, deserving of a book-length treatment, which, in fact, has already been undertaken.[5] First of all, how should one proceed? If we target the main arguments against cessationism, one must immediately ask, "Which brand of cessationism?" Do we seek to refute the arguments of B. B. Warfield in his classic work, *Counterfeit Miracles*,[6] as Jon Ruthven did?[7] Some contend, however, that such arguments are not the best that the cessationists have

---

3. In Peter's prophetic speech at Pentecost one immediately notes Luke's repetition of the words "shall prophesy" after the quote from Joel 2:28–29. This forms an inclusio for emphasis. For a book-length treatment of this thesis, see Stronstad, *The Prophethood of All Believers*.

4. Unless otherwise indicated, all Scripture quotations are taken from the *New American Standard Bible*. More will be said in conjunction with Acts 2:39 in the major apologetic section of the essay.

5. See Deere, *Surprised by the Power of the Spirit*, and his sequel, *Surprised by the Voice of the Spirit*; also see Grieg and Springer, *The Kingdom and the Power*.

6. See Warfield, *Counterfeit Miracles*.

7 See Ruthven, *On the Cessation of the Charismata*.

to offer.[8] Perhaps, we should strike out against the numerous objections of John MacArthur, a more recent antagonist to the validity of modern-day charismatic phenomena.[9] Then again, we might address the more exegetically informed arguments of cessationist, Richard Gaffin, as does Douglas Oss.[10] All these options are negative in their approach, and the agenda is restricted to the refutation of the major objections to "continuationism." Thus, the apologist for contemporary charismata finds himself jumping around from text to text, argument to argument, attempting to present a more cogent exegesis or theological explanation.[11] In such an approach it is possible to teach far more about the cessationist position than continuationism. The results are often disjointed and lack coherence. They do not present a theological paradigm or context for understanding the continuationist position.

In this present work I have chosen *not* to take the negative approach but a positive one. Here again there are a number of different apologetic options. One could take the approach of demonstrating the claim that charismatic gifts of the Spirit ceased at the end of the apostolic period is not sustainable in view of the historical evidence. For example, Ronald Kydd's historical survey of charismata in the early church provides a plethora of references to the presence of spiritual gifts in the first three centuries of the church.[12] In 1981, before the publication of Kydd's work, this author recalls a class taken at a Lutheran seminary on the Ante-Nicene Fathers. To the chagrin of my professor I turned in a term paper entitled, "Charismata in the Early Church ca. AD 95–250." Using little more than the indices of the Early Church Fathers in the *Library of Christian Classics* and a few other standard reference works, I found and documented references to the charismata in 13 separate works within this period.[13] My

8. Gaffin, "A Cessationist View," 28–29.

9. See MacArthur, *Charismatic Chaos*. For a response to and refutation of many of MacArthur's objections, see Williams, "Following Christ's Example."

10. See Gaffin Jr., "A Cessationist View," and Oss, "A Pentecostal/Charismatic View."

11. Wayne Grudem takes this apologetic approach for the purpose of demonstrating that the best arguments for cessationism are at best equivocal. See his article, "Should Christians Expect Miracles Today?"

12. See Kydd, *Charismatic Gifts in the Early Church*.

13. My essay dealt selectively with clear references to the charismata in the writings of Clement of Rome, Ignatius, the Didachē, the Shepherd of Hermas, the Epistle of Barnabus, Justin Martyr, Tatian, Irenaeus, Tertullian, Hippolytus, Cyprian, Origen, and Novatian. In addition my appendices included additional quotations and references from

research revealed that Pentecostal and charismatic scholars had long been mining the Early Church Fathers for evidence against the cessationist position.[14] Moreover, I was surprised to discover that scholars not of my tradition had weighed in against that position as well.[15] Needless to say, granting the reliability of the Early Church Fathers, one is not at a loss to find historical evidence for the presence of the charismata in the post-apostolic church.

Another apologetic approach is to argue from contemporary Christian experience. Essentially this is the approach of Jack Deere in *Surprised by the Power of the Spirit*. It is not as though Deere derives his justification of contemporary charismatic phenomena from experience alone. Rather, his book is a protracted testimonial of how God's sovereign invasion into his life forced him to rethink and intensely re-examine the teaching of Scripture on whether God was still manifesting his power and presence through the gifts of the Spirit.[16] Nevertheless, this approach is hindered by its initial appeal to experience for its subsequent understanding of Scripture. For so many who revere the Reformation principle of *Sola Scriptura*, this approach smacks of exegeting one's experience rather than the Scriptures.

---

some of the same Church Fathers and others such as Papias (quoted by Eusebius) and Athenagorus.

14. Some notable works uncovered were: Hurtado, "The Function and Pattern of Signs and Wonders in the Apostolic and Sub-apostolic Period;" Floris, "Didymus, Epiphanius and the Charismata," 26–31; Robeck, "The Gifts of the Spirit in the Ante-Nicene Literature." This author does not know if Robeck's paper was ever published in book form, but it no doubt served as a major resource for articles that subsequently appeared in the Pentecostal journal *Paraclete*. Among those articles were "Origen, Celsus and Prophetic Utterance," *Paraclete* 10 (1976) 19–23; "Ecclesiastical Authority and the Power of the Spirit," *Paraclete* 12 (1978) 17–23; "Montanism: A Problematic Spirit Movement," *Paraclete* 15 (1981) 24–29. See also Kydd, "Novatian's *De Trinitate* 29: Evidence of the Charismatic?" 313–18.

15. Piepkorn, "Charisma in the New Testament and Apostolic Fathers," 369–89; Quinn, "Charisma *Veritati Certum*: Irenaeus, *Adversus Haereses*, 520–25; Stam, "Charismatic Theology in the Apostolic Tradition of Hippolytus;" Stephanou, "Charismata in the Early Church Fathers," 125–46; Swete, *The Holy Spirit in the Ancient Church*.

16. In the second section of his book (cc 4-11), Deere carefully sifts through much of the New Testament evidence and shows that his prior commitment to cessationism was not grounded in a proper understanding of the Scriptures. Rather, it was derived by tradition and the fact that he had never before 1986 been confronted with a miraculous gift of the Spirit. See Deere, *Surprised by the Power*, 45–86.

Instead, I have chosen to put forth a redemptive-historical apologetic for the continuance of the charismata in our day. My strategy is threefold. First, by conducting a biblical theological analysis of the messianic fulfillment of the Davidic covenant, I will attempt to show that that fulfillment comes not only through the earthly ministry of Jesus Christ but also through his resurrection and exaltation, and extends to the outpouring of the Spirit on the day of Pentecost. I will elaborate on the abiding significance that Pentecost has for the NT people of God. Second, I will seek to demonstrate that in both the Old and New Testaments the work of the Spirit is not limited to an inner transformational work but includes empowerment for service. Finally, I want to show that the eschatological framework of NT theology views and even demands that the charismata be viewed as God's abiding empowerment of the church until the *parousia* at the end of the age.

THE MESSIANIC SIGNIFICANCE OF THE DAVIDIC COVENANT [17]

There is little debate or conflict over the fact that the Davidic covenant finds its ultimate and soteriological significance in Jesus the Messiah. Jews in Jesus's day already anticipated that the Messiah would be a descendant of David. Jesus played on this well-known expectation when he asked, "How *is it that* the scribes say that the Christ is the son of David?" (Mark 12:35) But Jesus's follow-up question clearly demonstrated that the Messiah held a status and identity that could not be explained by the mere equation—descendant of David. Nevertheless, Jews had arrived at an identification of the Messiah with David's descendent, no doubt in part from the Old Testament Scriptures. God's covenant with David included these words:

> I will raise up your descendant after you, who will come forth from you, and I will establish his kingdom. He shall build a house for My name, and I will establish the throne of his kingdom forever . . . Your house and your kingdom shall endure before Me forever; your throne shall be established forever. (2 Sam 7:12–13, 16)

17. I have Dr Douglas Oss and his work in *Are Miraculous Gifts for Today?* to thank, not only for suggesting that the redemptive-historical approach is the most convincing apologetic for the continuance of the charismata but in drawing the connection between Pentecost and the Davidic covenant. See p. 245–57.

Some might have looked for fulfillment in David's son, Solomon, who built the temple, but those hopes were soon dashed with the division of the kingdom, a succession of unrighteous kings, and a national apostasy that ended with the exile of both the northern and southern kingdoms into Assyrian and Babylonian captivities. But Israel's hope was kept alive by the prophets. Isaiah prophesied the coming of "a shoot . . . from the stem of Jesse," a "branch from his roots" that would be identified by two unmistakable features. First, on him would rest the manifold and manifest presence of God's Spirit.[18] Second, his judgment, contrary to so many corrupt and wicked kings, would be one of righteousness (Isa 11:1–5). On the eve of the southern kingdom's captivity, Jeremiah would reiterate this hope:

> "Behold, *the* days are coming," declares the LORD, "When I will raise up for David a righteous Branch. And He will reign as king and act wisely and do justice and righteousness in the land. In His days Judah will be saved, and Israel will dwell securely; and this is His name by which He will be called, 'The LORD our righteousness.'" (Jer 23:5–6 cf. 33:15–17)

One can only imagine how Israel clung to that hope during their captivity and longed for its realization in their return from exile. Zechariah gave expression to a hope of restoration that would transcend Israel's post-exilic temple: "Thus says the LORD of hosts, 'Behold, a man whose name is Branch, for He will branch out from where He is; and He will build the temple of the LORD'" (Zech 6:12).

The NT authors understood that Jesus was the fulfillment of the long-anticipated Davidic messiah-king. This is evident in Matthew's genealogy, which overtly labors to trace the lineage of Jesus as "*the Messiah, the son of David*" (1:1).[19] However, to fully grasp how they understood this identification we need to go back to David's anointing as king by Samuel in 1 Samuel 16. It reads: "Then Samuel took the horn of oil and anointed him in the midst of his brothers; and the Spirit of the LORD came *might-*

---

18. Note that Isaiah describes the Spirit with seven qualifiers: 1) of the Lord; 2) of wisdom; 3) of understanding; 4) of counsel; 5) of strength; 6) of knowledge; and 7) of the fear of the Lord. The number seven suggests a full or complete anointing, undiminished or limited.

19. Emphasis mine in *italics*. Scholars have long noted the three sets of fourteen generations that Matthew may have underscored Jesus' Davidic lineage by repeating the number fourteen, the Hebrew numerical equivalent for David.

ily upon David from that day forward" (v.13).[20] After Solomon's reign and apostasy, the kingdom was divided. Although twenty descendants of David would ascend to the throne, this Davidic anointing with the Spirit of the Lord is never again repeated. As Stanley Horton observes, the Spirit is mentioned in Kings and Chronicles only "in connection with the prophets."[21] The powerful Davidic anointing[22] was not repeated for any of the successive kings of Judah.[23] What then became of God's promise to David in 2 Samuel 7? The NT authors saw that, in Jesus of Nazareth, God had raised up his Anointed One from the line of David through whom the everlasting kingdom promised to David would be realized.

Of course the genealogies provided by Matthew and Luke both establish the legitimacy of Jesus as an heir to the Davidic throne.[24] However, in one sense, it is Luke who emphasizes more clearly that Jesus was that messianic heir. He highlights the supernatural work of the Spirit that occasions his miraculous birth (1:35) and the numerous Spirit-led, prophetic predictions and announcements of his birth.[25] Luke strikingly underscores the powerful anointing of the Spirit that marked the inauguration of Jesus's messianic ministry. The Holy Spirit descends upon him in the form of a dove at his baptism (3:21), followed by a heavenly voice declaring, "You are My beloved, Son, in You I am well-pleased" (v. 22).[26] Following his

20. It should be noted that Israel's monarchy began with the powerful anointing of Saul with the Spirit of the Lord (1 Sam 10:6 cf. 11:6), but the author of 1 Samuel makes it clear that it is God's choice of David to replace Saul as king, by the removal of this anointing from Saul and the Spirit's anointing on David (1 Sam 16:13–14).

21. Horton, *What the Bible Says About the Holy Spirit*, 51.

22. Literally the Hebrew text says that the Spirit of the Lord "rush" on or into David.

23. Not even once upon any of the eight kings who "did right in the sight of the Lord." See for example: Asa (1 Kgs 15:11), Jehoshaphat (1 Kgs 22:43), Joash/Jehoash (2 Kgs 12:2), Amaziah (2 Kgs 14:3), Uzziah/Azariah (2 Kgs 15:3), Jotham (2 Kgs 15:34), Hezekiah (2 Kgs 18:3), and Josiah (2 Kgs 22:2).

24. The question of the differing genealogies in Matthew and Luke is complex but it seems that Matthew follows Joseph's descent as the husband of Mary. Thus, Jesus would be his adopted Son and legal heir to David's throne. Luke, on the other hand, seems to follow the genealogical line of Mary through Nathan, a son of Bathsheba (1 Chr 3:5). This would likewise argue for the natural or physical descent of Jesus back to David. See Archer, *Encyclopedia of Bible Difficulties*, 315.

25. Luke's Gospel opens with a concentration of Spirit-filled prophetic spokespersons anticipating God's promised salvation in Christ: Elizabeth (1:41ff), Mary (1:46ff), Zacharias (1:67ff), Simeon (2:25ff), Anna (2:36ff), and John the Baptist (3:4ff).

26. This quotation of a royal Davidic psalm (Ps 2:7), used in the coronation cer-

baptism, Jesus is led by the Spirit into the wilderness where he is tempted by the devil for forty days. Upon his victory over Satan's temptations, Luke records the commencement of his public messianic ministry with these words, "And Jesus returned to Galilee in the power of the Spirit" (4:14). The narrative takes us immediately to the synagogue of Nazareth where Jesus takes a scroll and reads from Isaiah 61:1–2, "The Spirit of the Lord is upon Me because He anointed Me to preach the gospel to the poor. He has sent Me to proclaim release to the captives, and recovery of sight to the blind, to set free those who are oppressed, to proclaim the favorable year of the Lord" (vv. 18–19). Following this reading is his announcement that that Scripture had been fulfilled in the hearing of the people (v. 21). The narrative that follows includes accounts of demonic deliverances and numerous healings (4:31—5:26).

Luke makes crystal clear that what identified Jesus as the messianic Davidic heir was the anointing of the Spirit, which marked and empowered his messianic ministry. What has all this to do with the continuation of the charismata? To borrow a Pauline phrase, "much in every respect." Jesus came not only to declare the arrival of the kingdom of God (Mark 1:15) and preach and teach about the kingdom (Matt 5–7, 13) but was in his person the presence of the kingdom. He said, "If I cast out demons by the Spirit of God, then the kingdom of God has come upon you" (Matt 12:28). We note that it is the Spirit-empowered works of the Messiah that testifies to the presence of God's kingdom. This motif could be amply illustrated from any of the Synoptic Gospels, but for the sake of time, fast forward to the post-resurrection period of Jesus' earthly ministry in Luke's Gospel. After appearing to the disciples on the road to Emmaus and teaching them the necessity and significance of his sufferings (24:13–32), Jesus appeared to the eleven disciples and gave them similar instructions, but then issues a promise and a command: "And behold, I am sending forth the promise of My Father upon you; but you are to stay in the city until you are clothed with power from on high" (v. 49). In the book of Acts, Luke picks up this narrative and repeats the same command and promise (Acts 1:4–5). His elaboration includes the prediction that they

---

emonies for Israelite kings, is conflated with Isaiah 42:1, a part of one of four "servant songs" in Isaiah (42:1–7; 49:1–13; 50:4–11; 52:13—53:12). In these "servant songs" the servant (Heb. *ebed*) of the Lord is the Messiah. For a discussion of interpretive options and rationale for seeing these songs as messianic, see Hummel, *The Word Becoming Flesh*, 218–24.

will soon be "baptized with / in the Holy Spirit" (v. 5). This Spirit-baptism will result in the reception of power to be witnesses to the resurrected Christ in the entire world (v. 8).

That the promised anointing of the Holy Spirit was delivered when the Spirit was poured out on the day of Pentecost seems clear and incontestable. However, the significance of that outpouring of the Spirit is what is debated. How does Pentecost argue for the continuance of supernatural charismata in the church today? The answer lies in the purpose of Jesus's promise of the Spirit. There is the transference of the Spirit that empowered Jesus in his earthly ministry to his disciples gathered on the day of Pentecost. This has an Old Testament parallel with the transference of the Spirit that rested on Moses to the seventy elders, allowing the burden of ministry to be shared (Num 11:11–17). The connection is strengthened when we examine the prophetic explanation Peter gives to the Pentecostal outpouring of the Spirit. The *glossalalia*/tongues, which were mocked by the bystanders, constituted the fulfillment of Joel's prophesy that in the last days God would pour out his Spirit on all humanity. The result is that all categories of people would prophesy or receive prophetic revelation. The repetition of the words, "and they shall prophesy" (v. 17), is Luke's addition and forms an *inclusio*, a literary device that repeats words at the beginning and end of a passage for emphasis. The outpouring of the Spirit has marked God's end-time people as a prophetic community. The Spirit's prophetic anointing and empowerment in the Old Testament was limited, sporadic, and individual. But *this* eschatological prophetic anointing "democratizes" the Spirit, making his power available to all of God's people. Pentecost is, in fact, the fulfillment of Moses's wish in Numbers 11:29, "Would that all the LORD's people were prophets, that the LORD would put His Spirit upon them!"

The significance of Pentecost needs to be connected to the theme with which I began—the Davidic covenant. In quoting Psalm 16:8–11, Peter tells his audience that David's words spoke of Jesus's resurrection and certainly did not apply to himself (Acts 2:29). Nevertheless, "because he was a prophet and knew that God had sworn to him with an oath to seat one of his descendants *on his throne*, he looked ahead and spoke of the resurrection of the Christ" (vv. 30–31 cf. 2 Sam 7:12f).[27] Then we read Peter's climatic conclusion in verses 33–36. It begins with, "Therefore

27. Emphasis mine in *italics*.

having been exalted to the right hand of God, and having received from the Father the promise of the Holy Spirit, He has poured forth this which you both see and hear" (v. 33). It concludes with, "Therefore let all the house of Israel know for certain that God has made Him both Lord and Christ—this Jesus whom you crucified" (v. 36). Jesus is declared to be the Messianic, Davidic king who fulfills the covenantal promise God made to David. The resurrected Jesus, now exalted to his heavenly throne at the right hand of God, has poured forth the Spirit upon the spiritual heirs of David—the new covenant people of God. The kingly anointing of David has been extended and shared with all those who through faith in Jesus Christ have entered the kingdom of God.

The implication for our present concern seems clear. Is this kingdom anointing, which is grounded in the Davidic covenant and fulfilled in Christ, limited to the believers of the first century? Acts 2:33 makes it clear that Peter is referring to the Pentecostal outpouring of the Spirit. A few verses later he refers to it as the "gift of the Spirit" and adds, "For the promise is for you and your children and for all who are far off, as many as the Lord our God will call to Himself" (vv. 38–39). We cannot limit the adjective *makran* ("far off") to physical distance, as if Peter was referring only to Gentiles or Jews in the Diaspora, because neither the immediate context nor the word itself will allow it.[28] That the promise embraces future generations of believers seems clear unless one contends that God stopped calling people to himself after the first century!

It is significant that Peter recognizes that David's anointing with the Spirit, received as Israel's new king, resulted in prophecy (Acts 2:30). This dovetails with the point above. The effusion of the Spirit at Pentecost resulted in prophecy by all on whom the Spirit fell. The promise of the Father that Jesus had predicted would empower them to be prophetic witnesses to the resurrected and exalted Christ (1:8). But the continuity between Jesus and his followers consisted in more than just the empowered proclamation of the gospel (as in the case of Peter). It immediately resulted in signs, wonders, miracles, and healings at the hands of the apostles and other disciples.[29] This, Jesus himself predicted: "Truly, truly, I say to you,

---

28. Both the adjective *makran* and the adjective *makros* have temporal uses. See Liddle and Scott, *An Intermediate Greek-English Lexicon*, 484–5.

29. Most cessationists limit such supernatural manifestations to the apostles. I will later show this restriction to be unsustainable from the New Testament evidence.

he who believes in Me, the works that I do, he will do also; and greater *works* than these he will do; because I go to the Father" (John 14:12).

THE WORK OF THE SPIRIT
IN THE OLD AND NEW TESTAMENTS

A cessationist might be willing to concede this last point but still contend that such supernatural phenomena was necessary to establish the church, being an authentication of apostolic preaching that eventually produced the NT canon.[30] For example, in the thinking of Gaffin, Pentecost is a unique and non-repeatable slice of salvation history that produced the church. It is, in fact, the culmination of Jesus's redemptive work.[31] No Pentecostal or charismatic would necessarily disagree. To say that Pentecost as salvation history is non-repeatable is one thing, but to say that the dynamic *effects* that Pentecost provided for the church is restricted to its foundational period is quite another matter. The conflict arises when the cessationist understands the Pentecostal outpouring of the Spirit, or Jesus's prophesy of a baptism in/with the Holy Spirit (Acts 1:5), as exclusively soteriological. Before demonstrating that this restriction is unsustainable, a brief biblical theological sketch of the Spirit's work needs to be conducted.[32]

In the Old Testament

A comprehensive survey of the Old Testament (hereafter OT) would yield a wide range of activities of the Spirit and a diversity of functions.[33] Basically they can be listed under two broad categories: *transformational* and *empowerment*. Under the latter category we run into individuals who

30. See Gaffin, "A Cessationist View," 42–49.

31. Ibid., 36.

32. My colleague, Douglas Oss, should be credited with pointing out the need to conduct such a survey if one is to argue from a redemptive-historical approach that supports Pentecostal pneumatology. See Oss, "A Pentecostal/Charismatic View," 245.

33. Although a popular work, written for non-academics, Stanley M. Horton's *What the Bible Says About the Holy Spirit* is informed by a careful inductive study of all relevant texts that describe the Spirit's activities in the Old Testament. Roger Stronstad surveys the Septuagint and finds more than 20 verbs that describe the "charismatic activity" in the Old Testament. See Stronstad, *The Charismatic Theology of St. Luke*, 18–21.

were empowered (or some prefer "inspired") to prophesy,[31] judge, lead,[35] deliver God's people,[36] perform supernatural feats (usually related to the deliverance of Israel),[37] and practice feats of wisdom.[38] By far the preponderance of references to the activity of the Spirit relate to the inspiration of the prophets who were "men of the Spirit" and spoke for God (2 Pet 1:21).[39] This leads us to safely conclude that even if the Spirit is not explicitly mentioned, he is responsible for prophecy throughout the OT. Nevertheless, as alluded to earlier, the "charismatic"[40] empowerment of the Spirit in the OT is limited. The anointing falls on individuals, usually for a season to accomplish a given task. But as we saw in Numbers 11:29, Moses's prophetic wish anticipated the "democratization" of the Spirit at Pentecost.

The OT also gives evidence of the inner transforming work of the Spirit. This activity results in various changes of a person's inward nature or even personality. For example, when the Spirit mightily came upon Saul, he became "very angry" with the zeal of God (1 Sam 11:6). Earlier Samuel had prophesied that when the Spirit of the Lord came upon Saul, he would prophesy and be changed "into another man" (10:6). The question of whether and to what extent the Spirit effected a moral-spiritual transformation in the OT is debatable. However, David's prayer for purification and a clean heart, juxtaposed to a reference to the Spirit (Ps 51:7, 10–11), certainly suggests that David assumed that connection. Similarly, God's command that Israel "circumcise their hearts" speaks of an inner work that would produce repentance and consecration to God (Lev 26:41;

---

34. E.g., Moses, Eldad, Medad, and the 70 elders (Num 11:25–27); Saul (1 Sam 10:6, 10); Saul's messengers (1 Sam 19:6) et al. Cf. 2 Sam 23:2 (David); 2 Kgs 2:9, 15 (Elijah and Elisha).

35. E.g., Othniel, (Judg 3:10); Gideon (Judg 6:34); Jephthah (Judg 11:29), and of course David (1 Sam 16:13).

36. E.g., Moses (Num 11:17); Joshua (Num 27:18).

37. E.g., Samson (Judg 14:6, 19; 15:14–17).

38. E.g., Bezaleel and Aholiab (Exod 31:1–2; 35:30–34).

39. Horton notes that in Exodus 4:16 and 7:1 the words "prophet" and "spokesman" are used interchangeably. See Horton, *What the Bible Says*, 24.

40. Using the term "charismatic" in reference to the Spirit's work in the Old Testament may be subject to the charge of biblical anachronism. It is true that the term *charisma* is not found in the Old Testament and apart from 1 Peter 1:4, is found only in the writings of Paul. See Schatzmann, *A Pauline Theology of Charismata*. However, Stronstad and I (and others) use the term here to draw a parallel with the empowering aspect of the Spirit's work, which find ready parallels in the Old Testament.

Deut 10:16). Parallel to David's experience, the Israelites are described as having grieved the Holy Spirit in the wilderness (Isa 63:10–11).[41] But as Oss observes, "the inner transformation, both required by God and desired by David, is not described as a universal experience in this period."[42]

Yet the OT yields a prophetic longing for a future work of the Spirit in regard to this inner transformation. Jeremiah looked to a future day under a *new covenant* when God would write his law on the hearts of his people (Jer 31:33 cf. Heb 8:7–13). Ezekiel, anticipating the same day, describes this inner transformation. God will put *a new spirit* within them after removing from his people a heart of stone (Ezek 36:26). The agent used to produce this transformation is God's own Spirit (v. 27). Both David and Ezekiel describe an inward transformation that results in obedience to God's law. The universality of the provision is anticipated by Jeremiah when he writes, "They will not teach again, each man his neighbor and each man his brother, saying, 'Know the LORD,' for they will all know Me, from the least of them to the greatest of them, declares the LORD, for I will forgive their iniquity, and their sin I will remember no more" (Jer 31:34).

In the New Testament

One has only to read the third chapter of 2 Corinthians to realize that Jeremiah and Ezekiel foresaw the new covenant provision of the Spirit who imparts life (v. 6), true spiritual freedom (v. 17), and the power of inner transformation into the image of God's glory (v. 18). NT theologians of all stripes recognize this transformational work of the Spirit under the new covenant. It is identified with the new birth (John 3:3–8), regeneration (Titus 3:5), and sanctification (Rom 8:2–9 cf. Gal 5:13–18), all effected by the indwelling presence of the Spirit. The debate is not over this aspect of the Spirit's work but over what Roger Stronstad calls "the vocational" or "charismatic activity" of the Spirit.[43] That is, does this charismatic work of the Spirit show continuity with the Spirit's work of empowerment in the OT? I contend that the NT evidence answers that question in the affirmative.

---

41. It is instructive to note that Paul speaks of the inward transformation provided by the Spirit and experience by Christian believers as an inner "circumcision," that is, "of the heart" (Rom 2:28–29).

42. Oss, "A Pentecostal/Charismatic View," 246.

43. Stronstad, *Charismatic Theology*, 23–24.

As earlier stated, the outpouring of the Spirit at Pentecost resulted not only in transformed individuals (which it certainly did) but a church that was empowered to be a witness of the risen Christ (Acts 1:8). When we compare the charismatic activity in the OT with that of the Spirit in the post-Pentecost church, there are numerous parallels. On the day of Pentecost the Spirit empowers Peter's prophetic sermon (Acts 2:14).[44] The apostles (but not exclusively), like their Lord (Acts 10:38), are used to perform miracles, signs, and wonders,[45] heal the sick,[46] raise the dead,[47] and cast out demons.[48] By the Spirit they received revelations of human hearts[49] and prophetic knowledge they did not possess.[50] Beyond these extraordinary supernatural works, the first church experienced Spirit-empowered boldness for preaching (Acts 4:31–33), wisdom for service (Acts 6:3), guidance (Acts 16:7–8 cf. 19:21), the courage to face martyrdom (Acts 7:55–60), and comfort and joy (Acts 9:31; 13:52). The depiction of the early church in Acts leaves no question that it was a Spirit empowered, Spirit-gifted church. The only question that remains is whether God intended that power, that "giftedness," to mark the NT church for all time or only in the foundational period of the first century.

CHARISMATA AND THE ESCHATON

Earlier I drew attention to Peter's sermon on the day of Pentecost. In quoting Joel 2:28–32, Peter changed the Hebrew text from "and afterwards" (Heb. *achar ken*) to "in the last days" (Gk. *en tais eschatais hēmerais*). Under prophetic inspiration, Peter identified the outpouring of the Spirit as an eschatological sign that God's promised day of salvation had arrived (Acts 2:20–21). Following the Septuagint of Joel, Peter referred to it as "the great and glorious day of the Lord." A clear inference can and should be

---

44. There is little doubt as to the prophetic nature of this sermon given Luke's use of the rare verb *apophthengomai*, here and in 2:4, which is used of prophesy in the Old Testament (1 Chr 25:1) and is only used of speech inspired by God's Spirit or in connection with pagan prophesy (Mic 5:12).

45. Acts 2:43; 4:30–33; 5:12; 6:8 (Stephen); 14:1; 15:12; Rom 15:19; 2 Cor 12:12; Heb 10:4 (by those who heard, v. 3).

46. Acts 3:7; 4:14, 22, 30; 5:15; 8:7; 9:17; 28:8.

47. Acts 9:40–41; 20:9–12.

48. Acts 5:16; 8:7; 16:16–18.

49. Acts 5 3; 8:20–23 cf. Mark 2:6–8.

50. Acts 10:19 cf. John 1:48–49.

made. The church now exists in the end-time period called by theologians the *eschaton*—the epoch that is the "end of time" before the Lord returns. The second coming, or *parousia* of Christ, will conclude and consummate the *eschaton* and usher in the final events preceding the millennium[51] and the eternal age to come.[52]

But what is the nature of the church, and how did God intend it to function and fulfill the Great Commission "until the end of the age" (Matt 28:20)? It is my conviction that the NT evidence teaches that the church, by design and fundamental nature, is *charismatic*. That is, the church at Pentecost was endowed with the eschatological gift of the Spirit, in whom the panoply of spiritual gifts resides. The Spirit himself *is* that gift promised by the Father to all who repent and are baptized in the name of Jesus Christ for the forgiveness of sins (Luke 24:49; Acts 1:8; 2:38). As stated earlier, this eschatological gift was promised to "all who are far off, as many as the Lord our God will call to Himself" (Acts 2:39). Luke (nor any other NT author for that matter) nowhere even remotely suggests that after the founding of the church the reception of the Spirit brings only the transformational-soteriological work of the Spirit but not his empowerment. If such were the case, Paul's teaching on the nature of the church would have to be denied. Moreover, the Spirit, as Paul teaches, is the "earnest" (Gk. *arrabōn*) of our inheritance, an inheritance that includes the salvific and charismatic work of the Spirit.

In 1 Corinthians 12:4–31, Paul, taking the body metaphor, makes it clear that the church is fundamentally charismatic. It is comprised of members who are endowed with "varieties of gifts . . . by the one Spirit" who distributes them to each member of the body "individually just as He wills" (vv. 9, 11). He makes it abundantly clear that such a design, despite its diversity of expression, is unified by its source—the Triune God (vv. 4–6). Divine orchestration of the gifts guarantees the vital function of each gifted member in Christ's body.[53] A line of equations emerges. The

---

51. This is of course assuming a premillennial eschatology. However, my arguments for the continuance of the charismata works equally as well within amillennialism or postmillennialism.

52. For a complete discussion of the eschatological framework of the New Testament, see Ladd, *A Theology of the New Testament*, 550–68; Pate, *The End of the Age Has Come*, 217–35.

53. Note that the charismata are Spirit-effected as "one and the same Spirit works all these things" (12:11). They are sovereignly orchestrated, placed by God in the body "just as He desired" (12:18), and divinely ordered—God having "appointed" these gifts in the church (12:28).

body of Christ is comprised of many members who are part of one body. Each member of the body has a vital function to perform within the body. To empower that function each member is divinely gifted with a *charisma* from the Triune God. The functions described in this passage include ministries that are patently present in the church today and accepted by all Christians, even cessationists.[54]

Indeed, most cessationists are only "partial" cessationists, usually holding to the demise of certain revelatory gifts of the Spirit.[55] But we must ask the exegetical question: Where in the context of Paul's passage does he indicate that only some of the charismata were to endure in the church, while others were destined for either disuse or obsolescence? The cessationist, who reaches for 1 Corinthians 13:8–13 as a proof text, grasps exegetical straws and proffers the most tenuous of evidence. It is true that a time will come when spiritual gifts will cease. Paul specifically mentions prophecy, tongues, and knowledge (v. 8). But when is *that* time? Paul's answer: when "that which is perfect (Gk. *to teleion*) has come" (v. 10 NKJV). Those that see here a reference to the completion of the NT canon or the spiritual maturity of the church are hard pressed to support their views from the context of the passage.[56] Clearly the partial knowledge and impaired vision or understanding will be lifted only when we see "face to face" and when we shall "know fully just as [we] also have been fully known" (v. 12). As Deere points out, Paul's expression is used of the OT people who had a personal

---

54. E.g., teachers, helps, administrations (1 Cor 12:28), pastors and evangelists (Eph 4:11), and service, exhortation, giving, leadership, and mercy (Rom 12:7–8).

55. As with Gaffin, "A Cessationist View," 41-60. Gaffin argues that the revelatory gifts render the uniqueness of the New Testament canonical writings a moot point because there is nothing in the New Testament that helps us distinguish, for example, canonical and non-canonical prophesy. This present project is too brief to deal substantively with Gaffin's objection or to answer it. Full-length works that have done so are Jack Deere's *Surprised By the Voice of the Spirit* and Wayne Grudem's *The Gift of Prophecy in the New Testament Today*.

56. If the "childish things" that are put away (v. 11) refer to spiritual gifts, then partial cessationists cannot use this verse as support for their position. Some see the "perfection" as referring to the New Testament canon. Not only is that view nowhere even remotely suggested by the context, but defies reason and reality. Who today, with a complete New Testament canon, would say that we no longer have need for knowledge, or that we no longer know "in part" (v. 9)? Who would hold that we no longer "see in a mirror dimly" but rather "face to face," or that we now "know fully just as [we] also have been fully known (v. 12)?"

revelation of God.[57] This can only be an oblique reference to the *parousia*, which the apostle John makes more explicit when he writes, "Beloved, now we are children of God, and it has not appeared as yet what we will be. We know that when He appears, we will be like Him, because we will see Him just as He is. And everyone who has this hope *fixed* on Him purifies himself, just as He is pure" (1 John 3:2–3).

When a fair and careful reading of the NT evidence is conducted, we must agree with Grieg and Springer that "not a shred of evidence in the New Testament demonstrates or even suggests that any gift of the Spirit should or would cease in the Church until the second coming of Christ."[58] The reason is obvious—the Spirit is God's eschatological gift to the church. The gifts of the Spirit are an integral part of that package. That is why Paul could use the presence and miraculous work of the Spirit in Galatia as his evidence for justification by faith (Gal 3:5). Salvation, along with the reception of the Spirit and its attendant charismatic empowerment, came to them "by/through" faith, not works of law. Similarly, the author of Hebrews—in warning against apostasy—describes believers as those "who have once been enlightened and have tasted of the heavenly gift and have been made partakers of the Holy Spirit, and have tasted the good word of God and the powers of *the age to come*" (Heb 6:4–5).[59]

Thus, from the view of salvation history, the charismata belong to the *eschaton* and will not cease until the *parousia* of Christ. The Spirit comes as the partial inheritance of our salvation, as the pledge of its eschatological completion (Eph 1:13–14). He comes to deliver not only the transformational work of salvation but also the church's charismatic empowerment. This is nothing less than the divine in breaking of the kingdom of God on earth. While the kingdom awaits eschatological consummation at the *parousia*, the kingdom is also present and manifests itself in the church and its global mission on earth. That mission centers around the preaching of the gospel and the making of disciples (Matt 28:19; Mark 16:15). But that mission includes bearing witness to the reality of the kingdom of

57. Deere, *Surprised By the Power*, 142.

58. Grieg and Springer, *Kingdom and the Power*, 405–6.

59. Emphasis mine in *italics*. We acknowledge that much debate exists over whether those described in these verses are true or apparent Christians. While we cannot pursue this debate here, it is worth noting the clear connection between the Holy Spirit and power, all within an eschatological framework. It is then fair and instructive to ask whether such a description could ever be applied to non-believers by a New Testament author.

God in power. Mark makes this clear in his Gospel. Jesus begins his public messianic ministry by "preaching the gospel of God" and announcing that the "kingdom of God is at hand" (Mark 1:14–15). Then, in Capernaum, he amazes the people with his authoritative teaching in the synagogue and is immediately confronted by a demon-possessed man. His first supernatural deed in Mark, after announcing the coming of the kingdom, was to cast out an unclean spirit. The amazement of the people now escalates to include not only his teaching but also the demonstration of divine power, the authoritative power of the kingdom of God (Mark 1:23–27).

Paul understood this connection between preaching the gospel and God's kingdom revealed in power. As he contends, the kingdom of God does not consist in words but *in power* (1 Cor 4:20 cf. 2:4–5). For him, to "fully preach the gospel" included doing so "in the power of signs and wonders" and "in the power of the Spirit" (Rom 15:19).

CONCLUDING REMARKS

"This gospel of the kingdom shall be preached in the whole world as a testimony to all the nations, and then the end will come" (Matt 24:14). These words of Jesus state plainly that preaching the gospel of the kingdom is a task that belongs to the age of the church until the end of this age (the *eschaton*). I have one final question for the cessationist: Why would Jesus commission his church to preach the gospel of the kingdom of God devoid of the miraculous power that (1) characterized his own ministry (Luke 4:14; Acts 10:38),[60] (2) was promised to his church (Luke 24:49; Acts 1:8), and (3) he had predicted would follow the disciples' ministry (John 5:20 cf. Mark 16:17–20)?

If one still holds to the view that such a ministry was necessary to launch the church but not after its establishment, a whole host of nagging questions arise: Is Jesus still building his church and establishing his kingdom on earth? If so, why is there no longer any need for the demonstration of his kingdom *in power*? Have all the demons of Satan been cast out, no longer inhabiting those in need of rescue from "the domain of darkness" (Col 1:13)? Are there no longer any sick in need of Jesus's compassionate healing touch? Are there no places or populations on earth that

---

60. Especially in view of the fact that we are enjoined to imitate him (1 John 2:6). See Hernando, "Imitation Language in Paul," 1–26.

are as yet unevangelized?[61] Do not these situations call for a validation of both the message and the messenger by miraculous signs and wonders that marked the early church? Why should we assume that the needs met through charismata in the first church are either no longer relevant or no longer require the charismatic work of the Spirit to meet them?

These questions are rhetorical to be sure but are offered to suggest that there is situational continuity between the first church and the church of every generation throughout church history. Each generation has been entrusted with the same commission, faces the same challenges, and requires the same empowerment until the end of the age.

61. In fact, in recent years my own denomination has had part in the evangelization of areas of Mongolia where there was virtually no Christian presence. In 1993 the first Assemblies of God missionaries entered Mongolia. In 1994 the first Good News Crusade was held in the capital city of Ulan Bator. Over 500 Mongolians accepted Christ as their Savior. Not surprisingly, the missionaries also gave testimony to miraculous healings, signs, and wonders. See Houlihan, "Taking a New Territory," 26; "Pentecost now—in Mongolia," 12–13.

A Cessationist Response

Willem Berends

FROM THE OUTSET I want to make it clear that I value Dr. James Hernando's defense of continuationism as a well-reasoned and valuable contribution to the discussion. I especially appreciate his efforts to cover some new ground instead of merely repeating all the arguments of former debates, though he rightly draws our attention to them in copious footnotes. I will also try to avoid the older arguments in my response and give attention to the new materials brought forward. Here I will concentrate on the points I interpret differently than Dr. Hernando. By focusing on the differences I want to avoid two misunderstandings. First, I am not wishing to enter a "point-scoring" exercise but to help the readers see the other side of the question. Second, despite these differences I am in agreement with most of what Dr. Hernando has to say.

I also want to mention that I believe the charismatic movement has helped the older churches recognize once again the role of the Holy Spirit in empowering God's people to ministry. Creeds and confessions from early church and Reformation times recognize the Spirit's role in revealing God's will, calling God's people to faith, giving them a new life, and nurturing and sustaining them in that new life, but they are perhaps weak on the Spirit's role in empowering people for the ministry to which God calls us. Despite this, I do want to question Dr. Hernando's conclusion when he asks the cessationists: ". . . why is there no longer any need for the demonstration of his [Christ's] kingdom *in power*?" (p. 229) Most cessationists do recognize the continuing power shown in the Spirit's miraculous works and would add that the kingdom can advance by no other power (Zech 4:6; Acts 4:31; 1 Thess 1:5). The issue is not whether the kingdom is advanced through the miraculous power of God's Spirit but how God channels this power. Does God do this through gifts of miracles or in other miraculous as well as non-miraculous ways?

Perhaps I can best illustrate this with reference to my work in western Africa where my wife and I were called to begin a mission work among a pocket of pagans in a strongly Muslim state. Many people, both local and expatriate, Christians and Muslims, advised us that we were wasting our time because permission to start a new work would never be given. Humanly speaking they were right, but through a divinely directed series of events we were not only given permission but were welcomed by the very people who would normally have opposed us. We witnessed numerous other events of a providential and miraculous nature in our ministry, which caused people to turn to God and follow Jesus (cf. Gal 3:5; Heb 2:4). Despite this, we do not believe God granted us what he gave to Paul, "the things that mark an apostle—signs, wonders and miracles" (2 Cor 12:12).

THE MARK OF AN APOSTLE

In the Bible the words "signs," "wonders," and "miracles" are often used synonymously, though they stress different aspects of God's supernatural work.[62] The word "sign" reminds us that God's wondrous displays of power are meant to *signify, point to,* or *testify to* something. Here we include first, God's glory (Exod 15:11; Ps.118:23; Matt 9:8); second, God's saving grace in Christ (Matt 12:28; Luke 11:20; Heb 2:3–4); and third, messengers appointed by God (Exod 4:1–9; 1 Kgs 18:36; John 3:2; Acts 2:22). It is especially the last of these purposes of miracles that concerns us here. Where God gave specific people the gift to perform miracles, he invariably did this to testify to their special calling. In the passages cited above, Moses, Elijah, and Christ are said to do miracles in affirmation of their divine appointment. Thus, Peter appeals to Christ's miracles in this way: "Men of Israel, listen to this: Jesus of Nazareth was a man accredited by God to you by miracles, wonders and signs, which God did among you *through him,* as you yourselves know" (Acts 2:22).[63]

It is in this last sense that we must also understand the signs, wonders, and miracles in the ministry of Christ's apostles. God did his won-

---

62. The words used in both the Greek and Hebrew literally translate as *signs, powers,* and *wonders.*

63. Emphasis mine in *italics.*

ders *through* them to "mark" apostles (2 Cor 12:12).[64] This marking was necessary because there were also false apostles, with false teachings that would lead the church astray (2 Cor 11:13; Rev 2:2). Significantly, it was not just miracles done through the apostles that confirmed their status but especially their ability to bestow similar gifts on others through the laying on of hands. It was this ability that set the apostles apart from others who claimed miraculous powers, like Simon the magician (Acts 8:18–19). Simon and the Samaritans were led to conversion through the ministry of Philip, one of *the seven*. These seven were chosen to help the apostles because they were "full of the Spirit" (Acts 6:3). Yet they are not mentioned as doing any wonders or miraculous signs before the apostles placed their hands on them (Acts 6:6, 8). And though Philip's witness and miracles led the Samaritans to conversion, the Holy Spirit did not come upon the Samaritans with power until the apostles, Peter and John, laid their hands on them (Acts 8:17).

As stated in my essay, the apostolic office needed affirmation because apostles had a foundational function in setting up the church of Christ. No Christian has a comparable function today, and it is not individual Christians who need affirmation by God, but rather, the gospel they preach. Thus, the gospel continues to come with power, attested by signs, wonders, and miracles, but these occur in response to prayer, not through the exercise of a gift. Messengers do not need personal affirmation where the message itself comes with power. As with John the Baptist, the ones who bring the Word must decrease so that the Word might increase (John 3:30). This is expedient because where people are believed to have the gift of miracles there is the danger that these people will receive the glory that belongs to God. That this danger is real can be learned from history. The veneration of saints grew out of the belief that they could (and still can) perform miracles. Until today, some Christian traditions continue to identify and canonize saints on the basis of the miracles they are alleged to have performed.

THE GIFT OF PROPHECY AND THE ANOINTING OF THE SPIRIT

I fully endorse Dr. Hernando's salvation history approach and with him trace the Davidic blessings to Christ and the kingdom. But I fail to see

---

64. The Greek word *sēmeia* here is the same as that used for *signs*.

how recognition of the bestowal of the gift of prophecy on David implies that at Pentecost this "resulted in prophecy by all on whom the Spirit fell" (p. 221). This is claiming too much. In Acts 2 there is no mention that those who received the Spirit also prophesied. They miraculously spoke in tongues, "declaring the wonders of God" in the languages of the people represented there (v. 11). As I pointed out in my essay, this fitted in precisely with the first century Jewish understanding of Pentecost. They celebrated the feast to remember the covenant God made with them at Sinai, where they believed God himself spoke the words of the law in seventy languages.[65] The emphasis is on the tongues, and it is only when Peter identifies the events with Joel's predictions that prophecy is mentioned, along with dreams, visions, blood, fire, and smoke.

We can use the word "prophecy" to describe what happened at Pentecost if we use it in the sense of "declaring the wonders of God." The Greek verb to prophesy (prophēteuō) can mean "to proclaim" or "declare," as well as to "foretell" or "reveal."[66] Cessationists never had a problem in recognizing continuing prophecy by the first of these definitions. In fact, during the Elizabethan Reformation and Puritan times the word "prophesyings" was used to refer to the preaching of the word outside of formal church services. Elizabeth discouraged preaching at Sunday services, which tended to be highly liturgical. The prophesyings appear to be a reaction to this situation, possibly in application of 1 Thessalonians 5:19–20, "Quenche not the sprete. Despise not prophesyinge" (Tyndale's translation). As mentioned in my essay, cessationists do not recognize any "prophecy" in the sense of a new "revelation" additional to the will of God given in Scripture.

Most cessationists are in complete agreement that the Spirit anoints everyone who belongs to the kingdom. The tradition I belong to has long recognized the anointing of all those who recognize Jesus as Lord (1 Cor 12:3) and likens their anointing to that of prophets, priests, and kings.[67] While this speaks of the empowering of the Spirit to help Christians in their general calling rather than in specific tasks, no cessationist would suggest that this anointing is limited to the first century, as Dr. Hernando surmises. Neither must the scope of the Spirit's anointing be confused

65. See Weinfeld, "Pentecost as Festival of the Giving of the Law," 14–15.
66. Danker, *A Greek-English Lexicon of the New Testament*.
67. See *The Heidelberg Catechism*, L.D. 12, cf. 1 Peter 2:9.

with the scope of the gifts bestowed by the Spirit. The recognition that
all Christians receive the Holy Spirit, now as in apostolic times, does not
really answer the question as to which gifts Christ bestows on his people
today. The Spirit is given to all believers, but the gifts are distributed according to the needs of the church of the time (1 Cor 12:1–6).

The issue dividing cessationists and continuationists is not the question of whether God bestows his Spirit on the church today, nor even
whether the church is "fundamentally charismatic" (p. 226), but whether
all the gifts manifested in the first generation of Christians continue
on today. One of these gifts is the apostolic office (Eph 4:11). That the
apostles were limited in number is indicated in numerous places.[68] Jesus
chose twelve men to be his apostles (Matt 10:2), and this number was
maintained when one apostle was elected to replace Judas as a witness
to the resurrection (Acts 1:21–22). The number twelve here is the New
Testament counterpart to the twelve tribes of Israel, as can be clearly seen
in the description of the "new Jerusalem." Even as this city has twelve
gates with the names of the twelve tribes, it has twelve foundation stones
bearing the names of the twelve apostles (Rev 21:12, 14).

The church is also pictured as being built on the foundation laid
by the apostles and prophets, with Christ as the chief cornerstone (Eph
2:20). Together with the apostles, the prophets that Paul speaks of in this
verse must similarly be seen as foundational and no longer in the church
today. Paul is not speaking here of people who "prophesy" in the sense
of proclaiming God's marvelous deeds, or of prophets like Agabus who
predicted coming events, but of people given "insight into the mystery
of Christ, which was not made known to men in other generations as it
has now been revealed by the Spirit to God's holy apostles and prophets"
(Eph 3:4–5). In other words, these were the people the Spirit inspired to
write Holy Scripture (2 Tim 3:16; 2 Pet 1:20–21). When, a little further on,
prophets are listed with the apostles as God's gift (*charis*) to the church
(Eph 4:7, 11), we must conclude that such prophets are also no longer to
be found in the church today.

---

68. I am here speaking of the word "apostle" used in its narrow sense; the word is also
used in a wider sense to mean "missionary."

CLOSING REMARKS

If there are at least these two gifts no longer in operation today, is it not reasonable to ask whether there are other gifts associated with these offices? We believe that *signs, wonders, and miracles*, as gifts that "mark an apostle," disappeared along with that office. That is not to say that there are no signs, wonders, and miracles to be seen in the church today but to recognize that these are now worked sovereignly by God in answer to prayer. So in answer to Dr. Hernando's closing questions: Yes, there is a "need for the demonstration of his kingdom *in power*" and there are situations that "call for validation of both the message and the messenger by miraculous signs and wonders that marked the early church." We know this because it is happening. But there is a difference in the way it happens. It is no longer happening by gifts of miracles given to individuals like the apostles but as God's sovereign confirmation of the church they have established that all the glory may go to him alone.

Counter Response

James D. Hernando

I WANT TO THANK Dr. Berends for his response and the courteous and respectful way he frames his disagreements with my views. I am also delighted to learn of a "softer" cessationism that affirms much of what I presented in my essay, especially concerning the charismatic nature and empowerment of the New Testament church. Our main point of departure centers on the continuance of certain specific gifts, which Dr. Berends believes are, providentially I assume, no longer in operation today. These are the gifts associated with the foundational apostles and prophets (Eph 4:7, 11): "signs, wonders, and miracles," and prophecy that would provide "new 'revelation' additional to the will of God given in Scripture" (p. 234).

I hasten to reassure Dr. Berends that most Pentecostals likewise reject charismatic prophecy that claims to provide revelation augmenting canonical Scripture or a status of collateral authority. Obviously not all charismatic prophecy experienced in the apostolic church resulted in canonical Scripture as seen in the cases of Agabus and Philip's daughters (Acts 11:28; 21:9–10). Yet, in the case of Agabus, we have an example of what Berends most strenuously objects to—*revelational* prophecy. In the main, Pentecostals view such prophecy as "subordinate" to the Scriptures.[69] Despite the aberrant excesses abhorred by all evangelical Christians, it is possible for such prophecy to exist without threatening the pre-eminent and normative status of Scripture. To this both the New Testament itself and church history attest.[70]

---

69. See Lee, "Pentecostals and Subordinate Revelation," 9–11; Williams, *Renewal Theology*, 43–44. Williams clearly states that charismatic prophecy is "not new truth that goes beyond the special revelation" of the Scriptures.

70. I regret that Dr. Berends failed to indicate clearly if he viewed all revelational

A second major reservation of Dr. Berends concerns *signs, wonders, and miracles*, as present in the ministry of the apostles. He concludes that these are among the gifts that do not continue on today, except as "worked sovereignly by God in answer to prayer" (p. 236). But this distinction is an unnecessary one as Paul credits the distribution of all charismata to the sovereign will of the Spirit (1 Cor 12:11). Berends objects to individuals claiming the apostolic gift and ability to confer such gifts upon others as did the first apostles. Two corrective points are in order. First, such gifts did not exclusively validate the ministry of the apostles, as those who practiced them were not all apostles (e.g., Philip and Stephen).[71] To argue that they only practiced the miraculous after the apostles laid hands on them is not only an argument from silence but it also ignores the presence of such gifts in the sub-apostolic church (Heb 2:3–4). Second, while the "foundational" apostles, like Paul, were used to impart spiritual gifts (Rom 1:11), it is not at all clear from the New Testament evidence that apostles possessed either the power or authority to dispense the charismata *at will*. It is more likely that Paul's apostolic presence and teaching became the occasion for the sovereign work of the Spirit in blessing the church with charismata (cf. Heb 2:4).

Finally, I regret that Dr. Berends did not substantively address the New Testament evidence I presented in response to the *partial cessation* view of the charismata. His arguments, though well intentioned, leave no substantive challenge to the assessment of Grieg and Springer who wrote, "not a shred of evidence in the New Testament demonstrates or even suggests that any gift of the Spirit should or would cease in the Church until the second coming of Christ."[72]

---

prophecy recorded in post-apostolic church history as false.

71. In neither case does it say that the laying of hands by the Apostles conferred upon them the gift of miracles, signs and wonders. In fact, the purpose for this rite, symbolizing their anointing and consecration, is in reference to the task of administering benevolences in the church (Acts 6:3).

72. Grieg and Springer, *Kingdom and the Power*, 405–6.

13

Women Leadership: The Traditional View

INTRODUCTION

I AM A RELUCTANT participant in the discussion of women in ministry. I wish to be a peacemaker in the body of Christ, yet this issue continues to cause disagreements and divisions. Even those of us who agree about the inspiration and inerrancy of the Bible and desire to handle accurately the word of truth can disagree on what the Bible teaches about women and ministry.

In talking with other Christian women, I find that many are struggling to understand what the Bible teaches about their ministry in the church. As they have posed questions to me, I have actually had to begin to look deeper into this issue. I am indebted to many learned men and women who, through their books, lectures, commentaries, and counsel, have helped me come to a better understanding of the biblical teaching on this subject.

A brief word about my church affiliation: I am a member of the Presbyterian Church in America (PCA). The form of church government in the PCA is representative or presbyterian. The officers of the PCA are the elders and the deacons. There are two types of elders: teaching and ruling. The elders jointly are responsible for the government and spiritual oversight of the church. Only those elders who are gifted, called, and trained by God to preach may serve as teaching elders (pastors). Ruling elders are encouraged to zealously cultivate their own ability to teach the Bible. The deacon's area of ministry is one of service, after the example of the Lord Jesus. Our denomination believes Scripture teaches that only men should fill these offices of elder and deacon.[1]

There have been many books written about the subject of women in ministry, and there is so much that could be said here. In these few pages, I will state what I believe the Bible teaches. In order to guide our discussion about women in ministry, I will look at two passages in Scripture—1 Corinthians 14:33b–36 and 1 Timothy 2:11–14—and conclude with a discussion on the roles of women in the church.

DISCUSSION ON 1 CORINTHIANS 14:33B–36

[33b]As in all the congregations of the saints, [34]women should remain silent in the churches. They are not allowed to speak, but must be in submission, as the Law says. [35]If they want to inquire about something, they should ask their own husbands at home; for it is disgraceful for a woman to speak in the church. [36]Did the word of God originate with you? Or are you the only people it has reached?[2]

The context for this passage is the worshipping church. In the church both men and women have many gifts. First Corinthians 14:26 states, "Whenever you come together, each of you has a psalm, has a teaching, has a tongue, has a revelation, has an interpretation" (NKJV). But there is a proper order that must be maintained during the church worship. Women may prophesy, as we read in 1 Corinthians 11:5, but here in 1 Corinthians 14:34 Paul is saying that the women should remain silent in the church—in this church or any other church.

The question arises: Isn't it inconsistent for Paul to allow women to exercise their gifts, yet to remain silent? We do not expect Paul to contradict himself. I concur with Dan Doriani who states, "When Paul says women must remain silent, he means silent during the testing of prophecy."[3] The testing of prophecy is the theme of 1 Corinthians 14:29–35.

I do not believe that it is inconsistent for Paul to permit women to prophesy and then to forbid them to weigh prophecies. D. A. Carson com-

---

1. *Book of Church Order of the Presbyterian Church in America*, chaps. 8–9.

2. Unless otherwise indicated, all Scripture quotations are taken from the *New International Version*.

3. Doriani, *Women and Ministry*, 82. Dr. Doriani was my lecturer at Covenant Theological Seminary in St. Louis, Missouri, USA. Much of his discussion in this book was originally part of lectures he gave while I was at seminary.

ments that the Spirit-prompted utterances were not automatically given divine authority, so they were in need of evaluation (1 Cor 14:29), and, therefore, inferior in authority to Scripture as Paul states in 1 Corinthians 14:37–38.[4] Priests, not prophets, were the regular authoritative teachers in the Old Testament. In the New Testament, apostles and elders, not prophets, were the prime authorities. It is necessary to test prophecy because not everyone who says he is a prophet of God actually speaks for God. Thus, it is fitting for women to prophesy but neither to preach nor test prophecy. Women are not told to remain silent at all times, but, rather, during the testing of prophecies. The evaluation of prophecies is under the authority of the elders, especially the teaching elders. "Everyone should be discerning, but elders are especially responsible to guide the church to true doctrine (Acts 15:1–35; 20:17–31)."[5] According to Titus 1:6 and 1 Timothy 3:2 these elders are men since they must be "the husband of one wife."

I believe that Carson is correct when he says, "In certain respects, then, it is perfectly proper for Paul to elevate teaching above prophecy, especially if the teaching is considered part of the non-negotiable apostolic deposit that serves in part as one of the touchstones enabling the congregation to weigh the prophecies that are granted to the church, and especially if the prophecies themselves, unlike the apostolic deposit, are subject to ecclesiastical appraisal."[6] Of course, teaching also needs to be evaluated. The church is responsible to evaluate teaching (1 Tim 1:3; 6:3–5; Titus 1:9–14; Heb 13:9; 2 Pet 2:1). Carson goes on to say, "But it does mean that prophecy cannot escape such evaluation, and it presupposes that there is a deposit of apostolic teaching, a given content, that is non-negotiable and that can serve as the criterion both of further teaching and of prophecy."[7] So I believe that careful study of 1 Corinthians 14 supports the view that women may prophesy (11:5) but then must remain silent when prophecy is tested (14:34). Paul encourages women to use their gifts but also orders the use of the gifts so that women are silent during a specific time while prophecy is tested.

In continuing our study, we read at the end of verse 34, "as the Law says." Carson explains:

---

4. Carson, "Silent in the Churches," 153.

5. Doriani, *Women and Ministry*, 85.

6. Carson, "Silent in the Churches," 153.

7. Ibid.

By this clause, Paul is probably not referring to Genesis 3:16, as many suggest, but to the creation order in Genesis 2:20b–24, for it is to that Scripture that Paul explicitly turns on two other occasions when he discusses female roles (i.e. 1 Corinthians 11:8,9). The passage from Genesis 2 does not enjoin silence, of course, but it does suggest that because man was made first and woman was made for man, some kind of pattern has been laid down regarding the roles the two play. Paul understands from this creation order that woman is to be subject to man—or at least that wife is to be subject to husband.[8]

So I believe that Paul's reference to the law means that Adam must lead Eve. Paul goes on to say in 1 Corinthians 14:35 that the women are to ask their husbands at home about the testing of prophecies and the elders' assessment.

Scholars suggest that the Greek word Paul uses for "silence" means that the women's silence is not absolute. Doriani states, "Greek words for silence overlap, and we must not exaggerate differences between them. But our word here, *sigao*, rarely means total speechlessness. It can mean to keep something to oneself (Luke 20:26), to listen (Acts 15:12), or to be silent after speaking (Luke 20:26; Acts 15:13). The word appears in 1 Corinthians 14:28, 14:30, and 14:34. In 14:34, while prophecy is tested, Paul says women should temporarily stop speaking."[9]

In a Greek public meeting from this era, women were not allowed to speak at all. "By contrast, women in the Christian *ekklesia*, borne along by the Spirit, were encouraged to do so. In that sense Paul was not trapped by the social customs of Corinth: the gospel, in his view, truly freed women from certain cultural restrictions. But that does not mean that all distinctions in roles are thereby abolished."[10] These distinctions in men and women's roles were created for our good so that we can be a blessing to others as we live and work within our God-created roles.

When we consider the flow of thought in 1 Corinthians chapter 14, the gifts as they are used in the church, and the focus in the second part of chapter 14 on tongues and prophecy, verses 33b–36 fall in line with this discussion. As verse 36 says, the Corinthians were not to follow their own ideas about how to conduct worship but should conform to God's word.

8. Ibid., 152.

9. Doriani, *Women and Ministry*, 83.

10. Carson, "Silent in the Churches," 153.

The Corinthians should not separate themselves from the standard of all churches (14:33b). "This is part and parcel of Paul's frequent insistence in this letter that the Corinthian church return to the common practice and perspective of the other churches (1:2; 4:17; 7:17; 11:16; 14:33) and to wholehearted submission to apostolic authority (14:37–38)."[11]

DISCUSSION ON 1 TIMOTHY 2:11–14

> 11A woman should learn in quietness and full submission. 12I do not permit a woman to teach or to have authority over a man; she must be silent. 13For Adam was formed first, then Eve. 14And Adam was not the one deceived; it was the woman who was deceived and became a sinner.

Paul said that he wrote First Timothy "so that you will know how one ought to conduct himself in the household of God, which is the church of the living God" (1 Tim 3:15 NASB).

First-century Greek and Jewish cultures generally considered women mentally inferior. Therefore, they did not encourage women to learn. The Mishnah advised men not to talk much to women. But Paul encouraged women to listen and to learn. "Quietly receive instruction" means in a quiet manner—the relative silence that is a virtue for students, not in absolute silence.[12] "Submission" means that they obediently accept the doctrine taught by the church leaders. This type of learning only makes sense whether it be men or women learners.

Because the verb *permit* in 1 Timothy 2:12 is in the present tense, some say that it only prohibits teaching in the present, when women were uneducated. Once educated, they could teach. However, it is not correct to say that the present tense of "I do not permit" means a temporary state. As Doriani explains:

> Prohibitions ordinarily stand 1) until further notice, and 2) unless something in the context shows that the prohibition is temporary. When Paul says, "I do not permit a woman to teach," he delivers a permanent principle, not a temporary preference. But here Paul is not forbidding all teaching, only public, authoritative instruction in doctrine. Three factors indicate this. Firstly, other Scriptures show women teaching, but none show them preaching or teaching

11. Ibid., 151.

12. Doriani, *Women and Ministry*, 89.

the assembly of believers. Secondly, the context is worship in the church. Thirdly, Paul's language suggests that he forbids women to teach doctrine and to exercise ruling authority in the church.[13]

First Timothy does refer to women learning, and so it is right and proper that women can teach what they are learning, as Abigail and Priscilla did.[14] It is good for women to function as teachers in order to edify others. But because of 1 Timothy 2:12, women may learn but they may not teach or exercise authority over men.[15]

The following verses, however, explain why women are not allowed to teach men, and it has nothing to do with a lack of education. In fact, some women in the first century were educated, especially the wealthier women. Paul refers us to the order of creation, not a lack of education, in explaining why women are not permitted to teach or exercise authority over a man—"for Adam was formed first, then Eve" (v. 13). Thus, "male leadership is part of God's original plan. It rests on God's created order, not the Fall or the curse. The appeal to creation indicates that male leadership rests on something essential to men and women."[16]

I believe that Genesis 1 and 2 are vital portions of Scripture in understanding women's role in ministry. The principle of primogeniture—leadership by the firstborn—is evident here and additionally found throughout Scripture. In naming Eve, Adam was stating his authority over her, demonstrating his God-given leadership. Genesis shows that male leadership and authority are a result of God's original plan, and not a consequence of the Fall or later cultural pressures. Leadership by the firstborn is assumed throughout the Bible. As Douglas Moo writes:

> For Paul, the man's priority in the order of creation is indicative of the headship that man is to have over woman. The woman being created after man, as his helper, shows the position of submission that God intended as inherent in the woman's relation to the man, a submission that is violated if a woman teaches doctrine or exercises authority over a man . . . His reason for the prohibitions of verse 12 is the created role relationship of man and woman, and we

13. Ibid., 90–91.
14. See 1 Samuel 25 and Acts 18.
15. Doriani, *Women and Ministry*, 89.
16. Ibid., 93.

may justly conclude that these prohibitions are applicable as long as this reason remains true.[17]

I agree with Moo that these created role relationships of man and woman are a general teaching in Scripture. Paul is not creating a new teaching in 1 Timothy 2:12 but rather continuing to apply a principle that had its beginning in creation. Moo continues:

> The activities involved in 1 Timothy 2:12 are transcultural in the sense that they are permanent ministries of the Christian church, and the prohibitions of 1 Timothy 2:12 are grounded in theology. When we add to these factors the fact that the New Testament teaching on these matters is consistent, we are justified in requiring very good reasons *from the text itself* to limit the application of this text in any way. We find no such reasons. Therefore, we must conclude that the restrictions imposed by Paul in 1 Timothy 2:12 are valid for Christians in all places and all times.[18]

These restrictions continue even though Galatians 3:28 says, "There is neither Jew nor Greek, there is neither slave nor free man, there is neither male nor female; for you are all one in Christ Jesus" (NASB). Doriani rightly comments, "Scripture also says the order of creation will not change until Jesus returns to judge and restore creation. We are equal in redemption, in value, and in purpose, but we have different gifts and roles."[19] I believe that God would be pleased for us to willingly and obediently accept these roles, which he has created for us.

Looking now at 1 Timothy 2:14, we see that once again Paul takes us back to creation. Man was created first. Man named Eve. Eve was created to be a helper suitable for man. A woman's submission is inherent in the creation account. Therefore, it is not in God's plan that a woman should have authority over a man by teaching doctrine. "By rooting these prohibitions in the circumstances of creation rather than in the circumstances of the fall, Paul shows that he does not consider these restrictions to be the product of the curse and presumably, therefore, to be phased out by redemption."[20] Paul's reason for women not to teach or exercise authority over a man is the created role relationship of man and woman. His reason

---

17. Moo, "What does It Mean Not to Teach or Have Authority Over Men?" 190.

18. Ibid., 193.

19. Doriani, *Women and Ministry*, 94.

20. Moo, "What does It Mean," 190.

is not because he believes that women are so easily deceived. If women are so deceived, Paul wouldn't say in Titus 2:3–5 that older women should encourage the young women. There is a lot to be said in this discussion, but basically I believe that God created different roles for men and women and has ordained that men should lead.

The New Testament specifies that the leaders of the church must be male (Acts 1:21–23; 1 Tim 2:12—3:15; Titus 1:5-9). In replacing Judas, the apostles looked to one of the men who had been with them the whole time, believing that Jesus's choice of twelve male apostles was a precedent: "Therefore it is necessary to choose one of the men who have been with us the whole time" (Acts 1:21). "In the original (of Acts 1:21), the word for 'men' is not *anthropos*, the Greek term for a 'human,' but *aner*, the Greek term for a male."[21] Later on, this precedent was once again followed when the church chose seven males (*aner*) to oversee the church's mercy ministry (Acts 6:1–6).

I believe that Doriani states it well when he says:

> The pattern is clear. Women instructed men privately but did not deliver formal addresses to crowds gathered for instruction. They advised and rebuked men, great and small, but did not issue decrees that bound Israel or the church. Women counseled men, who listened and adopted their ideas. Women taught and prophesied, giving messages with theological content. But Scripture has no example of a woman doing what we today call "preaching." Women led beside men in Israel and the church, but no woman approached the rank of Abraham, Moses, David, Elijah, Isaiah, Peter, or Paul as a principal leader. Women led alongside men but ranked beneath them in authority, not beside them as absolute peers. When Miriam aspired to equality with Moses, God rebuked her. When Barak tried to avoid leadership, Deborah urged him on.[22]

Some feminists say that in the first-century culture, it would have been offensive if Jesus had chosen women as disciples and traveling companions. I think that Doriani's response to this is exactly right, "Yes, but Jesus violated cultural conventions whenever he saw fit. He touched lepers. He called tax collectors and prostitutes his friends. He healed Gentiles. He violated customs for the Sabbath . . . He shattered so many conventions; why should he quail at one more? Besides, when moral issues were at

21. Doriani, *Women and Ministry*, 50.
22. Ibid., 36.

stake, Jesus did not bend to social pressure."[23] Some say that it was because women were uneducated that Jesus chose men. But the twelve Jesus chose were not well educated (Acts 4:13), and yet the early Christian church accepted their leadership.[24]

I believe Scripture teaches that in the church, it is normative for men to be in the leadership roles. Some examples of men in leadership are Israel's priests, all monarchs, and the twelve apostles Jesus called. Many women were associated with Jesus and played important roles in the New Testament. Yet Jesus chose and trained twelve men, and no women, to be his apostles. There are occasions when women were appointed as prophetesses and judges, but in these positions they were not public preachers or teachers. They spoke for God but did not have the same kind of authority as kings, priests, or apostles. In Scripture women occasionally teach and lead, but they do not hold a permanent public Bible teaching office exercising authority over men.

DISCUSSION ON ROLES OF WOMEN IN THE CHURCH

Christian men and women have been given spiritual gifts (1 Cor 12:7–11). But it is interesting to note that from the earliest days of the apostolic church most orthodox Christians have agreed that there are restrictions to the ministry of women. The Bible gives us many examples of women in ministry. In Israel and in the church, women do many things but not everything. Women had great influence at times and many were honored. We see that women worked alongside men. We also see that women taught in private. Women were not public preachers or teachers. Women were prophetesses, but in Israel regular teaching authority lay with the law, not prophecy. The words of the prophets always had to be tested because prophets did not have formal authority as teachers in Israel. Women taught and led in the family, but we do not see them holding a permanent public teaching office.[25] In Scripture we read that God has given men the ordained offices of teaching and leading the church. As long as women do not exercise authority over the male leaders in the church, there are many things that women can do to be a blessing to the church family.

23. Ibid., 48.

24. Ibid.

25. Ibid., 35.

There is a biblical place for a ruling function exercised under God by some Christians over others (1 Thess 5:12; Heb 13:17). "In the pastoral epistles, this governing activity is ascribed to the elders (1 Tim 3:5; 5:17). Clearly then Paul's prohibition of women having authority over a man would exclude a woman from becoming an elder in the way this office is described in the pastoral epistles."[26] By extension, then, women would not be allowed to hold any position in a church that would be equivalent to the pastoral epistles' ruling elder (for instance, a deacon). Paul's concern is that a woman does not exercise authority in the church over any man.

Women never took ongoing leadership positions in Israel or the church. Women counseled, taught, and judged, but almost always privately. Women led alongside men. Women may join any ministry except those that are distinctive to elders or deacons.

Worship Services

First Corinthians 14:26 says that everyone has a hymn or a word of instruction. Women can be song leaders, sing in the choir, sing a solo, share a testimony, read Scripture, greet at the door, usher, and do many more ministries. If you are in a church that designates a particular job to an elder or deacon, then a woman should not be permitted to participate in that particular ministry. I concur with Doriani as he states:

> In today's terms, women may testify or teach informally. But the task of preaching and guarding the Word belongs to male elders . . . A woman who prophesies, having her words weighed, is like a woman who teaches occasionally at the invitation of church leaders . . . speaking without supplanting men who promote and guard doctrine . . . So then women exercise vital gifts, but do not hold final authority.[27]

Christian Ministries

Women can work in all ways within the *Women in the Church* (the name of our church's women's group). Women can work in all ways within the children's ministry of the church. Women also can work alongside men in the teenage ministry in the church. However, for one-on-one discipleship it would not be appropriate for a woman to disciple a male teenager.

26. Moo, "What does It Mean," 187.

27. Doriani, *Women and Ministry*, 86.

Women are free to work in Christian schools associated with the church, in mercy ministries, music ministries, church administration, writing and performing, missions, evangelism—the list goes on and on—as long as the woman does not usurp authority from the male leadership of a church.

How about women teaching a mixed Sunday School class? Scripture shows that women taught privately but not groups of men in a formal, regular way. If a woman is invited by the church to speak as a guest lecturer on a specific topic for a time or two, I think that would be scriptural, as long as there is a man in a church leadership position who has planned her topic and asked her to speak, has set the schedule and time limit of the talk, introduces her, and closes with his remarks. She should not continue teaching week after week. Soon her position as "regular" teacher brings with it a level of authority.

Women as Deacons?

The first seven deacons were men (Acts 6). Still, Phoebe was called a deacon (Gk. *diakonos*) in Romans 16:1, "but we cannot be sure she had an office, since Romans 16 does not focus on church order and since the word *diakonos* is often nontechnical in the New Testament."[28] *Diakonos* can mean either a servant or a formal deacon. Greek scholars say that it is difficult to determine in 1 Timothy 3:11 whether Paul is using *diakonos* to refer to deacons' wives or deaconesses. But because 1 Timothy 3:11 is in the midst of the context of Paul's instructions to men deacons, I believe that *diakonos* here is referring to deacons' wives.

I believe that our church denomination is correct in having only men as deacons. In our church it is an office that has a leadership role over the entire church. In our denomination, men are often deacons first and then elders. The women in our church hold offices in our *Women in the Church* organization and many of their duties are to assist the deacons. But we always work under the authority of an elder or deacon. There is active communication between the officers of the women's group and the elders and deacons. Wisdom from both men and women is shared for the building up of the body of believers and the glory of God. Under this system, women have no reason to feel that their wisdom is not needed or used. The women are actively involved in church life but are not in

28. Ibid., 181.

ultimate authority. I believe that this system falls in line with the teaching of the whole of Scripture.

Women on the Mission Field?

The question is often asked about women's roles on the mission field. I believe that everything I have said in this essay also applies to the mission field, no matter where it is. If there are only women on the mission station without men leadership, especially in a church planting situation, I would not want to be a part of the ministry. If there were an established national church with national men in leadership positions, then I would fall under their authority and could work on that mission field. I know that one could come up with various scenarios about mission field experience. Yet the biblical example of men in leadership is vital, even (and especially) on the mission field. Women could teach men privately and occasionally, but it would be an important goal to have a spiritually mature and biblically qualified man to be in the leadership position. I do not believe that it is ever God's will to go against scriptural principles.

IN SUMMARY

"Virtually without exception for nineteen centuries, orthodox Christian theologians said that women ought to learn quietly and submissively. Women could teach informally but not authoritatively. God fashioned men and women and ordained a structure for their relationships. He appointed men to lead the church and home."[29] If Jesus can subordinate himself to the authority of the Father, then women can choose to subordinate themselves to the authority of the male leadership in the church. I believe that in doing so, women are following the teaching in Scripture and bringing glory to God. We need to be faithful in our God-given roles.

AVOIDING MISREPRESENTATIONS

The egalitarian author, Alvera Mickelsen, writes about the use of women's gifts being often limited in the traditional view.[30] I do not think that God gives us a gift and then limits it. I believe that a woman can use her gifts to full potential and still adhere to the traditional view. The author links

29. Ibid., 147.
30. Mickelsen, "An Egalitarian View," 174.

this with women not having important leadership roles in the church. I again believe that she is misrepresenting the traditional view. To me she is saying that leading women and children, along with many other roles women have, are not important leadership roles; in other words, a woman only has an important leadership role if she is teaching men or is a pastor of a church!

Mickelsen says that we believe in "male supremacy" and that women are not equal in worth to men.[31] However, we believe that God created both man and women in his image—men and women are equal in worth to God because each one is created in his image. Also, in Galatians 3:28 we see, as the NIV text note says, "Unity in Christ transcends ethnic, social and sexual distinctions."[32] Therefore, we do not believe in male supremacy. When a man is in a leadership position, he should be a humble servant to everyone he leads. The Bible doesn't teach that men in leadership should put on a "male supremacy" attitude.

31. Ibid., 183–84. Also see 195–96, 199.
32. Barker, *NIV Study Bible*, 1785.

An Egalitarian Response

Diana Valerie Clark

I T WAS WITH APPRECIATION that I read Barbara Wannemacher's argument for the traditional point of view regarding women in ministry, and many of her points were indeed cogently made. Her obvious commitment to ministry within her own paradigm is highly commendable.

I would, however, like to make a few comments in response even though I feel that all of Barbara's arguments have been dealt with in my essay.[33]

1. Barbara's argument is from a Reformed Presbyterian perspective and seems consistent within its own paradigm, but it sounds alien for those who read the Bible from the perspective of a Pentecostal revivalist paradigm (which, after all, we argue the church of Acts was)!

2. Barbara's interpretation of 1 Corinthians 14 is rather obscure. Her view that women should keep silent "during the testing of prophecies" (p. 241) is not consistent with Paul's overall teaching in this section, beginning at 1 Corinthians 11:5, which speaks of women praying and prophesying. Rather, it should be noted that there is a symmetry in the entire section of 1 Corinthians 11 to 1 Corinthians 14, in Paul's return to the theme of disorderly women.

The creation order of Genesis 2:24 and Genesis 3:16 speaks of God's order between husband and wife. In the church context, Paul uses it again because churches are, after all, made up of husbands, wives, and children. He uses it again in Ephesians 5:22–26 to compare Christ and his bride. If a woman was used in prophecy or prayer during a church service, as

---

33. Again let me state that I am no advocate of the Women's Liberation Movement.

is indicated in 1 Corinthians 11:5, it does not mean that she was being insubordinate to her husband. For a woman to be used by the Lord in such a ministry is not indicative of grabbing authority from a man. She is simply being an obedient servant of the Lord, using gifts of ministry bestowed on her by the Lord.

Furthermore, Paul speaks of a head-covering for the women, indicating that they were under the authority of men. He thus diffused any criticism that the pagan world might have brought against the church in a patriarchal social context in which the only "autonomous" women (i.e., without head-covering) were prostitutes and pagan priestesses. In 1 Corinthians 11 Paul is reproving the women for their social irresponsibility with regard to dress. In 1 Corinthians 14:34 he urges modesty in public. This reproof is grounded on the subjection of women to men in the order of creation, and not the fact that a woman is praying or prophesying in church. Paul was not prohibiting praying and prophesying by women but reprehending the manner in which they were doing it; in other words, with uncovered heads.

Barbara says that women must keep silent when it comes to weighing "carefully what is said" (1 Cor 14:29). And, according to her, that job was left to the teachers of the church who were all men. In response to this, I would say that according to Acts 18:26 they were *not* all men. Aquila *and* Priscilla taught Apollos: "they took him unto *them*, and expounded unto him the way of God more perfectly."[34] In Romans 16:3 Paul lists their names as his helpers in Christ: "Greet Priscilla and Aquila my helpers in Christ Jesus." It is significant that he mentions Priscilla's name first, contrary to the local custom of placing the man above the woman in importance. Indications are that Priscilla was an accepted teacher in the things of the Lord.

In 1 Corinthians 14:34, there is reference to women keeping silent in church and being in obedience "as also saith the law." One would need to ask the question: Which law is Paul referring to? Is it Genesis 3:16? A man was indeed the head of his household and of his wife. In church there was no sudden change: a woman did not suddenly try to usurp authority by prophesying, and so on. Paul is saying to women: Be modest in all your ways, have your head covered, and be of a submissive and quiet spirit, not brazen and outspoken.

34. Unless otherwise indicated, all Scripture quotations are taken from the *King James Version*. Emphasis mine in *italics*.

3. In 1 Timothy 2:12–14 Paul says he does not allow a woman to teach or to usurp authority over a man. However, one needs to understand the situation at Ephesus where Timothy was the acting pastor. The goddess Diana (or Artemis) dominated the religious life of the city and pagan women were conspicuous in their roles as priestesses and prostitutes, displaying both bold behavior and an authoritative attitude toward men-worshippers. Paul stresses that Christian women were not to be like them. Paul is making a distinction between Christian women, who share like redemption with men, and the same women who live in a society where their conduct needs to be above reproach.

However, Paul is obviously not generally against a woman teaching. After all, Priscilla and Aquila took Apollos to one side and taught him, thus enriching his life and ministry (Acts 18:26). Apollos was not just anybody: he was not a new convert or a reinstated Christian—he was the leader of the church at Corinth!

4. Barbara mentions that there is no record of women taking an official lead in the New Testament, for example, as apostles (p. 247). But this is simply because of pragmatic considerations: they did not enjoy the protection, respect, and entrance to audiences that the men of the time were able to enjoy. In social terms, a respectable woman with a good reputation was not able to travel or participate in public events without the presence and protection of a man.

5. In her opinion that the words of the Old Testament prophets had to be tested against the law, Barbara's standpoint can be questioned (p. 241). Their words, prophesied at the command of the Lord, had simply to be obeyed even if it meant going against the will of the king and priests (see Amos 7:10–17).

6. Concerning women in missions, Barbara makes the statement that all women missionaries should be under male supervision, albeit remote supervision (p. 250). This may be true in many cases, but *on* the field the woman-missionary is a leader, an apostle, a church-planter, and a church-builder. Remote supervision is hardly helpful. Revivalist movements have known too many lady church-planters and builders for this point to be able to stand.

It is not good to see anyone, woman *or* man, usurp authority and grab leadership where God has not indicated it. However, God often does and has used women to teach, to establish churches, and to preach where the need has arisen. Thus, women should not be discriminated against because of their gender. Ministry—teaching, preaching, praying, prophesying, and so on—need not be confused with leadership or usurping of authority. And if a woman like Margaret Thatcher could lead the nation of Britain for a double-term of office and make a success of it, why should God not use *his* women to bless churches and to fulfill his vision of a changed community and a changed world?

14

Women Leadership: The Egalitarian View

Diana Valerie Clark

INTRODUCTION

IN TODAY'S POSTMODERN WORLD, where women confidently and competently fulfill the roles of doctor, lawyer, lecturer, politician, manager, pilot, and countless other positions, it is baffling to comprehend the church's discriminatory attitude toward women in leadership ministry. Although I am not a supporter of the women's liberation movement and am happy to be submissive to my husband, I do think that *tradition* and *the male chauvinist attitude* have contributed to the fact that women are rarely accepted in church leadership positions.

The constitution of The Apostolic Faith Mission of South Africa—a Pentecostal denomination that I represent—makes no gender suppositions or distinctions in its legislation, and, thus, contains no gender comments. A man (or woman) called of God to full-time ministry may study, qualify, and be ordained as a pastor in the AFM Church. Once ordained, they (men or women) may be called or elected to a congregation or organization in whatever role the "callers" wish to receive them. They may, therefore, be called as a senior pastor, associate pastor, junior pastor, or assistant pastor; the congregations make the decision. Unlike, for example, the sacramental churches, the pastor of the Pentecostal or charismatic church is *not* a priestly intermediary between God and the people. Ordination is rather the church's recognition of a calling by God and a setting aside for ministry under the anointing of the Spirit. Dr. Mathew S. Clark of the AFM Church says, "The community of believers cannot 'ordain' a minister in the sense of 'granting' a ministry: rather, the community by ordination *recognizes* the ministry of the individual."[1] If *God* then gives ministry to a woman, who or what is the church that they should ignore it?

It is true to state that at this present time there are few, if any, women fulfilling the role of senior pastor in an AFM church. Prejudice against women in an authoritative ministry still prevails. Church-men are afraid to relinquish their "rights" and position of supreme "power" and authority to make decisions regarding the church to women—those created beings who are "inferior to the male species." Yet women featured prominently at every level of Christian ministry in the early years of the Pentecostal movement.

HISTORICAL BACKGROUND TO 1 CORINTHIANS 14 AND 1 TIMOTHY 2

> Let your women keep silent in the churches, for they are not permit-
> ted to speak (1 Cor. 14:34); And I do not permit a woman to teach or
> to have authority over a man, but to be in silence (1 Tim 2:12).[2]

These Scriptures have been used to argue against the official recognition of women in ministry. However, in 1 Corinthians 11 Paul had already approved public prayer and prophecy by women: "But every woman who *prays or prophesies* with her head uncovered dishonours her head." (v. 5)[3] Therefore, his further comments in 1 Corinthians 14 must surely indicate regulation in terms of order. Thus, when writing to Timothy, it must be realized that his words were a local ruling for the situation there at Ephesus. The Corinthian and Ephesian heathen religions were centered round the major role that the priestesses and prostitutes played. Paul, leaving the church in young Timothy's hands, said, "I don't allow women to teach," indicating that it was a personal view and not "of the Lord" (cf. 1 Cor 7:10–12). This was very likely because Ephesus was the center of Artimas–worship (Diana of the Ephesians) and pagan women held a dominant role in the local region. On an island not far from Ephesus, Aphrodite was worshipped too, also giving pagan women dominance. Paul did not want

---

1. Clark, "The Role of Women in the Early Church," 27–34.

2. Unless otherwise indicated, all Scripture quotations are taken from the *New King James Version*.

3. Emphasis mine in *italics*.

young Timothy to be overwhelmed by women dominance in this particular church. He was saying that in that specific atmosphere and milieu, he did not want the church to be confused with paganism. Clark says, "Paul appears to be stressing the position of women in the order of creation, as opposed to their liberty in the order of redemption. The text of 1 Timothy 2 may thus only be normative in the context of the historical situation that evoked it."[4]

The Greek women were not educated and did not enjoy the freedom of the Roman women. Converts in Corinth were from the lower orders of society, and probably their behavior was less than modest in the meetings. First Corinthians 14's proscription is not a blanket denial to women of participation and ministry in public worship; it is a command not to chatter and be disturbing. Says Clark regarding the traditional reading of 1 Corinthians 14 and 1 Timothy 2, "these appear to militate against the inclusion of women in public ministry . . . Many of the current discussions on this issue assert confidently that women were wilfully excluded by the church Fathers who were inimical to their progress on grossly sexist grounds."[5]

WOMEN LEADERS IN THE OLD TESTAMENT

It is important to look at God's calling and anointing on women in the Old Testament. Jesus often referred to, and quoted from, the Old Testament, thus endorsing these Scriptures. Peter too quoted from the Old Testament on the day of Pentecost, using Joel's words, "I will pour out My Spirit on all flesh; your sons and your *daughters* shall prophesy . . . And also on My menservants and on My *maidservants*" (Joel 2:28).[6]

Two Old Testament prophetesses that come to mind are Huldah: ". . . and she answered them, "Thus says the LORD God of Israel . . ." (2 Chr. 34:23); and Deborah who "was judging Israel at that time" (Judg 4:4).

At Jesus's birth, Anna the prophetess was awaiting the news in the temple where she served the Lord night and day (Luke 2:36–38).

---

4. Clark, "The Role of Women," 31.

5. Ibid.

6. Emphasis mine in *italics*.

WOMEN LEADERS IN THE NEW TESTAMENT

Paul would have been aware of the role played by charismatic women in the Old Testament and would have struggled to find ruling against women in ministry on scriptural grounds. The discussion would be pointless if Paul intended that women were never to speak in church. First Corinthians should be given its due place in such a debate; women in the early church were clearly not excluded from any position of Christian ministry. The New Testament Scriptures, as well as the writings of the Fathers, appear to confirm though that women were involved in both the ministry of elder and of teacher.

Priscilla was a teacher, and she had a church in her home. She and her husband expounded the Scriptures more fully to Apollos (Acts 18:26; Rom 16:3–5). Priscilla would have been a Roman citizen and thus had more freedom and education opportunity than her Corinthian sisters.

Lydia, who began a church in her home in Philippi, was a renowned businesswoman (Acts 16:14–15). Philippi, being a Roman colony, also allowed women greater freedom. Paul refers to the women there as being "team-mates" with him in ministry (Phil 4:3). The Greek word here is *sunergos: a fellow-labourer, associate;*[7] and is linked to the verb *sunathlew: to contend on the side of anyone; to co-operate vigorously with a person.*[8] They were thus fellow wrestlers with Paul for the cause of the gospel.

Junia,[9] with Andronicus, her husband, is referred to as an apostle (Gk. *apostolos*) (Rom 16:7), which is a primary ministry given in the church (Eph 4:11). John Chrysostom, an early church writer who portrayed a negative attitude toward women in ministry, agreed that Junia was a woman and is said to have marveled at Paul's description of her as "apostle."[10]

Three women are mentioned in Romans 16:12 who "laboured much in the Lord." The Greek word *kopiaw* is used here: *spent with labour, faint from weariness.*[11] This same word is used by Paul to describe his own apostolic ministry (Gal 1:1). Tryphena, Tryphose, and Persis are mentioned

---

7. Perschbacher, *The New Analytical Greek Lexicon*, 392.

8. Ibid., 388.

9. A common Latin female name.

10. Chrysostom said, "Oh! how great is the devotion of this woman, that she should be even counted worthy of the appellation of apostle!" (*Homilies on the Epistle of St. Paul*, xxxi.7, quoted in Piper and Grudem, *Recovering Biblical Manhood & Womanhood*, 80).

11. Perschbacher, *The New Analytical Greek Lexicon*, 244.

by name. Phoebe was a minister or servant of the church in Cenchrea (Rom 16:1). House-church leaders were Chloe (1 Cor 1:11) and Apphia (Philem. 2). Women made up nearly 20 percent of Paul's coworkers, and he treated all these women as equals in the ministry. With him they risked their lives for the sake of the gospel. In all, Paul mentions thirteen women by name. "There can be little doubt that women were involved as ministers in church-planting, teaching and evangelising."[12]

Joel's prophecy, affirmed by Peter on the day of Pentecost, states that God promised to pour out his Spirit on all flesh: sons and daughters; male servants and female servants (Acts 2:17–18). Note that in Acts 21:9 Philip's four daughters "prophesied." If prophecy is equivalent to preaching, as some fundamentalists claim—the same who do not believe in women preaching the word—then his daughters were preachers.

LIBERATION OF WOMEN IN THE CHURCH: NEITHER MALE NOR FEMALE

For too long, historical attitudes, biased translations and two small Scriptures taken out of context have held women in a bondage God never intended for them.[13]

The politically correct beliefs of our society are moving increasingly toward the 'unisex' position—that gender is irrelevant and should not be considered a factor in any job-qualification. This is forcing the church to take a new look at what the Bible says about women and men in the church.[14]

Women can be well suited to the role of a pastor in the church. This is because women are generally more caring and compassionate (toward the congregation), more efficient, organized, and dedicated. Furthermore, a woman is accustomed to "juggling" many activities in her life, whereas a man finds it difficult to do more than one thing at a time. According to a newspaper report by Iris Kallin, researchers maintain that women have learned to make snap decisions: "Their lives are much more complex due to a wide range of demands at work, at home, and in the family."[15]

12. Clark, "The Role of Women," 30.

13. Boone et al., "The Women Speak Out!" 46–47.

14. Parr, "The Woman Question," 45–50.

15. "When push comes to shove, women pilot shopping trolley" (publication unknown, n.d.).

It is interesting to note that for the past 150 years or more, women have received the blessing of the church (thus, of the men) to go into the far, dark, lonely parts of the world as missionaries.[16] There they have lived and toiled among foreign people, faithfully sharing the gospel message and starting Christian churches, often risking and losing their lives. They have fulfilled the fivefold ministry of apostle, prophet, evangelist, pastor, and teacher "for the equipping of the saints for the work of ministry, for the edifying of the body of Christ" (Eph 4:11–12). It is claimed that at least two-thirds of ground-breaking work done in foreign mission fields has been accomplished by women in the nineteenth and twentieth centuries. Ruth A. Tucker refers to William Booth, founder of the Salvation Army, and his reflections on the "soldiers" in the ranks of the organization. He said, "My best men are women," and indeed there was no position too difficult, no place too dangerous for these women who went anywhere and everywhere for the sake of the gospel.[17]

The Pentecostals have their roots in Methodism and, before that, in the Anabaptists. These revivalists recognized and blessed the ministry of women. Susanna Wesley, mother of John and Charles Wesley, was not only a devoted homemaker but also a powerful preacher. When her husband was away, she conducted the Sunday services that overflowed the parsonage. Her motive was primarily the spiritual well-being of her own family—nineteen children in all! Says Tucker again, "It was the Wesleyan movement, more than any other, that opened the floodgates for women to participate in public ministry across denominational lines."[18]

Pastor David Yonggi Cho of South Korea says that he uses women in his church because they "are often more spiritual than men, they frequently have more time, and they are more willing to visit people in their homes."[19] Today's church needs to recognize that women are not "barefoot and pregnant in the kitchen," as the popular saying goes. In a speech, one of South Africa's previous deputy ministers of trade and industry, Lindiwe Hendricks, said, "A woman's place is no longer in the kitchen but in the

16. See Landman, *Digging up our Foremothers*.

17. Tucker, "A Historical Overview of Women in Ministry," 3–7.

18. Ibid., 6.

19. Parr, "The Woman Question," 46.

boardroom. This is not merely rhetoric but an important comment on women's productive role in developing our economy."[20]

We live in a modern world and women are modern women. If women contribute substantially to the fiscal well-being of a country's economy and consequently contribute to the financial benefit of the church, should she not have a say in the decisions of the church?

Colleen Benson stated that "by the year 2000, some women will have 25–30 years of business experience, qualifying them to be CEO's of large corporations and, hopefully, taking them through the 'glass ceiling.'"[21] Because today's young women do not expect any barriers blocking their role or advancement in their jobs, it is no surprise that they will not tolerate barriers to serving in any of the ministries of Christ and his church. However well-defined theologically, such double standards are unacceptable to the modern woman. Jean Steffenson said, "I believe the social acceptance of women in ministry has gotten better over the last 10 years, and some of this might be attributed to the women's liberation movement. It is a shame the church did not take the lead in liberating women by recognizing and calling them to ministry within the church."[22]

Cathy Lechner wrote, "Just because the Scriptures give no examples of women in the role of senior pastor or bishop does not mean the Bible is against it."[23] Paul worked with women in a multicultural context, with Hebrews, Greeks, and Romans. He had reason to know them and their cultural backgrounds; he valued their contribution to the gospel ministry. In confirmation that Paul did not oppose women in ministry, we note his classic words, "For as many of you as were baptized into Christ have put on Christ. There is neither Jew nor Greek, there is neither slave nor free, there is neither *male nor female*; for you are all one in Christ Jesus" (Gal 3:27–28).[24] Is it not clear, then, that we are "a priesthood of believers"?

WHAT ABOUT MALE HEADSHIP?

Male headship, as spoken of by Paul in 1 Corinthians 11:2–16 and Ephesians 5:22, states clearly that a woman is to be submissive and under

20. "Women reach for their slice of the pie," *The Star* newspaper (n.d.).

21. Benson, "The Mindset of Women Today," 13–17.

22. Boone et al., "The Women Speak Out!" 47.

23. Ibid., 46.

24. Emphasis mine in *italics*.

the authority of her *own husband.* Does this mean, then, that she should be expected to be under the authority of someone else's husband? I think not. What she does not understand in church she may ask for an explanation from her own husband (1 Cor 14:35). Again, mention must be made that in both Corinth and Ephesus the heathen women played a prominent role in the religions of the day. Paul was protecting the Christian women from being associated with them in any way. At a time of heretical sedition in the church, Paul was trying to deal with every appearance of unnecessary provocation.

Ephesians 5:22–23 must be seen in the context of household, domestic order and not social order: "Wives, submit to your own husbands, as to the Lord. For the husband is head of the wife, as also Christ is head of the church." Paul does not set aside the creation order in which the man in the marriage functions as head of the woman in the home but emphasizes rather the spirit of servanthood and love that Christ exemplified.

In 1 Corinthians 11 the issue is not whether a woman may or may not take part in public worship but rather what her demeanor and attitude should be when she prays or prophesies. A woman's bearing and attitude should be different to that of a man. This was based upon the order of creation. Any distinction between man and woman was based on the Genesis order and the claims of common decency. Paul wanted women to further the witness of the gospel of Christ and not to hinder it by any aggressive assertiveness.

Each Scripture must therefore be interpreted in the light of the other Scriptures.

CULTURE AND THEOLOGY

Gordon Kirk states that every man and woman carries around *cultural baggage*—traditions that have been a part of our lives—and also *ecclesiastical baggage*, which has to do with denominational or ordinational issues. We all see life through our own particular lens. Kirk says, "Apart from the Bible and apart from our culture, we also see major transitional views between rural backgrounds and urban settings. We need to recognize which of our views of male and female relationships are traditional and which are biblical—which are cultural and which are theological."[25]

---

25. Kirk, "A Consideration of Biblical Versus Cultural Issues," 18–19.

Clark gives the example of a church building erected in 1994, to the then value of R400 000 (US$120,000), in an African tribal area of South Africa. Male church leaders of all races gathered to dedicate the building. In an impoverished homeland, this church was a miracle. "And the pastor, church-builder, and building-builder? A Black woman."[26]

CONCLUSION

The question that needs to be asked is, "The Great Commission: Was it only for male-believers, and not for females?" It should be noted that women were the first to be given the resurrection news and commissioned to pass it on (Matt 28:7–8).

I personally believe that Christian women do not want to usurp the authority of a man. I am perfectly happy to work under the authority and umbrella of a man's protection, but too often incapable, disorganized men are chosen for a leadership position over a woman, *simply because of their gender*. Some people would rather have a bumbling, incompetent man do a job than an efficient, dynamic woman.

> The Spirit of God is certainly grieved when men rail against women in ministry while they themselves are insubordinate and unwilling to be accountable to any other leaders . . . Meanwhile, church history reveals a fascinating principle: In times of revival and spiritual awakening, gender distinctions are minimized; in times of spiritual decline, we are more aware of our differences and come up with regulations to keep everyone in their places.[27]

AVOIDING MISREPRESENTATIONS

The idea by some traditionalists that women teaching men is "unbiblical" and a form of "Gnosticism" holds no ground.[28] First of all, the "creation order" mentioned in Genesis 2:24 and Genesis 3:16 speaks of the order between husband and wife: "Your desire shall be for your husband, and he shall rule over you" (Gen 3:16). This is reiterated in Ephesians 5:22–24 where Paul is speaking of the *home* situation where a wife is to be in sub-

26. Clark, "The Role of Women," 34.

27. Parr, "The Woman Question," 50, 55.

28. A traditionalist has written that the egalitarian view attempts to "blur and destroy the order God has ordained in creation," and that it has its "historical antecedents in Gnosticism" ("The Bible vs. Egalitarianism," unpublished study notes [August 2003]).

mission to her *own husband*—not to someone else's husband, and there-fore, not to another man. She is not to usurp authority over her husband, and thus, the passage concerns the *domestic ruling* for Christian women (cf. 1 Pet 3:1–7). However, as I've explained above, the situation in the church is different.

Second, traditional Gnosticism follows the teaching of dualism that sees the spirit and flesh as two separate entities: the spirit is good and righteous, but the flesh is evil and ungodly.[29] Some say that Paul's words to Timothy regarding a woman teaching (1 Tim 2:12) refer to certain Gnostic ideas that the woman was responsible for the creation of man and therefore superior to man. However, the Bible shows clearly in the Genesis references that God's creation order is that man was made first, and *then* the woman. However, in reality, Gnostic dualism was more likely to denigrate women. After all, it was women who gave birth in the flesh to humans in the flesh and, according to Gnostic dualism, flesh is evil.

---

29. Added to this is the teaching that some humans are supernaturally empowered by God (the anointed ones), while others (the common ones) must pay special homage to these 'spirituals.' Today it is known as neo-Gnosticism.

A Traditionalist Response

Barbara Wannemacher

I AM GREATLY ENCOURAGED to read Diana Valerie Clark's statement that wives should be submissive to their husbands (p. 263). It is not easy to stand firm in this belief, and I am so pleased to see this position affirmed in her essay. Submission to husbands is not a popular topic in today's culture.

However, I believe that Mrs. Clark has allowed the changing culture to influence her position in the role of women in the church. Genesis 1–3 has been the determining factor in understanding the entire manhood/womanhood debate for centuries and continues to be relevant today. All the other biblical texts need to be interpreted consistently with Genesis 1–3. God created male and female equally in his image, but he also created the man as head and the woman as helper. God gave Adam headship responsibility in marriage and he stamped "the helper" design onto the woman. This was established by God before the Fall and was not a result of sin.

The reason that women are not to have authority over men in the church is not due to prejudice or women being an inferior species, rather it is because of God's direction for the church as set forth in Scripture. Our position in Christ determines our worth. But a person's role in the church does not determine the worth and value of that person. I agree that women throughout New Testament history were valuable members of churches, yet women never took ongoing leadership positions in Israel or the church. Women counseled, taught, and judged, but almost always privately. Nevertheless, the task of preaching and guarding the word of God belonged to male elders.[30] It is true that many women missionaries have

30. Doriani, *Women and Ministry*, 86.

266

done wonderful works for God on the mission field. But we don't build our theology on this. Women working on the mission field without being under the authority of male church leadership is not the model. Nevertheless, God does use a willing vessel and can choose to bless the work.

Additionally, our role in society also does not determine our worth. "Stay at home" mothers are of equal value and worth as boardroom executives. Sunday school teachers and women Bible study leaders of women's groups have equal worth as the pastor. Distinctions in masculine and feminine roles are ordained by God as part of the created order. At the same time there can be equality and differences between persons! This is where we look to the Trinity to see modeled for us ontological equality as well as functional differences. The "Ontological Trinity" is defined as three persons of the Godhead who are fully equal in divinity, power, and glory. Yet within the Holy Trinity, the Father leads, the Son submits to him, and the Spirit submits to both (i.e., the "Economic Trinity"). Christ submitted to the Father's will and instructed his disciples that it was good for him to go, that he might send the comforter, that is, the Holy Spirit (John 14:16). Certainly, in our theology we agree that all three persons of the Trinity—Father, Son, and Holy Spirit—are co-equal, co-eternal, and co-substantial although they function totally differently. Likewise, men and women are equal in personhood and value, but functionally they have been assigned different roles. They complement one another, and the created order works according to God's design for us, which does not change with time, culture, or any other factor. This is not to argue against women in positions of leadership outside the home and church. But within these God-ordained institutions, and through the history of God's people, the roles of men and women remain different, complementing one another as God has prescribed in Holy Scripture.

In conclusion, I find some of the wording used in her essay very troubling: "women in bondage," "church's discriminatory attitude towards women in leadership," "women are generally more caring and compassionate, more efficient, organized, and dedicated," "[women] will not tolerate barriers to serving in any of the ministries of Christ and his church," "liberating women." Although Mrs. Clark has stated that she is not a supporter of the women's liberation movement, I am concerned that she may have been more influenced by it than she realizes. We must take our direction from God through his word, not from a secular liberation movement. Feminism has led women into seeking self-fulfillment as opposed to seeking to glorify God. Feminism insists that personal role and personal worth go together. This leads the woman's liberation followers to believe that a limitation in roles reduces personal worth. This is the world's reasoning, not the teaching of Scripture.

Our pattern should be the "biblical woman" as set forth in Scripture. I do not believe that following the women's liberation movement is a step in the right direction. Choosing to adapt some of women's liberation ideology is a slide down a slippery slope. What seems initially to be small choices, starting with denying gender differences, too easily leads to having a pride in female differences, then on to women competing against men, and ending up with women feeling superior to men. This can eventually lead to male hating. I believe that it is a departure from the plain teaching of Scripture on the role of men and women.

Appendix A

"Our Unity in the Essentials" Document

1. We believe in one God, the LORD, creator of heaven and earth, who is holy and righteous. God is also love, "a gracious and compassionate God, slow to anger and abounding in love" (Jonah 4:2).

2. We believe that God exists as three distinct Persons—the Father, the Son (Jesus Christ), and the Holy Spirit—who are one in essence/being. Therefore, God is a Trinity.

3. We believe that human beings are created in God's image: in knowledge, holiness, and righteousness (Eph 4:24; Col 3:10). However, "just as sin entered the world through one man [Adam], and death through sin, and in this way death came to all men, because all sinned" (Rom 5:12).

4. We believe in Jesus the Christ, the Son of God, the Savior of the world. He is the Word who existed from eternity with God the Father.

5. We believe that in the fullness of time God sent his Son, born of a woman, born under law, who lived a sinless life and died as an atoning sacrifice for our sins. Moreover, he was raised to life for our justification and ascended to the right hand of the Father.

6. We believe that everyone who hears the gospel and responds to God's grace by repenting of sin and believing in Jesus Christ will receive eternal life. Salvation cannot be earned or merited by works or obedience to the law of God. We are freed from guilt and declared righteous in God's sight by faith.

7. We believe in the Holy Spirit who convicts people of their sinfulness, gives them new life in Christ, and creates in them a new heart and nature. He lives within believers, enabling them to live a holy life in Christ.

8. We believe that all believers in Christ are members of one body. As Christ's body, we are called to manifest the gifts and the fruit of the Spirit, which is love, joy, peace, etc. (1 Cor 12–14; Gal 5:22–23)

9. We believe that the Bible is the inspired word of God, "and is profitable for doctrine, for reproof, for correction, for instruction in righteousness: that the man of God may be perfect, thoroughly furnished unto all good works" (2 Tim 3:16–17).

10. We believe in the return of Jesus Christ, a resurrection of both the righteous and the wicked, and a final judgment where the wicked will go away to eternal punishment, but the righteous to eternal life (Matt 25:46; Acts 24:15).

Michael J. Meiring	*Benjamin R. Webb*
Diana Valerie Clark	*Colin Maxwell*
Adrio König	*Eric Severson*
Jim Hernando	*Bill Berends*
Barbara Wannemacher	*Dereck Stone*
L.L. (Don) Veinot Jr.	*Craig Branch*

Appendix B

About the Authors

ADRIO KÖNIG

Dr. Adrio König has been professor of Systematic Theology with the *University of South Africa* since the late 1960s. He is a minister of the Dutch Reformed Church and has published widely in the area of theology, some of his titles include *Here Am I! A Christian Reflection on God* (M. Morgan & Scott, 1982) and *The Eclipse of Christ in Eschatology* (Eerdmans, 1989). In 2006 he published an Afrikaans dictionary on the key words of the Christian faith (*Die Groot Geloofswoordeboek*). He is married to Hermien and they have three children and four grandchildren.

BARBARA WANNEMACHER

Mrs. Barbara Wannemacher is a member of the Presbyterian Church in America (PCA). She and her husband, Bruce, serve in South Africa with *Mission to the World*—the missionary arm of the PCA. They are both lecturers at *The Bible Institute of South Africa* in Kalk Bay, where Barbara teaches women students, as well as being involved in "Titus 2" mentoring relationships with younger women. She attended *Covenant Theological Seminary* in St. Louis, Missouri, USA and received a Master's degree in Theology. She is the mother of two grown children.

BENJAMIN R. WEBB JR.

Mr. Benjamin Webb is an Electronics Tester/Technician for Raytheon, with an Associate's degree in Electronics Technology. He has also studied dispensationalism for over a quarter of a century and is the current editor for the "dispensationalism category," along with various sub-categories for the *Open Directory Project* (ODP). In a continuing effort to promote the understanding of dispensational theology, Benjamin has added over 200 sites and articles to the ODP. His website, "The Dispensational Berean," compares differing views among dispensationalists.

COLIN MAXWELL

Pastor Colin Maxwell is a full time missionary with the Free Presbyterian Church of Ulster. He graduated from the Missionary Course of *The Whitefield College of the Bible* in 1986 and has labored in Cork, in the Republic of Ireland, since September 1987. He has contributed articles for the *Let the Bible Speak* magazine and the *British Church Newspaper*. Colin enjoys spiritual and doctrinal debate with those of other positions, both within and without the Christian church. Colin is happily married to Olive, and they have two children.

CRAIG BRANCH

Rev. Craig Branch is director of the *Apologetics Resource Center*, ordained in the Evangelical Church Alliance, and is a ruling elder in the Presbyterian Church in America. Craig is on the faculty of the *Birmingham Theological Seminary* where he earned his Masters in Religious Education. He is senior editor of the Center's bimonthly *Aeropagus Journal*. Craig is the co-author of *Thieves of Innocence: Protecting our Children from New Age and Occult Practices* (Harvest House, 1993) and is a frequent conference and seminar speaker. Craig is married and has three children (and a son-in-law).

DERECK F. STONE

Pastor Dereck Stone trained at the *Baptist Theological College* in South Africa. He has pastored Baptist churches for 35 years, taught on *Radio Pulpit* on the program, "A Firm Foundation," for 16 years, and led 19 tours to Israel and other Bible lands. He is the author of *Christian Tourists in Bible Lands*. In 2006 he retired from the senior pastorate and now serves as pastor of Cell Groups and Missions at the Waterkloof Baptist Church, Pretoria, as well as writing material for cell groups. He also serves as an international pastor for SIM. Dereck is married to Peggy, and they have four children and six grandchildren.

DIANA VALERIE CLARK

Pastor Diana Valerie Clark was born in Zimbabwe and married Rev. Dr. Mathew Clark in 1975, ministering with him in war-torn Rhodesia-Zimbabwe. Some years later they moved to South Africa where they raised two children and continued to be involved in Christian ministry. Valerie spent seven years in Christian radio broadcasting (*West Rand Stereo* and *Radio Pulpit*). In 2003 Valerie was ordained as a pastor in the Apostolic Faith Mission of South Africa. Today she holds a Masters degree in Theology, specializing in Church History, and lectures at various Bible schools.

ERIC SEVERSON

Professor Eric Severson teaches Philosophy, Ethics, and Theology at *Eastern Nazarene College* in Quincy, Massachusetts. He has recently finished editing a collection of primary readings from Christian history entitled, *The Least of These: Selected Readings from Christian History* (Cascade Books, 2007). Eric is completing his Ph.D. at *Boston University*, writing about the relationship between ethics and the philosophy of time. His journal publications range across the overlapping fields of philosophy and theology.

JAMES D. HERNANDO

Dr. Jim Hernando is an ordained minister with the Assemblies of God. He earned an M.Phil. and Ph. D. in Biblical Studies from *Drew University* with a concentration in the New Testament. He is currently Professor of New Testament and serves as chairperson of the *Bible and Theology Department at the Assemblies of God Theological Seminary*, where he began his teaching tenure in 1990. He has written a commentary on 2 Corinthians (Zondervan, 1997) and most recently *Dictionary of Hermeneutics* (Gospel Publishing House, 2005).

L. L. (DON) VEINOT JR.

Rev. Don Veinot is president of *Midwest Christian Outreach, Inc.*, an apologetics ministry to new religious movements based in Wonder Lake, IL. He, along with his wife of 37 years, Joy, has been involved in the discernment ministry since 1987. He is a frequent guest on various radio and television broadcasts and is co-author of *A Matter of Basic Principles: Bill Gothard and the Christian Life* (2003). In 1997 he was ordained to the ministry by West Suburban Community Church in Jerusalem. Don is also the current president of *Evangelical Ministries to New Religions*—a consortium of United States counter cults ministries.

MICHAEL J. MEIRING

Mr. Michael Meiring is a member of the Uniting Presbyterian Church in South Africa. Along with his wife, Wilna, he graduated from *The Bible Institute of South Africa* with a B.A. and Licentiate in Theology (2003). He also earned an Honors degree in Theology, specializing in Church History and Contemporary Theological Issues. Michael has edited and co-written a "four views" book, *The Four Keys to the Millennium* (Sola Fide, 2004). He is completing his Masters in Theology at the *University of Stellenbosch*, writing on evangelical fundamentalism.

WILLEM BERENDS

Dr. Willem (Bill) Berends lectures in Theology & Ethics at the *Reformed Theological College* in Geelong, Australia. He did his doctoral work on the theology of culture. Before that he and his wife, Henny, spent 15 years in Nigeria and two more in Kenya in the employ of the *Christian Reformed World Missions*. Bill is the editor of *Vox Reformata* and regularly contributes to this and other journals. Several teaching stints in the Solomon Islands have prompted him to write a theology textbook in simple English, published in Honiara.

Bibliography

Alexander, Charles D. "Moses or Christ? Paul's Reply to Dispensational Error." No pages. Online: http://www.geocities.com/Heartland/9170/ALEX1.HTM.

Alexander, T. D, and Brian S. Rosner. *New Dictionary of Biblical Theology*. Leicester: IVP, 2000.

Archer, Gleason. *Encyclopedia of Bible Difficulties*. Grand Rapids, MI: Zondervan, 1982.

Arminius, James. *The Writings of Arminius*, 2 vols. Translated by James Nichols. Grand Rapids, MI: Baker, 1956.

Augustine, St. *The Confessions of Saint Augustine*. Translated by John K. Ryan. New York, NY: Doubleday, 1969.

Avrigo, Rosita. *Spiritual Bathing: Healing Rituals and Traditions from Around the World*. Berkeley: Celetrial Arts, 2002.

Baker, Charles. *A Dispensational Theology*. Grand Rapids, MI: Grace Bible College, 1971.

Barclay, William. *The Letters of James and Peter: Daily Study Bible Series*. Rev. ed. Philadelphia: Westminster, 1976.

Barker, Kenneth L., ed. *The NIV Study Bible*. Grand Rapids, MI: Zondervan, 1995.

Basinger, David and Randall Basinger, eds. *Predestination & Free Will: Four Views of Divine Sovereignty & Human Freedom*. Downers Grove, IL: IVP, 1986.

Beale, G. K. "An Exegetical and Theological Consideration of the Hardening of Pharaoh's Heart in Exodus 4–14 and Romans 9," *Trinity Journal* 5 NS, no. 2 (Autumn 1984): 152. Quoted in Cottrell, Jack W, "The Nature of the Divine Sovereignty." In *The Grace of God and the Will of Man*, edited by Clark H. Pinnock, 97–119. Minneapolis, MN: Bethany, 1995.

Beare, F. W. *The First Epistle of Peter*. Oxford: Basil Blackwell, 1947.

Beker, J. C. *Paul the Apostle*. Philadelphia: Fortress Press, 1980.

Benson, Colleen. "The Mindset of Women Today." *Theology, News and Notes* 42/1 (1995): 13–17.

Berends, Willem. "Cessationism." *Vox Reformata* 60 (1995): 44–54. Also available online at http://www.pastornet.net.au/rtc/cessatn.htm.

———. "Prophecy in the Reformation Tradition." *Vox Reformata* 60 (1995): 30–43. Also available online at http://www.pastornet.net.au/rtc/prophecy.htm.

———. "What Do We Celebrate at Pentecost?" *Vox Reformata* 63 (1998): 42–66. Also available online at http://www.pastornet.net.au/rtc/pentecost.htm.

Berkhof, Louis. *Systematic Theology*. England: Banner of Truth, 1981.

Berkouwer, G. C. *De Wederkomst van Christus II*. Kampen: Kok, 1963.

Bernard, J. H. *International Critical Commentary on St. John*. Vol. 2. Edinburgh: T&T Clark, 1928.

Bittlinger, Arnold. *Gifts and Ministries*. Grand Rapids, MI: Eerdmans, 1975.

Blocher, Henri. *Original Sin: Illuminating the Riddle*. Leicester, England: Apollos, 1997.

Boettner, Loraine. *The Reformed Doctrine of Predestination*. Phillipsburg, NJ: Presbyterian & Reformed, 1932.

Book of Church Order of the Presbyterian Church in America. Atlanta: The Office of the Stated Clerk of the General Assembly of the Presbyterian Church in America, 1997.

Boone, Corinthia, et al. "The Women Speak Out!" *Ministries Today* (September–October 1995): 46–47.

Bounds, E. M. *Power through Prayer*. Grand Rapids, MI: Baker, n.d.

Bowman Jr., Robert M. *Orthodoxy and Heresy: A Biblical Guide to Doctrinal Discernment*. Grand Rapids, MI: Baker, 1992.

Boyd, Gregory. "The Open Theism View." In *Divine Foreknowledge: Four Views*, edited by J. Beilby and P. Eddy, 13–47. Downers Grove, IL: IVP, 2001.

Bromiley, G. W. *The Unity and Disunity of the Church*. Grand Rapids, MI: Eerdmans, 1958.

Bullinger, E. W. *The Foundations of Dispensational Truth*. London: Samuel Bagster & Sons, 1972.

Burchett, Dave. *When Bad Christians Happen to Good People*. Colorado Springs: WaterBrook Press, 2002.

Calver, Clive and Rob Warner, *Together We Stand: Evangelical Convictions, Unity and Vision*. London: Hodder & Stoughton, 1996.

Calvin, John. *Commentary on Acts I*. Edinburgh, Scotland: Calvin Translation Society, n.d. Reprint, Grand Rapids, MI: Baker, 1981.

———. *Commentary on Isaiah* 2 vols. In *The John Calvin Collection*, vol. 7. Rio, WI: AGES Library CD-ROM.

———. *Commentary on Jonah-Nahum*. Edinburgh, Scotland: Calvin Translation Society, n.d. Reprint, Grand Rapids, MI: Baker, 1981.

———. *Genesis: Crossway Classic Commentaries*. Wheaton, IL: Crossway Books, 2001.

———. *Institutes of the Christian Religion*. Edited by John McNeill. Philadelphia: The Westminster Press, n.d.

———. *Letters of John Calvin*. Edinburgh: Banner of Truth Trust, 1980.

———. "Secret Providence of God." In *The John Calvin Collection*. Rio, WI: AGES Library CD-ROM.

———. *Synoptic Gospels III*. Edinburgh, Scotland: Calvin Translation Society, n.d. Reprint, Grand Rapids, MI: Baker, 1981.

Caputo, John D., and Michael J. Scanlon. *God the Gift and Postmodernism*. Bloomington and Indianapolis: Indiana University Press, 1999.

Carson, D. A. *Showing of the Spirit*. Grand Rapids, MI: Baker, 1987.

———. "Silent in the Churches: On the Role of Women in 1 Corinthians 14:33b–36." In *Recovering Biblical Manhood and Womanhood*, edited by J. Piper and W. Grudem, 140–53. Wheaton, IL: Good News Publishers, 1991.

Chrysostom, John. *Homilies on the Epistle of St. Paul the Apostle to the Romans*. In *A Select Library of the Nicene and Post-Nicene Fathers of the Christian Church*, edited by Philip Schaff, 11:555. Grand Rapids, MI: Eerdmans, 1956. Quoted in Piper, John and Wayne Grudem, *Recovering Biblical Manhood & Womanhood: A Response to Evangelical Feminism*. Wheaton, IL: Good News, 1991.

Clark, Mathew S. "The Role of Women in the Early Church: Indications from the New Testament for the Practice of a Modern Spirit Movement." *Acta Patristica et Byzanatina* (1995): 27–34.

Clines, David. "Predestination in the Old Testament." In *Grace Unlimited*, edited by Clark H. Pinnock, 110–26. 2nd ed. Eugene, OR: Wipf and Stock, 1998.

Cottrell, Jack W. "The Classical Arminian View of Election." In *Perspectives on Election: Five Views*, edited by Chad Brand, 70–134. Nashville, TN: Broadman & Holman, 2006.

———. "Conditional Election." In *Grace Unlimited*, edited by Clark H. Pinnock, 51–73. 2nd ed. Eugene, OR: Wipf and Stock, 1998.

Craig, William L. "The Middle Knowledge View." In *Divine Foreknowledge: Four Views*, edited by J. Beilby and P. Eddy, 119–143. Downers Grove, IL: IVP, 2001.

Crockett, William, ed. *Four Views on Hell*. Grand Rapids, MI: Zondervan, 1996.

Culbertson, P., and H. Wiley. *Introduction to Christian Theology*. Kansas City, MS: Beacon Hill, 1964.

Danker, Frederick W. *A Greek-English Lexicon of the New Testament and other Early Christian Literature*. 3rd ed. Chicago: University of Chicago Press, 2000.

Deere, Jack. *Surprised by the Power of the Spirit*. Grand Rapids, MI: Zondervan, 1993.

———. *Surprised by the Voice of the Spirit*. Grand Rapids, MI: Zondervan, 1996.

Descartes, Rene. *Meditations on First Philosophy*. Indianapolis: Hackett Publishing Group, 1993.

Dix, Gregory. *The Treatise on the Apostolic Tradition of St. Hippolytus of Rome, Bishop and Martyr*. London: Curzon Press, 1995.

Domning, Daryl P. "Original Selfishness." *Science and Spirit* (Summer 2001).

Doriani, Dan. *Women and Ministry*. Wheaton, IL: Good News Publishers, 2003.

Eliade, Mircea. *The Sacred and the Profane*. San Diego: Harcourt Brace Jovanovich, 1987.

Eusebius. *The Ecclesiastical History of Eusebius Pamphilus*. Translated by Christian F. Cruse. Grand Rapids, MI: Baker, 1988.

Fee, Gordon D. *God's Empowering Presence*. Peabody, MA: Hendrickson, 1994.

Feinberg, John. "God Ordains All Things." In *Predestination and Free Will: Four Views of Divine Sovereignty and Human Freedom*, edited by D. Basinger and R. Basinger, 17–43. Downers Grove, IL: IVP, 1986.

Fisk, Samuel. *Election and Predestination*. Eugene, OR: Wipf and Stock, 2002.

Floris, Andrew T. "Didymus, Epiphanius and the Charismata." *Paraclete* 6 (1972): 26–31.

Frame, John. *No Other God: A Response to Open Theism*. Phillipsburg, NJ: P&R, 2001.

Furness, Victor Paul. *The Anchor Bible: II Corinthians*. Garden City: Doubleday, 1984.

Gabriel, Richard A. *God of our Fathers: The Memory of Egypt in Judaism and Christianity*. Westport, CN: Greenville Press, 2002.

Gaffin Jr., Richard B. "A Cessationist View." In *Are Miraculous Gifts for Today?*, edited by Wayne Grudem, 25–64. Grand Rapids, MI: Zondervan, 1996.

Gerstner, John. *A Primer on Dispensationalism*. Phillipsburg, NJ: P&R, 1982.

Gill, John. *Gill's Commentary*. Vol. 2. Grand Rapids, MI: Baker, 1980.

Gnilka, J. *Der Epheserbrief. Herders theologidcher Kommentar zum Neuen Testament*. Freiburg: Herder, 1971.

Goff Jr., J. R. "Parham, Charles Fox." In *Dictionary of Pentecostal and Charismatic Movements*, edited by Stan M. Burgess and Gary B. McGee. Grand Rapids, MI: Zondervan, 1988.

Good, Chris. "The Anabaptists and the Reformation: The Swiss Anabaptists (1523–1526)." No pages. Online: http://www.rbc.org.nz/library/anabap.htm

Green, V. *Luther and the Reformation*. London: New English Library, 1974.

Grieg, Gary S., and Kevin N. Springer. *The Kingdom and the Power*. Ventura, CA: Regal Books, 1993.

Grosheide, F. W. *De Brief van Paulus aan de Efesiërs*. Kampen: Kok, 1960.

Grudem, Wayne. *The Gift of Prophecy in the New Testament Today*. Wheaton, IL: Crossway Books, 1988.

———. "Should Christians Expect Miracles Today?" In *The Kingdom and the Power*, edited by Gary S. Greig and Kevin N. Spinger, 55–110. Ventura, CA: Regal Books, 1993.

———. *Systematic Theology*. Grand Rapids, MI: Zondervan, 1994.

Gundry, Stanley, ed. *Three Views on the Rapture*. Grand Rapids, MI: Zondervan, 1996.

Gustafson, Robert R. *Authors of Confusion*. Tapa: Grace Publishing Company, 1971.

Henry, Matthew. *Matthew Henry's Commentary in One Volume*. Edited by Leslie Church. Grand Rapids, MI: Zondervan, 1961.

Hernando, James D. "Imitatio Christi and the Character of Apostolic Ministry." In *He Gave Apostles*, edited by Edgar R. Lee, 69–91. Springfield, MO: The Assemblies of God Theological Seminary, 2005.

———. "Imitation Language in Paul: Implications for Discipleship and Ministerial Training." Lecture at The Assemblies of God Theological Seminary, Springfield, MO, 2003. Also available online at www.agts.edu.

———. "Paul and the Scope of Apostolic Authority." In *He Gave Apostles*, edited by Edgar R. Lee, 94–113. Springfield, MO: The Assemblies of God Theological Seminary, 2005.

Hill, Jonathan. *The History of Christian Thought*. Oxford, England: Lion, 2003.

Hippolytus. *The Apostolic Tradition of Hippolytus*. Translated by B. S. Easton. Cambridge: University Press, 1934.

Hodge, Charles. *An Exposition of the Second Epistle to the Corinthians*. Grand Rapids, MI: Eerdmans, 1973.

———. *Princeton Sermons*. England: Banner of Truth, 1979.

Hoekema, A. A. *The Bible and the Future*. Grand Rapids, MI: Eerdmans, 1979.

Horton, Stanley M. *What the Bible Says About the Holy Spirit*. Springfield, MO: Gospel Publishing, 1976.

Houlihan, Robert. "Pentecost now—in Mongolia." *Pentecostal Evangel* (November 1994): 12–13.

———. "Taking a New Territory." *Mountain Movers* (February 1994): 26.

Hummel, Horace D. *The Word Becoming Flesh*. St. Louis: Concordia, 1979.

Hunt, D., and J. White. *Debating Calvinism*. Sisters, OR: Multnomah, 2004.

Hurtado, Larry W. "The Function and Pattern of Signs and Wonders in the Apostolic and Sub-apostolic Period." MA thesis, Trinity Evangelical Divinity School, 1967.

Hutson, Curtis. *Why I Disagree with all Five Points of Calvinism*. Murfreesboro, TN: Sword of the Lord, 1980. No pages. Online: http://www.jesus-is-savior.com /False%20Doctrines/Calvinism/calvinism-hutson.htm.

Ice, T., and T. Demy. *Prophecy Watch*. Eugene: Harvest House, 1998.

Kearney, Richard. *The God Who May Be*. Bloomington: Indiana University Press, 2001.

Kelly, J. *Early Christian Doctrines*. 5th ed. London: A. and C. Black, 1977.

Kildal, John P. *The Psychology of Speaking in Tongues*. London: Hodder and Stoughton, 1972.

Kirk, Gordon. "A Consideration of Biblical Versus Cultural Issues." *Theology, News and Notes* 42/1 (1995): 18–19.

Koivisto, Rex A. *One Lord, One Faith: A Theology for Cross-denominational Renewal*. Wheaton, IL: Victor Books, 1993.

König, A. *The Eclipse of Christ in Eschatology: Towards a Christ-Centered Approach*. Grand Rapids, MI: Eerdmans, 1989.

———. *Gelowig Nagedink Deel 4 Oor die Wese van die Mens en die Sonde*. Pretoria: NGKB, 1991.

Kydd, Ronald A. N. *Charismatic Gifts in the Early Church: An Exploration of the Spirit During the First Three Centuries of the Christian Church*. Peabody, MA: Hendrickson, 1984.

———. "Novatian's *De Trinitate* 29: Evidence of the Charismatic?" *Scottish Journal of Theology* 30 (1977): 313–18.

Ladd, George Eldon. "A Historic Premillennial Response." In *The Meaning of the Millennium: Four Views*, edited by Robert G. Clouse, 93–94. Downers Grove, IL: IVP, 1977.

———. *A Theology of the New Testament*. Grand Rapids, MI: Eerdmans, 1974.

Landman, C. *Digging up our Foremothers: Stories of Women in Africa*. Pretoria: Unisa, 1996.

Lange, L. *History of Protestantism*, n.p., n.d. Quoted in Watson, T. E. *Should Infants be Baptized?* Rev. ed. Grand Rapids, MI: Guardian Press, 1976.

Larkin, Clarence. *Dispensational Truth*. Rev. ed. Glenside, PA: Rev. Clarence Larkin Est., 1920.

Lee, Edgar R. "Pentecostals and Subordinate Revelation." *Advamce* 30.6 (1994): 9–11.

Lewis, C. S. *Mere Christianity*. London: HarperCollins, 1997.

Liddle and Scott. *An Intermediate Greek-English Lexicon*. Oxford: The Clarendon Press, 1985.

Luther, Martin. *Born Slaves*. London: Grace, 1984.

Lutzer, Erwin W. *The Doctrines that Divide*. Grand Rapids, MI: Kregel Publications, 1989.

MacArthur, John. *Charismatic Chaos*. Grand Rapids, MI: Zondervan, 1992.

MacDonald, William. "The Spirit of Grace." In *Grace Unlimited*, edited by Clark H. Pinnock, 74–94. 2nd ed. Eugene, OR: Wipf and Stock, 1998.

Marshall, I. Howard. "Predestination in the New Testament." In *Grace Unlimited*, edited by Clark H. Pinnock, 127–43. 2nd ed. Eugene, OR: Wipf and Stock, 1998.

Masters, Peter, ed. *The Baptist Confession of Faith 1689*. London: Metropolitan Tabernacle, n.d.

McAfee Brown, Robert. *The Spirit of Protestantism*. New York: Oxford, 1961. Quoted in Calver, Clive and Rob Warner, *Together We Stand: Evangelical Convictions, Unity and Vision*. London: Hodder & Stoughton, 1996.

Mickelsen, Alvera. "An Egalitarian View: There is Neither Male nor Female in Christ." In *Women in Ministry: Four Views*, edited by B. Clouse and R. Clouse, 173–206. Downers Grove, IL: IVP, 1989.

Migliore, Daniel L. *Faith Seeking Understanding: An Introduction to Christian Theology*. Grand Rapids, MI: Eerdmans, 1991.

Moltmann, Jurgen. *The Church in the Power of the Spirit*. Translated by Margaret Kohl. London: SCM Press, 1977.

Moo, Douglas. "What does It Mean Not to Teach or Have Authority Over Men?" In *Recovering Biblical Manhood and Womanhood*, edited by J. Piper and W. Grudem, 179–93. Wheaton, IL: Good News Publishers, 1991.

Morris, Leon. *The First Epistle of Paul to the Corinthians*. London: Tyndale Press, 1958.

O'Donnell, J. J. "A common quotation from 'Augustine'?" No pages. Online: http://ccat.sas .upenn.edu/jod/augustine/quote.html

Origen. *Commentary on Romans*. Baltimore: Catholic University of America Press, 2001.

Oss, Douglas A. "A Pentecostal/Charismatic View." In *Are Miraculous Gifts For Today?* edited by Wayne Grudem, 237–83. Grand Rapids, MI: Zondervan, 1996.

Pache, R. *Die Wiederkunft Jesu Christi.* Wuppertal: Brockhaus Verlag, 1974.

Packer, J. I. *Evangelism and the Sovereignty of God.* Downers Grove, IL: IVP, 1991.

———, and Thomas C. Oden. *One Faith: The Evangelical Consensus.* Downer's Grove, IL: IVP, 2004.

Parr, Randall. "The Woman Question." *Ministries Today* (September–October 1995): 45–50.

Pate, C. Marvin. *The End of the Age Has Come: The Theology of Paul.* Grand Rapids, MI: Zondervan, 1995.

Perschbacher, Wesley J. *The New Analytical Greek Lexicon.* Peabody: Hendrickson, 1990.

Picirilli, Robert. *Grace, Faith, Free Will.* Nashville, TN: Randall House, 2002.

Piepkorn, A.C. "Charisma in the New Testament and Apostolic Fathers." *Concordia Theological Monthy* 42, 6 (1971): 369–89.

Pieters, Albert. *The Facts and Mysteries of the Christian Faith.* 3rd ed. Grand Rapids, MI: Eerdmans, 1939. Quoted in Fisk, Samuel. *Election and Predestination.* Eugene, OR: Wipf and Stock, 2002.

Pink, Arthur. *The Sovereignty of God.* Grand Rapids, MI: Baker, 1984.

Pinnock, Clark H. "God Limits his Knowledge." In *Predestination and Free Will: Four Views of Divine Sovereignty and Human Freedom*, edited by D. Basinger and R. Basinger, 141–62. Downers Grove, IL: IVP, 1986.

———. "Responsible Freedom and the Flow of Biblical History." In *Grace Unlimited*, edited by Clark H. Pinnock, 95–109. 2nd ed. Eugene, OR: Wipf and Stock, 1998.

Poythress, Vern S. *Symphonic Theology: The Validity of Multiple Perspectives in Theology.* Grand Rapids, MI: Zondervan, 1987.

Pratt, Richard. *He Gave us Stories: The Bible Student's Guide to Interpreting Old Testament Narratives.* Phillipsburg, NJ: Presbyterian & Reformed, 1990.

Price, R. *Jerusalem in Prophecy.* Eugene: Harvest House, 1998.

Quinn, Jerome D. "Charisma *Veritati Certum*: Irenaeus, *Adversus Haereses* 4, 26, 2." *Theological Studies* 39 (1978): 520–25.

Ratzinger, Joseph. *The Ratzinger Report.* Ft. Collins, CO: St. Ignatius Press, 1985.

Reichenbach, Bruce. "God Limits His Power." In *Predestination and Free Will: Four Views of Divine Sovereignty and Human Freedom*, edited by D. Basinger and R. Basinger, 99–124. Downers Grove, IL: IVP, 1986.

Rice, John R. *Hyper Calvinism: A False Doctrine.* Murfreesboro, TN: Sword of the Lord, 1970. Online: http://www.jesus-is-savior.com/Books,%20Tracts%20&%20Preaching/Printed%20Books/Dr%20John%20Rice/hypercalvinism.htm.

Ridderbos, H. *Aan de Romeinen.* Kampen: Kok, 1960.

———. *Paulus—Ontwerp van zijn Theologie.* Kampen: Kok, 1966.

Robeck, Jr., C. M. "Azusa Street Revival." In *Dictionary of Pentecostal and Charismatic Movements*, edited by Stan M. Burgess and Gary B. McGee. Grand Rapids, MI: Zondervan, 1988.

———. "Ecclesiastical Authority and the Power of the Spirit." *Paraclete* 12 (1978): 21.

———. "The Gifts of the Spirit in the Ante-Nicene Literature." Graduate paper, Fuller Theological Seminary, 1976.

Roberts, A. and J. Donaldson. *The Ante-Nicene Fathers*, 4 vols. Grand Rapids, MI: Eerdmans, 1956.

Robinson, Stephen E. *Are Mormons Christians?* Salt Lake City, UT: Bookcraft, 1991.

Roser, Mark. *God's Sovereignty: Restoring Truth for God's People to Trust Him More.* Cincinnati, OH: Uttermost, 2003.

Ruthven, Jon. *On the Cessation of the Charismata: The Protestant Polemic on Post-biblical Miracles*. Sheffield: Academic Press, 1993.

Sanders, John. "Inclusivism." In *What About Those Who Have Never Heard? Three Views on the Destiny of the Unevangelized*, edited by John Sanders, 21–55. Downer's Grove, IL: IVP, 1995.

Saucy, Robert L. "An Open but Cautious View." In *Are Miraculous Gifts for Today?* edited by Wayne Grudem, 95–148. Downers Grove, IL: IVP, 1996.

Schatzmann, Siegfried. *A Pauline Theology of Charismata*. Peabody MA: Hendrickson, 1987.

Schlier, H. *Der Brief an die Galater*. Göttingen: Vandenhoeck und Ruprecht, 1962.

Scott, James M. *New International Bible Commentary: 2 Corinthians*. Peabody: Hendrickson, 1998.

Seaton, W. J. *The Five Points of Calvinism*. Edinburgh: Banner of Truth, 1970.

Service Book And Ordinal of the Presbyterian Church of Southern Africa. N.p.: General Assembly, 1984.

Shiflet, R. B. "Ultradispensationalism: A Personal Testimony." No pages. Online: http://eleventhavenuechurch.com/ultra.html.

Simmons, Scott J. "John Calvin and Missions: A Historical Study." No pages. Online: http://aplacefortruth.org/calvin.missions1.htm.

Sproul, R. C. *Chosen by God*. Wheaton, IL: Tyndale House, 1986.

Spurgeon, Charles H. *Metropolitan Tabernacle Pulpit*, 56 vols. In *Charles H. Spurgeon Collection 2*, vol. 6. Rio, WI: AGES Library. CD-ROM.

Stam, J. E. "Charismatic Theology in the Apostolic Tradition of Hippolytus." In *Current Issues in Biblical and Patristic Interpretation*, edited by Gerald F. Hawthorne, 267–76. Grand Rapids, MI: Eerdmans, 1975.

Staples, Rob. *Outward Sign and Inward Grace*. Kansas City: Beacon Hill Press, 1991.

Steele, D., and C. Thomas. *The Five Points of Calvinism: Defined, Defended, Documented*. Phillipsburg, NJ: Presbyterian & Reformed, 1963.

Stephanou, Eusebius A. "Charismata in the Early Church Fathers." *The Greek Orthodox Theological Review* 21 (1976): 125–46.

Stookey, Laurence Hull. *Baptism: Christ's Act in the Church*. Nashville: Abingdon, 1982.

Storms, C. Samuel. "Prayer and Evangelism under God's Sovereignty." In *Still Sovereign*, edited by T. Schreiner and C. Ware, 307–23. 2nd ed. Grand Rapids, MI: Baker, 2000.

———. "A Third Wave Response to Richard B. Gaffin, Jr." In *Are Miraculous Gifts For Today? Four Views*, edited by Wayne A. Grudem, 72–85. Grand Rapids, MI: Zondervan, 1996.

Stott, John. *Evangelical Truth: A Personal Plea for Unity, Integrity and Faithfulness*. Leicester, England: IVP, 2003.

Stronstad, Roger. *The Charismatic Theology of St. Luke*. Peabody, MA: Hendrickson, 1984.

———. *The Prophethood of All Believers: A Study of Luke's Charismatic Theology*. Sheffield, England: Sheffield Academic Press, 1999.

Swete, Henry Barclay. *The Holy Spirit in the Ancient Church*. Grand Rapids, MI: Baker, 1966.

Taylor, Vincent. *The Gospel According to Mark*. London: Macmillan, 1959.

Templeton, Charles. *Farewell to God: My Reasons for Rejecting the Christian Faith*. Toronto, Ontario: McClelland & Stewart, 1996.

Tertullian, *On Baptism*. Whitefish, MT: Kessinger, 2004.

Tucker, Ruth. "A Historical Overview of Women in Ministry." *Theology, News and Notes* 42/1 (1995): 3–7.

Turner, Max. *The Holy Spirit and Spiritual Gifts Then and Now.* Carlisle: Paternoster Press, 1966.

Tyler, Bennett. *The Doctrine of Election: the Only Ground of Encouragement to Preach the Gospel to Sinners.* From the Inheritance of our Fathers 32. Grand Rapids, MI: Inheritance, n.d.

Van der Meer, F. *Augustine, the Bishop.* Translated by B. Battershaw and G. R. Lamb. New York: Harper and Row, 1961.

Van Stempvoort, P. A. *De Brief van Paulus aan de Galaten.* Nijkerk: Callenbach, 1961.

Vance, Laurence M. *The Other Side of Calvinism: Calvinism and the Baptists.* Pensacola, FL: Vance Publications, 1999. Online: http://www.jesus-is-savior.com/False%20Doctrines /Calvinism/calvinism_and_baptists.htm.

Vedder, Henry C. *A Short History of the Baptists.* Valley Forge, USA: The Judson Press, 1967.

Walls, J., and J. Dongell. *Why I am not a Calvinist.* Downer's Grove, IL: IVP, 2004.

Walvoort, J. F. *Israel in Prophecy.* Grand Rapids, MI: Zondervan, 1962.

Warfield, Benjamin B. "Calvinism Today." No pages. Online: http://www.the-highway. com/caltoday_Warfield.html.

———. *Counterfeit Miracles.* Edinburgh: Banner of Truth, 1983.

———. *Miracles: Yesterday and Today, True and False.* Grand Rapids, MI: Eerdmans, 1954.

Weinfeld, Moshe. "Pentecost as Festival of the Giving of the Law." *Immanuel* 8 (1978): 14–15.

Wesley, John. *Wesley's Works,* 14 vols. In *The Master Christian Library,* vol. 5. Rio, WI: AGES Library. CD-ROM.

Westminster Confession of Faith. Glasgow: Free Presbyterian Publications, 1995.

White, James R. *Is the Mormon my Brother? Discerning the Differences Between Mormonism and Christianity.* Minneapolis, MN: Bethany House, 1997.

Wiersbe, Warren. *The Bible Exposition Commentary.* Vol. 1. Wheaton, IL: Victor Books, 1989.

Wiley, Tatha. *Original Sin: Origins, Developments, Contemporary Meanings.* New York: Paulist Press, 2002.

Wilken, Robert Louis. "Salvation in Early Christian Thought." In *Catholics and Evangelicals: Do They Share a Common Future?* edited by Thomas P. Rausch, 56–76. Downers Grove, IL: IVP, 2000.

Williams, Don. "Following Christ's Example: A Biblical View of Discipleship." In *The Kingdom and the Power,* edited by Gary S. Grieg and Kevin N. Springer, 175–96. Ventura, CA: Regal Books, 1993.

Williams, J. Rodman. *Renewal Theology: Systematic Theology from a Charismatic Perspective.* Grand Rapids, MI: Zondervan, 1996.

Wood, Nathan E. *The Person and Work of Jesus Christ: An Exposition of Christian Doctrine.* Philadelphia: American Baptist Publication Society, 1908. Quoted in Fisk, Samuel. *Election and Predestination.* Eugene, OR: Wipf and Stock, 2002.